TURNING TIDES

D1249236

TURNING TIDES

MODERN DUTCH & FLEMISH VERSE
IN ENGLISH VERSIONS
BY IRISH POETS

EDITED BY PETER VAN DE KAMP
ASSOCIATE EDITOR: FRANK VAN MEURS

WITH AN INTRODUCTION BY
PROFESSOR THEO D'HAEN

STORY LINE PRESS
1994

ISBN: 0-934257-70-1

Published by Story Line Press, Inc., Three Oaks Farm, Brownsville, OR 97327

This publication was made possible thanks in part to the generous support of the Nicholas Roerich Museum, the Andrew W. Mellon Foundation, individual contributors to Story Line Press.

We extend special thanks for the generous support of the Prins Bernhard Fonds, the Foundation for the Production and Translation of Dutch Literature, Administratie Kunst, and the Commission for the European Communities. The Dutch Government, through the Dutch Embassy in Ireland, gave support in the form of an LCP Cultural Grant of the Netherlands Embassy in Ireland.

Turning tides, their regularities!
What is the heart, that it ever was afraid,
Knowing as it must know spring's release,
Shining heart, heart constant as a tide.

(Seamus Heaney after J.C. Bloem)

For my late father & brother
and my sister & mother

EDITOR'S PREAMBLE

This anthology grew out of a seminar course in Translation Theory which I taught at Leiden University in 1986, and in which we progressed from theory to practise. Students transposed poetry from The Netherlands and Belgium into English by making 'cribs', literal or, to be precise *verbum de verbo* translations with notes on the syntax, style, rhetoric, prosody and semantics of the poems, and on their cultural and historical context.

In the classroom these served the purpose of showing the difference between translations and—what Valéry has termed—*versions*, between translating a poem and re-creating it in the cultural context of the target language. *Versions* leave room for all the liberties advocates of literal translation might frown upon, and may result in poetry which, being poetically acceptable in the target language, is in some respects a more immediate representation of the original.

Frank van Meurs and I had set our aims at producing an anthology which offered a representative selection of modern Dutch poetry through the medium of a fairly representative number of contemporary Irish poets. I therefore produced over 400 cribs; and, with help from Professor Augustine Martin, submitted selections to more than twenty Irish poets, according to—what Gus and I considered to be—their poetic preferences. Many poets proved cooperative. The network of contributors spread, and the anthology came close to reaching its present form.

The reader may notice that I have avoided using the word 'translations.' This book, it must be stressed, is *not* a collection of translations. Most of the Irish contributors do not know any Dutch. Their *versions* are 'after' the original in various ways: some are as close to the meaning of the Dutch *sensum sensu* as possible, others *verbum de verbo*, and some bear out a transcendental mimetic approach.

What this book intends to offer is a record of cultural cross-fertilization which may be of interest to two cultures. It presents over a century of Dutch and Flemish poetic experience, with its occasionally radical penchant for renewal, through the words and music of contemporary Irish poetry—which, rightly or wrongly, has been associated more with the mainstay of tradition.

At this stage of production, the anthology met all but one of our aims, to give *some* historically acceptable—albeit far from authoritative—representation of Modern Dutch and Flemish poetry. We liked the Irish look at Dutch poetry, but it made our Dutch eyes squint a bit. In the end, we decided that in order to prevent too great a misrepresentation of the Dutch and Flemish canon, a modicum of classic poems had to be incorporated. I have added these in versions of my own, with the assistance of Frank van Meurs. My main excuse for joining the ranks of Irish poets is that I have lived in Ireland since 1981, teaching, and writing about, Anglo-Irish literature. Besides, some of the Irish poets who declined to participate did so because they claimed my cribs could stand on their own as fully-fledged versions. And, on top of that, my publisher, Robert McDowell, advised me to do so. My additions consist, in the main, of poems which through the test of time have become accepted as 'classics', the selection becomes more adventurous, and more dictated by Irish taste, in the periods closest to the present. On the advice of van Meurs, I have also added my own, more "literal", versions to poems which had been traduced very freely.

The Netherlands and Belgium have always been dependent on outside influences, as is reflected in the literary movements which have been so dominant in this century's Dutch poetry. Any of the "isms" that became fashionable in literary Europe have had their exponents in the Lowlands. This has contributed to the dynamic nature of the Dutch and Flemish verse tradition in the periods covered by this book. In order to bear out the turning of the tides in modern Dutch language poetry, we have opted for a chronological—rather than a thematic—arrangement.

Like any chronological demarcation, the present division of some 100 years of Dutch verse into five periods is arbitrary. It is loosely based on major historical events that exerted an undeniable cultural impact. It does show how some poets, like Roland Holst, span a considerable period of Dutch poetry, and how others are representative of a single movement. Within each section, chronological rigidity has been sacrificed to the unity of personal expression; the sequence of poets is mainly determined by the year of publication of the first poem with which they are represented.

Dr. Peter van de Kamp
University of Leiden,
University College Dublin,
RTC Tralee
1986—1994

Acknowledgements

The production of this anthology would have been impossible without financial support. I am grateful for the support of the former Dutch Ambassador to Ireland, Eric Niehe, and the First Secretary, Joseph Damoiseaux. Personally, I am grateful for the support I received from the Ireland Fund in the form of a University College Dublin Newman Scholarship. I should particularly like to thank the former President of the college, Professor Patrick Masterson, and the Director of Postgraduate Studies, Professor Frank Hegarty. Dr. E.M. Joon offered welcome support, both with his perennial good humour and with his purse, in times of doubt about funding this project.

Emiel Fangmann of the *Leidsch Dagblad* helped gather biographical and bibliographical data. Dr. Tjebbe Westendorp, of the University of Leiden, helped collect some biographical material. Linda de Win and Kristien Bonneure, both of B.R.T. (Belgian radio), Hannie Rouweler and Elizabeth Dinet helped select Flemish poetry. Daisy Wolthers gave essential advice on Achterberg's work, and on getting funding.

The following colleagues, students and friends assisted in making crib translations: Hanneke Bos (Slauerhoff), Peter Both and Annette van het Erven (van Ostaijen), Erik Brus (Gorter), Annelies Burger (Marsman), Elizabeth Dinet (van de Woestijne), Thessa Dirksen (Couperus), Saskia Hoepman and Marten Vogelaar (Marsman), José Lanters (Vroman), Boudewijn van der Leck (I.K. Bonset, Koster), Dieke Rietkerk (Achterberg), Jacqueline Tordoir and Marco Goudzwaard (Nijhoff).

Dutch poets Mieke Tillema, Johanna Kruit and Levi

Weemoedt offered valuable support. Most Irish poets whom I consulted were very helpful. Desmond Egan deserves special mention; he offered over forty-five versions, not all of which, for obvious reasons, could be included in this book. Among the Irish poets who introduced me to various contributors, Dennis O'Driscoll and Theo Dorgan deserve special thanks. Joan McBreen found me the right publisher.

Peter Costello offered useful advice on production and publication. Stefan Gunarsson of Microsoft Ireland advised me about computer software. Marian Lovett, Odile Oomen, Daisy Wolthers and David Krop cast a critical eye over my unwieldy prose. Frank Hendriks and Lian van de Kamp put the computer facilities of their company, van de Kamp Voorschoten BV, at my disposal whenever I was in Holland.

The following poets and publishers, presented here in random order, have kindly granted permission to reprint copyright poems: Hester Knibbe (De Prom); Theo Sontrop, the estate of Jan Hanlo (Uitgeverij G.A. Van Oorschot), Hendrik de Vries, M. Vasalis, Hanny Michaelis, Rutger Kopland, the estates of Jan Emmens, Adriaan Roland Holst and Hans Lodeizen (through Uitgev-erij G.A. Van Oorschot); Bertus Aafjes, Rein Bloem, Maurice Gilliams, Ed. Hoornik, Anton Korteweg and Laurens Vancrevel (through Meulenhoff Nederland B.V.); Willem Jan Otten, Albert Verwey, J. Bernlef, Lenze L. Bouwers, Willem Elsschot, Han G. Hoekstra, K. Schippers, Toon TeTellegen, Christine D'haen, Leonard Nolens, Herman van den Bergh and Leo Vroman (through Em. Querido's Uitgeverij B.V.); J.C. Bloem, Ida Gerhardt, P.C. Boutens, Christine D'haen (Athenaeum-Polak & Van Gennep); Elma van Haren (Uitgeverij De Harmonie); Marga Kool (Stichting Het Drentse Boek); the estate of Gerrit Achterberg

(Daisy Wolthers); Martinus Nijhoff (Andreas Oosthoek); Charles Ducal, Anna Enquist, Eva Gerlach, Gerrit Komrij and Ed Leeflang and Jan Eijkelboom (through Uitgeverij De Arbeiderspers); Jan Arends, Cees Buddingh; Remco Campert, J.B. Charles, Hugo Claus, Hans Faverey, Lucebert, Adriaan Morrien, H.C. ten Berge, Miriam Van hee and Bert Voeten (through Uitgeverij De Bezige Bij); Patricia Lasoen, Jotie T' Hooft, Herman de Coninck and Victor Vroomkoning (through Uitgeversmij. A. Manteau n.v.); Paul Rodenko (through Uitgeverij De Harmonie); Ben Cami (through uitgeverij De Sikkel); Hans Andreus, Neeltje Maria Min and Renée van Riessen (through Uitgeverij Bert Bakker); Jan Elburg, Judith Herzberg, Johanna Kruit, Willem M. Roggeman, Leo Ross, Mieke Tillema, Job Degenaar, Judith Mok, Roland Jooris, Cees Nooteboom, Jana Beranová and Hannie Rouweler.

I should like to express my gratitude to these poets and to the staff in the Dutch and Flemish publishing houses who have approached them on my behalf, and who proved immensely helpful in supplying and verifying bibliographical and biographical details. Before I started this enterprise I had no idea that poets and publishers could be such great company.

I wish ceremony and custom would allow me to express my gratitude to my associate editor, Frank van Meurs: this is his book at least as much as it is mine.

TABLE OF CONTENTS

1914 –1940

1940 –1960

1960–1980

INTRODUCTION

The present anthology originally labeled itself as a collection of "modern Dutch verse." This "Dutch" label might well have been misleading to English-language readers, for whom this adjective applies exclusively to what in colloquial English is referred to as "Holland" and to what on offical maps is labelled "The Netherlands." The language of this specific geographical and political unit, though, is also that of Flanders, the northern half of present-day Belgium. It has long been a bone of contention in Dutch-language literary history, and it has often been a subject of bitter polemic in criticism, whether the literary products of the two regions should be dealt with as one undivisible whole, or whether they should be treated separately. The problem poses itself most acutely with regard to the post-1600 period in which Holland and Flanders, except for a very brief period between 1815 and 1830, have had completely separate histories. Literary developments in these regions have not always followed the same track, nor have they always shown the same speed. The present anthology incorporates texts from the entire Dutch-language area in Europe. With some twenty million speakers in all—over 14 million Dutch and 6 million Flemings—Dutch is one of the middle-sized languages of Europe in terms of numbers: considerably less than French, German or Italian, sizably more than any of the Scandinavian languages.

The present anthology provides glances into modern Dutch poetry; the poems here offered, though all significant in their own right, were not selected to form a representative sample illustrating the entire development of Dutch-language poetry in the period 1880–1990. Rather, they should be seen as choices made by the editor and the "translators" according to their own sympathies and affinities. Therefore, it might not be a bad idea to offer the English-language reader a brief preliminary survey of modern Dutch-language poetry. He or she can then read the specific poems presented in the anthology against this survey.

The 1880s mark the advent in Dutch poetry of "modern" concerns. From the eighteenth century on, in fact ever since the end of the Dutch so-called Golden Age in the late seventeenth century, Dutch literature had been prattling away modestly on the backburner of European literature. The Romantic movement, wreaking havoc in most other European literatures, had largely passed Holland by. True, a number of younger Dutch poets had introduced Byron in Dutch literature in the 1820s and 1830s, translating selections from his works. However, the vogue—for it never grew beyond this—rapidly passed, and the most prominent of these poets went on to become the leading "parson-poets" of the ensuing decades, endlessly grinding out utterly conventional domestic and patriotic rhymes. It is against the tyranny of this kind of poetry that the so-called Eighties Poets revolted. Though each of the members of the "Movement of 80" would soon go his own separate way, they initially all clustered around the magazine *De Nieuwe*

Gids (*The New Guide*), founded in opposition to the older *De Gids* (*The Guide*). The initiator and main theoretician of the movement was Willem Kloos (1859–1938). He coined the catch-phrases "form and content are one" and "poetry is the most extremely individual expression of the most extremely individual emotion." Significant for the state of Dutch poetry at the time is that Kloos, and with him his fellow Eighties Poets Frederik van Eeden (1860–1932), Herman Gorter (1864–1927), and Albert Verwey (1865–1937), found most of their inspiration with the English Romantics of the beginning of the century, especially Wordsworth, Shelley and Keats. Even then, theirs is a softened version of the Romantics' poetics. As such, it is a prime example of how Dutch literature, until the second half of the twentieth century, follows international literary developments "from afar," both chronologically—though the gap narrows constantly over the following century—and in intensity.

If anything, the state in which Dutch-language poetry lingered in Flanders until the end of the nineteenth century was even worse than in Holland. For centuries Flanders had been ruled by foreigners: the Spanish, the Austrians, and the French. The language of the court, of the nobility, of the elite, and partly also of the administration, was French, while the language of the people was Dutch. Obviously, such a situation did not provide fertile ground for the development of an important literature in Dutch, especially during the (Neo) Classicist period when the influence of French literature was predominant throughout (at least continental) Europe anyway, and folk language and literature were spurned. The period of unification with Holland in the Verenigde Nederlanden (United Netherlands) between 1815 and 1830 was too short to turn the tide. And after Belgian independence was achieved by an alliance of the Catholic clergy, the nobility, the bourgeoisie, and the Walloon industrialists (from the southern and Francophone part of Belgium), who all for their own reasons preferred an independent and French-speaking Belgium, matters only got worse still. It is all the more surprising, then, that in the second half of the century there arose in the extreme western part of Flanders (the area next to the sea, around Bruges, Ypres and Roeselare) a poet totally unlike anything ever seen in Dutch-language poetry. Guido Gezelle (1830–99) was a veritable magician of language, who bent and played his West-Flemish dialect to effects that would only be repeated, though perhaps not even equalled, much later by a major modernist poet like Paul van Ostaijen. Gezelle was a Catholic priest, who all his life suffered the discipline of the church. He corresponded with, and translated, the American poet Longfellow. His own poetry, though, remains virtually untranslatable.

Even if they borrowed much of their poetics from the Romantics, in other respects the Eighties Poets were closer to the French "Symbolistes," especially in their ivory tower mentality, their extreme individualism, and their shunning of moral or social responsibilities. This has led some critics to consider them as the Dutch branch of international Symbolism. Yet, things are not quite so simple. Gorter, for instance, though some of his early verse might qualify as close to Symbolism, quickly developed into a radically and powerfully social poet. The term can perhaps with more justice be applied to Verwey, who pursued the typically Symbolist goal of serving some remote and elevated "idea" or "ideal," comparable perhaps to Mallarmé's *livre sacr.* Verwey was also influenced by the poetry of Stefan George. It may with equal justice be applied to J. H. Leopold (1865–1925) and P.C. Boutens (1870–1943), both of whom partly took their cue from Gorter's early verse. In turn, J.A. Dèr Mouw (1862–1919), who wrote under the name of "Adwaita", and A. Roland Holst (1888–1976) have been called Post-Symbolists. Of all these poets, A. Roland Holst is probably the most interesting for the English-language reader. Roland Holst spent part of his early manhood in England, where he became acquainted with the work of Yeats and with Irish literature in general. His entire work was to show the traces of this encounter. J.C. Bloem (1887–1966) on the other hand could be called an anti-Symbolist in his insistence on the everyday and the commonplace. In Flanders, French Symbolism found a much less ambiguous follower than in Holland in the figure of Karel van de Woestijne (1878–1929).

In Dutch literary history, the year 1916 is often taken as marking the turning point of Dutch poetry joining international developments rather than following them from a (respectable) distance. This same year saw the creation of a journal that would gather a number of the poets that would dominate the interbellum in Dutch poetry, *Het Getij,* as well as the first publication of the poet who, certainly in retrospect, looms largest among them, Martinus Nijhoff (1894–1953). With Nijhoff, who translated T.S. Eliot, Dutch poetry turns resolutely Modernist. For the inflated and stilted poetic diction of his Symbolist predecessors Nijhoff substitutes a colloquial idiom. To their Romantic and decadent *poète maudit* image he prefers that of the poet-craftsman. And like Eliot he aspired to "impersonalism" in his poetry. Whereas Nijhoff is a Modernist in the Anglo-American sense of the word, his contemporaries often subscribed to the more extreme continental European -isms ruling the literature of the period. Hendrik de Vries (1896–1989), Herman van den Bergh (1897–1967) and Hendrik Marsman (1899–1940) took their cue from German Expressionism. Theo van Doesburg (1883–1931), who took the pseudonym of I.K. Bonset, allied himself with Cubism, Constructivism and Dadaism. He toured Holland with Kurt Schwitters, and wrote radically experimental poetry, innovative both in in its use of sound and of typography. Van Doesburg also founded and directed the famous magazine *De Stijl*, which played a major role in renewing European art and architecture immediately after World War I. In his theoretical pieces, Van Doesburg invoked the likes of Ezra Pound, August Stramm, Marinetti, and Alfred Döblin. At least as radical as Van Doesburg was the Flemish poet Paul van Ostaijen (1896–1928). Like Nijhoff he made his poetical debut in 1916 with staunchly Expressionist verse. During his brief career he rapidly developed into an astonishingly original experimentalist, comparable only to Apollinaire in his daring use of typography and lay-out in his collections of the early to mid-twenties, and to his nineteenth-century Flemish predecessor Guido Gezelle in the musicality and linguistic inventiveness of his later poetry. Like Van Doesburg, Van Ostaijen defended his own poetic practice in a number of closely reasoned theoretical essays, in which he showed himself to be very well up on wider European artistic and literary developments.

A position somewhat apart from the other poets of the first half of the twentieth century is occupied by

Jan Slauerhoff (1898–1936) and Gerrit Achterberg (1905–1962). Slauerhoff adopted the stance of the *poète maudit*, and wrote of basically romantic and nostalgic longings. He himself spent most of his adult life roaming the earth as a ship's medic. Achterberg wrote deceptively simple-looking poetry, often close to Surrealist poetry in its combination of technological imagery and dreamlike content. Fully as much alienated from, and disenchanted with, the world as were Slauerhoff and Achterberg, was Ed Hoornik (1910–70), but he chose to voice his alienation via a more "realist" poetry.

After World War II Dutch poetry, which until then had been following European developments rather from a distance, exploded in a veritably unique frenzy of experimentalism with the work of the so-called "Fifties Poets." The poets of this movement were politically on the far left, and they fulminated against what they perceived as traditional Dutch stolidness, mediocrity, and reserve. As examples they fastened upon the most experimental of contemporary and pre-War foreign poets: Pound, Eliot, Artaud, Char, Michaux, Eluard. The poem to them was an autonomous entity, a linguistic monument or sculpture with the needs of the linguistic material pre-empting or overtaking those of any previous "content." They preferred irrationality, spontaneity, and the language of the body to cool and intellectual rationalism. Many of their poems are self-referential process-poems detailing their own genesis, pondering their own being. A number of the most prominent Fifties Poets was also active as painter or sculptor, and the emergence of these poets is closely linked to the creation of the *COBRA*-movement (COpenhagen–BRussels–Amsterdam) in art. This is particularly true of the Flemish representative of the movement, Hugo Claus (1929), and of the Dutch poets Lucebert (1924-1994), penname of L. J. Swaanswijk, Jan G. Elburg (1919–1992), and Gerrit Kouwenaar (1923). Other Fifties Poets include Hans An-dreus (1926–77), pseudonym of J. W. van der Zant, and Jan Hanlo (1912–69).

Two important but isolated figures in post-War Dutch poetry are Ida Gerhardt (1905) and Leo Vroman (1915). Gerhardt is a classicist in form and themes, and draws upon Christian tradition. Vroman, in contrast, writes playful and absurdist poetry, with a sharp eye for detail often couched in scientific language or in neologisms. After the War, which he spent in a Japanese prisoners' camp in Indonesia, Vroman settled in the United States. It has been argued that it is the tension between his non-Dutch linguistic environment and his continuing to write in Dutch that makes for his often startling use of language.

Since 1960 Dutch poetry has basically followed three major roads. First, there are a number of poets continuing in the footsteps of the Fifties movement: experimental and self-reflexive poetry, though decidedly less exuberant than that of the original Fifties writers. Two names to be mentioned here are Hans Faverey (1933–1990), and H.C. ten Berge (1938). Then, there is a return to everyday reality. Often this takes the form of wry and ironic descriptions with twist endings, especially with representatives of the so-called "New Realism" movement in Flanders such as Herman de Coninck (1944) and Roland Jooris (1936). But also Dutch poets like Rutger Kopland (1934), penname of R. H. van den Hoofdakker, and Kees Ouwens (1944) can be seen in this light. Finally, there is what some critics have branded as a return to Romanticism, but what can perhaps more accurately be considered as a postmodern appropriation of earlier forms and diction, usually with ironic intent. This is particularly the case in the work of Gerrit Komrij (1944). No matter which particular directions contemporary poets are travelling in, however, the popular success of the two massive anthologies of both older, pre-1900, and more recent, post-1900, poetry which Komrij edited in 1986 and 1979, respectively, is proof that the Dutch and the Flemish continue to value both their rich poetic heritage and the contemporary poetic ferment revitalizing it.

Theo D'haen
University of Leiden

1880–1914

MOEDERKEN

't En is van u
hiernederwaard,
geschilderd of
    geschreven,
mij, moederken,
geen beeltenis,
geen beeld van u
    gebleven.

Geen tekening,
geen lichtdrukmaal,
geen beitelwerk
    van steene,
't en zij dat beeld
in mij, dat gij
gelaten hebt,
    alleene.

o Moge ik, u
onweerdig, nooit
die beeltenis
    bederven,
maar eerzaam laat
ze leven in
mij, eerzaam in
    mij sterven.

LITTLE MOTHER

Of you
my, little mother,
down here on earth,
painted or
   written,
no image,
no sign of you,
   remained.

No drawing,
no photograph,
no chisel-work
   of stone,
it's that sign
in me,
solely
that you
   have left.

o May I, you,
unworthy, never
corrupt
   this image,
but let it
live honourably
in me, honourably
   die in me.

(version by Mary O'Donnell)

EGO FLOS...

CANT.II

Ik ben een blomme
en bloeie vóór uwe oogen,
geweldig zonnelicht,
dat, eeuwig onontaard,
mij, nietig schepselken,
in 't leven wilt gedoogen
en, na dit leven, mij
het eeuwig leven spaart.

Ik ben een blomme
en doe des morgens open,
des avonds toe mijn blad,
om beurtelings, nadien,
wanneer gij, zonne, zult,
heropgestaan, mij nopen,
te ontwaken nog eens of
mijn hoofd den slaap te biên.

Mijn leven is
uw licht: mijn doen, mijn derven,
mijn' hope, mijn geluk
mijn éénigste en mijn al;
wat kan ik, zonder u,
als eeuwig, eeuwig sterven;
wat heb ik, zonder u,
dat ik beminnen zal?

'k Ben ver van u,
ofschoon gij, zoete bronne
van al dat leven is
of immer leven doet,
mij naast van al genaakt
en zendt, o lieve zonne,
tot in mijn diepste diep
uw aldoorgaanden gloed.

EGO FLOS...

CANTO II

I am a flower
and bloom before your eyes,
magnificent sunlight
that, for ever undeterred,
condones a paltry thing
like me to live its life,
and, after this life,
spares me eternal life.

I am a flower
and open up at morn,
and close my leaf at night,
that afterwards in turn
when you, sun, re-arise,
you'll prompt me wake once more
or tell my head to rest.

My life is
your light: my acts, my lack,
my hope, my luck, my sole,
my all; what can I do
without you but die
for ever and ever;
what have I, without you
that I shall ever love?

I am remote from you,
though you, sweet source of all
that's life or life can stir,
approaches me closest,
and sends, O sweetest sun,
within my deepest depth
your all-pervasive glow.

Haalt op, haalt af!...
ontbindt mijne aarsche boeien;
ontwortelt mij, ontdelft
mij...! Henen laat mij, ... laat
daar 't altijd zomer is
en zonnelicht mij sproeien
en daar gij, eeuwige, ééne,
alschoone blomme, staat.

Laat alles zijn
voorbij, gedaan, verleden,
dat afscheid tusschen ons
en diepe kloven spant;
laat morgen, avond, al
dat heenmoet, henentreden,
laat uw oneindig licht
mij zien, in 't Vaderland!

Dan zal ik vóór...
o neen, niet vóór uwe oogen
maar naast u, nevens u,
maar in uw bloeien zaan;
zoo gij mij, schepselken,
in 't leven wilt gedoogen;
zoo in uw eeuwig licht
me gij laat binnengaan!

Pull up, pull down!...
Undo my earthly chains;
uproot me, dig me up...!
Let me go thither, ... let
me sprout where it's summer
and sunlight for ever,
where you, the One, ever-
all-splendid flower, stand.

Let all that be
gone, done, past which divides us,
which makes deep crevices;
let morning, evening, all
that must go, tread thither,
let your unending light
show me the Fatherland.

Then shall I before...
No, not before your eyes
but beside you, by you,
but speed into your bloom;
if you condone me,
paltry thing, to live life;
then in your eternal light
you will let me enter.

(version by Peter van de kamp)

IRIS

Der eerwaarde jonkvrouwe Joanna C. B.

"Ik ben geboren uit zonnegloren
En een zucht van de ziedende zee,
Die omhoog is gestegen, op wieken van regen,
Gezwollen van wanhoop en wee.
Mijn gewaad is doorweven met parels, die beven
Als dauw aan de roos, die ontlook,
Wen de Dagbruid zich baadt, en voor 't schuchter gelaat
Een waaier van vlammen ontplook.—

Met tranen in 't oog, uit de diepte omhoog,
Buig ik ten kus naar beneden:
Mijn lichtende haren befloersen de baren
En mijn tranen lachen tevreden:
Want diep in zee splijt de bedding in twee,
Als mijn kus de golven doet gloren...
En de aarde is gekloofd en het lokkige hoofd
Van Zefier doemt lachend te voren.
Hij lacht... en zijn zucht blaast, mij arme, in de lucht
En een boog van tintlende kleuren
Is mijn spoor, als ik wijk naar het droomerig rijk,
Waar ik eenzaam om Zefier kan treuren.
Hij mint me als ik hém... maar zijn lach, zijn stem,
Zijn kus... is een zucht: wij zwerven
Omhoog, omlaag; wij wíllen gestaâg,
Maar wij kunnen nóch kussen, nóch sterven.—

De sterveling ziet mijn aanschijn niet,
Als ik uítschrei, hoog boven de wolken,
En de regenvlagen met ritselend klagen
Mijn onsterflijken weedom vertolken.
Dan drenkt mijn smart het dorstende hart
Van de bloem, die smacht naar mijn leed
En met dankenden blik naar mij opziet, als ik
Van weedom het weenen vergeet.
En dán verschijn ik door 't nevelgordijn—

IRIS

To the Honourable Lady Joanna C.B.

"I was born out of sun-rays
And a sigh of the seething sea,
Which rose up, on wings of rain,
Swollen with despair and woe.
My robe is interwoven with pearls that tremble
Like dew on the rose, which opened,
When the Day-bride bathes and before that demure face
A fan of flames enfurls.—

With tears in the eye, risen from depths,
I bend down to kiss:
My lightning hair shrouds the waves
And my tears smile satisfied:
For deep down in the sea the bed splits in two,
When my kiss makes the waves gleam...
And the earth is cleft and the curly head
Of Zephyr looms up laughing.
He laughs... and his sigh blows me into the sky
And an arc of sparkling colours
Is my track, as I recede into the dreamy realm
Where in solitude I can grieve for Zephyr.
He loves me as I love him... but his smile, his voice,
His kiss... is a sigh: we roam
Up, down; we yearn constantly,
But we can neither kiss nor die.—

A mortal does not see my countenance,
As I cry out, high above the clouds,
And the gusts of rain with rustling lament
Interpret my immortal woe.
Then my sorrow drenches the thirsting heart
Of the flower, which yearns for my grief,
And looks up with a grateful glance as I
Forget to weep out of woe.
And *then* I appear through the curtain of mist—

Dat mijn Zefier verscheurt, als hij vliegt—
Somber gekromd... tot de zonneschijn komt,
En op 't rag mijner wieken zich wiegt.
Dán zegt op aarde, wie mij ontwaarde:
"De goudene Iris lacht!"...
En stil oversprei ik de vale vallei
Met een gloed van zonnig smaragd.—

Mijn handen rusten op de uiterste kusten
Der aarde als, in roerloos peinzen,—
Eén' bonte gedachte — ik mijn liefde verwachte...
Die mij achter de zon zal doen deinzen.—
'k Zie 's nachts door mijne armen de sterren zwermen
En het donzige wolkengewemel
En de maan, die mij haat en zich koestert en baadt
In den zilveren lach van den hemel.—
Mijn pauwepronk... is de dos, dien mij schonk
De zon, om den stervling te sparen,
Wien mijn lichtlooze blik zou bleeken van schrik
En mijn droeve gestalte vervaren.
Nu omspan ik den trans met mijne armen van glans
Tot mij lokt Zefier's wapprend gewaad
En ik henenduister naar 't oord, waar de luister
Der lonkende zon mij verlaat.—

Ik ben geboren uit zonnegloren
En een vochtige zucht van de zee,
Die omhoog is gestegen, op wieken van regen,
Gezwollen van 't wereldsche wee.—
Mij is gemeenzaam, wie even eenzaam
Het leven verlangende slijt
En die in tranen zijn Vreugde zag tanen...
Doch liefelijk lacht, als hij lijdt!"—

Which my Zephyr rents as he flies —
Curled-up sombrely... till the sunshine comes
And rocks on the the web of my wings.
Then whoever sees me on earth says:
"The golden Iris smiles!"...
And silently I spread out over the pale valley
A glow of sunny smaragdine.—

My hands rest on the extreme coasts
Of the earth as, in motionless contemplation,—
—*One* colourful thought—I awaited my love...
Which will make me wince behind the sun.—
At night through my arms I watch the stars swarm
And the downy confusion of clouds
And the moon, who hates me and basks and bathes
In the silver light of the sky.—
My peacock's pride... is the attire,
Which the sun gave me, to save the mortal,
Whom my lightless glance would blanch with fear
And my sad figure would startle.
Now I span the firmament with arms that sparkle,
Till I'm enticed by Zephyr's wafting robes,
And I thither-dusk to the region where the lustre
Of the ogling sun deserts me.—

I was born out of sun-rays
And a damp sigh of the sea
Which rose up, on wings of rain,
Swollen with worldly woe.—
With those I'm united who spend life
As lonely in longing
And who in tears watched his Joy wane...
Yet smiles lovingly when he is in pain!"—

(version by Peter van de kamp)

BUI

Grimmig snellen rondgerolde wolken,
Eindeloos groote kluwens, aan door 't blauw;
Doodsche stilte.... toch, ze naderen gauw,
Scherp weerspiegeld in de molenkolken.

Schelle fonkeling van millioenen dolken....
Dan de donder; — en, van regen lauw,
Schudt de wind den hechten molenbouw,
Loeit het rund, dat wegvlucht ongemolken.

Zuiver, als geslepen edelsteenen
In een rand van donker goud gevat,
Spiedt de klaproos door de halmen henen,

Glanst de koornbloem helder na het bad;
En het paard, met glimmend stijve beenen,
Scheert de klaver, koel en druipend nat.

SHOWER

The passing clouds roll grimly on,
Endlessly moving through the blue.
Gravely silent! They approach with haste,
Reflecting in the water of the mill-pool,

Sparkling in a million shafts of light.
Then thunder rolls, and with it the lukewarm
Rain, and a wind that shakes the sturdy mill,
Or frightens the cow, scattering it away unmilked.

Pure, like a cut gem
Fastened in a rim of gold,
The poppy bursts through the stalk.

The corn-flower shines after the rain;
And the horse, with damp hooves,
Shears clover, cool and dripping wet.

(version by Tony Curtis)

AVOND

Nauw zichtbaar wiegen op een lichten zucht
De witte bloesems in de scheemring—ziet,
Hoe langs mijn venster nog, met rasch gerucht,
Een enkele, al te late vogel vliedt.

En ver, daar ginds, die zacht gekleurde lucht
Als perlemoer, waar ied're tint vervliet
In teêrheid... Rust—o, wonder-vreemd genucht!
Want alles is bij dag zóó innig niet.

Alle geluid, dat nog van verre sprak,
Verstierf—de wind, de wolken, alles gaat
Al zacht en zachter—alles wordt zoo stil...

En ik weet niet, hoe thans dit hart, zoo zwak,
Dat al zóó moê is, altijd luider slaat,
Altijd maar luider, en niet rusten wil.

SONNET

Ik ben een God in 't diepst van mijn gedachten,
En zit in 't binnenst van mijn ziel ten troon
Over mij-zelf en 't al, naar rijksgeboôn
Van eigen strijd en zege, uit eigen krachten,—

En als een heir van donker-wilde machten
Joelt aan mij op, en valt terug, gevloôn
Voor 't heffen van mijn hand en heldre kroon:
Ik ben een God in 't diepst van mijn gedachten.

EVENING

Hardly visible they rock, on a sigh of light,
White blossomings in the dusk—look
How by my window now, with quick whirring
One lone bird wings, already too late.

And far off there, the barely tinted sky,
Like mother-of-pearl where every tone vanishes
In fineness... O go to rest, wonderfully strange delight!
Since everything lacks this intensity by day.

Each sound that spoke, still, from a distance
Dies away—wind, cloud, it all passes
Softly, more softly—all falls so still...

And I don't understand why it's now my heart, so weak
Already so weary, begins to beat louder
Louder still, and will not rest.

(version by Desmond Egan)

SONNET

I am a God in the depths of my thought
And I rule from the centre of my being
Over my self and soul, according to commands
From my own forces, my own struggle and victory.

When a host of dark-wild forces
Howls up at me and falls away, fleeing
Before the raising of my hand and crown:
I am a God in the depths of my thought.

En tóch, zoo eind'loos smacht ik soms om rond
Uw overdierbre leên den arm te slaan,
En, luid uitsnikkende, met al mijn gloed

En trots en kalme glorie, te vergaan
Op úwe lippen in een wilden vloed
Van kussen, waar 'k niet langer woorden vond.

DE BOOMEN DORREN IN HET LAAT SEIZOEN

De boomen dorren in het laat seizoen,
En wachten roerloos den nabijen winter.
Wat is dat alles stil, doodstil.... ik vind er
Mijn eigen leven in, dat heen gaat spoên.

Ach, 'k had zoo graag heel, héél veel willen doen,
Wat Verzen en wat Liefde,—want wie mint er
Te sterven zonder dees? Maar wie ook wint er
Ter wereld iets door klagen of door woên?

Ik ga dan stil, tevreden en gedwee
En neem geen ding uit al dat Leven meê
Dan dees gedachte, gonzende in mij om:

Men moet niet van het lieve Dood-zijn ijzen.
De doode bloemen keeren niet weêrom,
Maar *Ik* zal heerlijk in mijn Vers herrijzen.

And yet, so interminably I yearn to
Fold my arms around your body
And cry with all my passion

For pride and glory to perish
On your lips in a wild torrent
Of kisses, where I'd be lost from words.

(version by Tony Curtis)

TREES, LATE IN THE SEASON

Trees, late in the season, bare
And waiting, motionless, for advancing winter...
How still it all is, dead still... here I discover
My own life which goes hurrying on.

Ah, so eagerly I had wanted, very *very* much
A little Verse and a little Love—and who wishes
To die without these? But who gains
Anything in this world by whinging or by rage?

So I go quietly, submissive and meek
Taking nothing with me out of my whole life
Other than this conclusion, droning around in me:

One must not shrink from this loved death-state:
Dead flowers do not return any more
But *I* shall enjoy glorious resurrection in my Verse!

(version by Desmond Egan)

ZELF-VERANDERING

Aan Trifouillard.

Ik ben te veel een ménsch geweest,
Een mensch, die gilde en klaagde en schreide.
Die dronk zijn glas en vierde feest
En díep-gevoelde dingen zeide.

Nú ben 'k een delikaat artiest,
Verliefde van zijn fantasieën,
Maar die zich 't áller-liefst verliest
In zijn kokette melancholieën....

Melancholie—om wie? om wat?....
Ik weet niets meer, kan niets meer voelen
Dan zoet gespeel met dit en dat
Van rijmen, zachte, klare, koele.

Self-Transformation

To Trifouillard.

Too much have I been a mere man —
A man who cried out, moaned, wept;
Who emptied his glass and lived it up
Though he also gave utterance to deeply-felt things.

Now I have become *a fastidious artist*!
The lover of his own imaginings
But even more, one who likes best of all to lose
Himself in teasing depressions...

Depressions: over whom? at what?
I know no more, can feel no more
Than pleasant dalliance with the ins and outs
Of poems, *gentle, simple, detached.*

(version by Desmond Egan)

DE NOORDEWIND.

De wind waait hoog en kent de menschen niet.

Hoog wil ik stijgen met den Noordewind,
boven 't gerucht der stemmen—boven 't licht
der volle straten. Weg! het warm gewoel,
de weeke druk van menschen om mij heen!

Ik wil ééns vrij zijn, ééns oneindig vrij,
dat er geen liefde en lachen om mij is,
geen zoete stem, geen blik van vrienden-oogen
geen weekheid en geen weemoed en geen lust.

'k Wil eenzaam stijgen in den Noordewind,
die in den killen nacht gestadig waait
groot en onwetend.
                    Stijgend wil ik neerzien
met kouden blik en onbewogen mond
op wat voor eeuwig wegzinkt onder mij.

En als de passies, die 'k heb liefgehad,
zich aan mijn kleedren hechten en 't gelaat
met schreien heffen en mij angstig vragen,
hen niet alleen te laten in den nacht....

dan zal ik zwijgend hun gekromde handen
losmaken van mijn kleed,—en als zij vallen
zal ik niet sidd'ren bij den doffen slag....

maar zingend rijzen in den kouden nacht.

THE NORTH WIND.

The wind blows high above the people's heads.

I want to be airborne with the north wind
Above cacophonous voices, busy streets,
Street lights, all that sweaty activity,
People who put me under pressure.

I want to be liberated, just for once,
Beyond the reach of love and laughter,
Seductive whispers, flirtatious glances,
My weak points, melancholia and lust.

I want to be carried away by the north wind
Which whistles in the dark, then bellows
Grandiloquently.
                    I shall look down
With indifference, with a cold eye
On what vanishes for ever beneath me.

When those I have loved most passionately
Try to buttonhole me, beseeching me
With terror-stricken, hysterical faces
Not to leave them on their own in the dark,

I shall escape from their desperate clutches,
And even when they collapse backwards
I shall not be deterred by the dull thuds,

But soar singing into the cold night.

(version by Michael Longley)

EEN SCHOOL VAN ZILV'REN MAANLICHTVISSEN VOLGT

Een school van zilv'ren maanlichtvisschen volgt
Waarlangs ik ga; zij rimp'len vroolijk op
Bij 't blazen van den dart'len avondwind.
Mijn schaduw schuift lang-donker voor mij uit,
En boven mij, bleek-schrijdend in den glans
Der maan, die hen verblindt en tanen doet,
Gaan stil de sterren. Rondom liggen breed
De weiden, kort van gras, in 't kalme licht,
Verwachtend warm'ren tijd en zomerzon
Om op te bloeien in hun bloemenpracht,
Nu rustig, groen-zwart; hier en daar een sloot,
Met flikkerlichten snijdend door hun vlak.
De boomen bladerloos nog, laten flauw
Hun teer-geknopte twijgen willig gaan
Op 't allegretto-rhythme van den wind.
En ver de stad, spelonkig-zwart en stom,
Wier macht'ge torenromp zich opwaarts werkt
Door mist'ge dampen, hangend om zijn lijf.
En even strijkt de maan langs 't koper heen
Van 't haantje, dat daar blikkert als een ster
Boven het somber-donk're huizenblok,
Waarvoor met vurige oogen, glurend-fel,
Slechts enk'le roode lichten loerend staan.

A SHOAL OF SILVER ANGELFISH

A shoal of silver angelfish
Follows where I go; they ripple
With the evening's fresh wind.
My dark shadow stretches before me,
It will wane with the glow
Of the moon, disappear
When stars appear. All around are
The barren fields, in a quiet light
They wait for warmer times, for Summer
Sun to herald in a host of flowers.
Quiet now, the earth is green-black, ditches
Cut its face with shimmering light.
Even the trees are leafless,
They let their new buds sway
With the movement of the wind.
Far away is the city, silent and cavernous-black,
Its mighty towers rise up
Through vapours, masking its body.
For a moment the moon skims the brass
Of the little cock, which glitters like a star
Above the sombre black of the houses,
In front of which, like fiery, prying eyes,
Red lights stand leering.

(version by Tony Curtis)

KOORTS-DEUN

't Is triestig dat het regent in den herfst,
dat het moe regent in den herfst, daar buiten.
—En wat de bloemen wégen in den herfst;
—en de óude regen lekend langs de ruiten...

Zwaai-stil staan grauwe boomen in het grijs,
de goede sidder-boomen, ritsel-weenend;
—en 't is de wind, en 't is een lamme wijs
van kreun-gezang in snakke tonen stenend...

—Nu moest me komen de oude drentel-tred;
nu moest me 't oude vreê-beeldje gaan komen,
mijn grijs goed troost-moedertje om 't diepe bed
waar zich de warme koorts een lícht dierf droomen,
en 't wegend wee in leede tranen berst...

...'t Is triestig dat mijn droefheid tháns moest komen,
en loomen in 't atone van de boomen;
—'t Is triestig dat het regent in den herfst...

FEVER TUNE

It's sad that it rains in the Autumn,
And, out here, it rains every Autumn day.
Sad how flowers stoop in Autumn;
How the same rain leaks down the window-panes.

Bare trees stand motionless against the grey,
The cold trembling trees, rustling, crying;
But it's only the wind sings a tiresome tune,
A low moan of tones laments.

Soon it should come, the quickening step,
Soon it should come to me, my peaceful memory;
My mother, sweet comforting, round the sunken bed
Where the warm fever dared dream of a light
And the pressing pain burst in bitter tears.

It's sad that my sorrow should come now,
And dull in the languor of the trees;
It's sad that it rains in the Autumn.

(version by Tony Curtis)

DE RIEMEN, ZWAAR VAN WIER

De riemen, zwaar van wier, ter ruste; in zwoele dampen,
ten zomp'gen zoom der zee het plompe zeil gereefd;
—en over de' ootmoed van hun aangezicht, de lampe
die na der dagen kamp weêr d'avond-monkel weeft.

Zij zijn ten disch. De stille, vriendelijke spijzen;
de slaap van 't kind, die moede en blijde, 't ruim
doorweegt;
de linzen en de visch; de rozige radijzen;
en van hun vrouwe de aêm die hare borst beweegt.

Zij zullen vredig rusten gaan na dage-take,
de vrome zomer-nacht gedeeld in liefde en slaap...
Voor mij? De moede troostloosheid der looden wake,
en loomende eenzaamheid die timmert aan mijn slaap.

THE OARS HEAVY WITH SEAWEED

The oars, heavy with seaweed, at rest in humid mists;
The home-made sail folded at the edge of the ocean;
And over their unassuming faces, lamp-light
That after a day's work is the soul of evening.

They are eating. Food spicy with peace and friendship;
The child's sleepy happiness soothing the hold;
The lentils and the fish and the rose-pink radishes;
The mother's breasts rising and falling as she breathes.

They will rest in peace after the daily routine,
The sacrament of a summer's night's love and sleep...
For me? Depression that never lifts, insomnia,
Loneliness like a lead weight dragging me under.

(version by Michael Longley)

EENZAME NACHT

Uw oogen waren er niet,
Uw stem was zoo ver, zoo ver,
Het was een avond zonder lied,
Nacht zonder ster.

De stilte was zoo diep, zoo groot,
Boven en onder en overal,
Dat iedre windeval
Moest brengen dood.

Mijn ziel was als een bloem naar u
Grootopen,
Weerloos als doodschaduw
Ze had beslopen...

Hoe heb ik wreed verstaan
In één stil even
De pijn van te vergaan
Uit dit schoon leven.

LONELY NIGHT

Your eyes were not there,
Your voice so far, so far,
It was an evening without song,
Night without star.

The silence was so deep, so still,
Above, below and all around,
That each breeze
Brought a little death.

My soul was like a flower to you,
Wide open,
Helpless if death's hand
Crept up on her ...

In that quiet moment
I cruelly understood
The pain of passing
From this beautiful life.

(version by Tony Curtis)

DE NOORDZEE

De Noordzee doet zijn gore golven dreunen
En laat ze op 't strand in lange lijnen breken.
Zijn voorjaarswater marmren groene streken
En schuim en zwart waaronder schelpen kreunen.

Zie van 't balkon mij naar den einder leunen
Met ogen die sints lang zo wijd niet keken:
Een droom in 't hart is me eer ik 't wist ontweken
En 't oog wil buiten me op iets komends steunen.

Hoe ben ik altijd weer vervuld, verlaten:
Vervuld van liefde en hoop en schoon geloven;
Verlaten als mijn dromen mij begeven.

Maar dan komt, o Natuur, langs alle straten,
Uw kracht, uw groei, uw dreiging, uw beloven—
Hoe klopt mijn hart van nieuw, van eeuwig leven.

THE NORTH-SEA

The murky water of the North-Sea
Drones onto the beach in pounding waves.
It's a water streaked marble green,
With foam and oil under which shells groan.

See me stare from my balcony towards the horizon
With eyes that haven't looked so far for so long:
Not since the dream in my heart abandoned me
And my eyes looked outside to rest on something nearing.

How often I am filled or deserted:
Filled with love, hope, fantastic belief:
Deserted as my dreams forsake me.

But, O Nature, you come passing along all streets,
Your power, your growth, your threat, your promise —
How my heart pounds with new, with eternal life.

(version by Tony Curtis)

MOEDER

Mijn moederken, ik kan het niet verkroppen
dat gij gekromd, verdroogd zijt en versleten,
zoals een pop waarin een hart zou kloppen,
door 't volk bij 't heengaan in een huis vergeten.

Ik zie uw knoken door uw kaken steken
en diep uw ogen in het hoofd gedrongen.
En ik ben gans ontroerd en kan niet spreken,
wanneer gij zegt 'komt zit aan tafel jongen'.

Ik hoor u 's avonds aan de muren vragen
of gij de vensters wel hebt toegesloten.
Gij kunt den mist niet uit uw hersens jagen.
Uw lied is uit, gij kreunt de laatste noten.

Daar in de verte wordt een put gegraven;
ik hoor zo goed het ploffen van de kluiten.
En achter 't huis zie ik een schimme draven:
hij staat waarachtig reeds op haar te fluiten.

—Kom in, Mijnheer, ik stel u voor aan Moeder.
—Vrees niets, kindlief, al heeft hij naakte benen:
hij is een vriend, een goede vriend, een broeder:
hij is niet ruw, hij wandelt op de tenen.

Tot weerziens dan. Ik kom vannacht of morgen.
Gij kunt gerust een onze-vader lezen,
en zet uw muts wat recht. Hij zal wel zorgen
dat gij geen kou vat en tevreê zult wezen.

MOTHER

My mother, I cannot endure
That you are bent, dried up and worn,
Like a doll in which a heart should beat
Left in a house by the departing crowd.

I see your bones stick through your cheeks
And your eyes set deep in your head.
And I am deeply moved and cannot speak
When you say 'dinner's ready, dear'.

I hear you ask the walls at night
If you have closed the shutters.
You cannot chase the mist out of your mind.
Your song is finished, you groan the last notes.

There in the distance a pit's being dug;
I can clearly hear the thuds of the clods.
And behind the house I see a shadow trot:
In fact, he's already whistling for her.

— Come in, Sir, may I introduce my Mother.
— Fear not, dear child, despite his naked legs:
He is a friend, and good friend, a brother:
He is not rough, he walks on his toes.

See you, so. I'll come tonight or tomorrow.
You might as well read Our Lord's Prayer,
And straighten your cap. He will make sure
That you won't catch a cold and will be content.

(verson by Peter van de Kamp)

HET LEVEN

Ik stond toen in mijmerij
aan het scheemrende strand van de zee—
de wereld was achter mij,
en de zon zonk voor mij naar zee—
en tussen de zon en mij
zong de grote zang van de zee—

Er kwamen toen mannen aan
en zij maakten muziek in een rij—
er kwamen ook kinderen aan,
die dansten er huppelend bij—
en ik hoorde de maat van het lied,
die was niet droef en niet blij
want eentonige lach en verdriet
dansten er zij aan zij.

O, dat was de vreemde mineur
van het eeuwige scheemrende wee—
en blij met die droeve mineur
dansten de kinderen mee—
en langzaam verging alle kleur
want de zon zonk in de zee—

Toen stierf ook de melodij
en de dans in de schemering mee—

ineens leek het jaren voorbij
dat lied en die dans bij de zee—

o, mijn woelende mijmerij
bij het ruisen dier eeuwige vree—

en de wereld was achter mij
en de zon zonk weg in de zee—

en tussen haar graf en mij
zong de grote stem van de zee—

BEING

So it came in a dream I was bound
on the twilit sands by the sea.
The world was left behind
when the sun fell into the sea;
to that grave all light was bound,
to the great song of the sea.

And I watched three fates draw near
making music, wave on wave.
And I watched the children draw near
dancing, stave on stave.
And I heard the beat of the song;
chant not of triumph nor wrong;
alike danced laughter and grief,
both seed and tumbling leaf.

O, that was the strange under score,
eternal blessing and curse.
Borne by the swell of its choir
each child was turned to dance,
the light leached from the shore
with the sun's slow cadence.

But it came the melody died
on the twilit sands by the sea,

the children cast on the tide
the music entered history.

Forever I'm cursed to dive
into the blesséd restless sea,

the world to be thrown aside
when the sun falls into the sea,

the grave of light beat wide,
dark the huge voice of the sea.

(*version by Paula Meehan*)

IK, DIE GEBOREN BEN

Ik, die geboren ben
uit uwe schoot,
voel mij verkoren en
klaar tot uw dood.
't Eind van mijn zwerven zal
zijn als ik sterven zal
weer in uw schoot.

Maar is mijn zwerven niet
zingen naar u?
Is al mijn derven niet
winnen van u?
't Einde der dingen is
eeuwig. —Mijn zingen is
sterven in u.

DE NACHT

Door 't waaiend maanlicht is zij weergekomen.
Snel en geluidloos liet zij 't lang gewaad
vallen—ik zag heur haren langs 't gelaat
goudelend naar de blanke borsten stromen.
Wij hebben 't leven in dien nacht genomen
tot waar het duizlend in den dood vergaat,
en samen stervend bleven we in een staat
van dieper lust en siddrender betomen.

Tot zij, ontwaakt, nam haar gewaad, en liep
door de open deur naar buiten en heur haren

I WHO WAS BORN

I who was born
from your womb
consider myself chosen and
marked until you die.
The end of my wandering
will come with my dying
again in your womb.

But isn't my wandering
a singing for you?
Isn't all my losing
to win you?
The end of everything
lasts forever. My song is
a dying in you.

(version by Desmond Egan)

NIGHT VISIT

Next time she came when the moon was windblown.
So surely, so silently let fall her blue robe.
Her hair uncauled was a stream of beaten gold
Against the starry face of night. The window
Cast white light to her breasts. We drank Life, kindled
Such fires that jealous Death lured us to the wild zone
And on and harder we rode demented to that cold
Fascination, rode the night out till the spell dwindled

And she, awakened, got up and put on her clothes,
Walked straight out my door hauling the moon behind her.

woeien in 't laatste maanlicht goudlend uit.
Ik zag haar na—een haan kraaide, en zij riep
van ver lachende woorden, en die waren
als een hel wonder van licht en geluid.

ZWERVERSLIEFDE

Laten wij zacht zijn voor elkander, kind—
want o, de maatloze verlatenheden,
die over onze moegezworven leden
onder de sterren waaie' in de oude wind.

O, laten wij maar zacht zijn, en maar niet
het trotse hoge woord van liefde spreken,
want hoeveel harten moesten daarom breken
onder den wind in hulpeloos verdriet.

Wij zijn maar als de blaren in den wind
ritselend langs de zoom van oude wouden,
en alles is onzeker, en hoe zouden
wij weten wat alleen de wind weet, kind—

En laten wij omdat wij eenzaam zijn
nu onze hoofden bij elkander neigen,
en wijl wij same' in 't oude waaien zwijgen
binnen één laatste droom gemeenzaam zijn.

Veel liefde ging verloren in den wind,
en wat de wind wil zullen wij nooit weten;
en daarom—voor we elkander weer vergeten—
laten wij zacht zijn voor elkander, kind.

The cock crowed, the wind moved through her, the sun rose
Simply on the morning. I watched her go further.
She tossed back strange words and faded into the shadows:
Words of light and sound I set down now, bright wonders.

(*version by Paula Meehan*)

BEGGAR LOVE

Let us be tender to each other, dear
because desolation that is unlimited
would destroy these world-weary limbs
out under the stars, that time-old wind.

O let us be more tender and never again
mention that proud, intolerable word, love
because any hearts must be broken by it
into hopeless anguish where the wind blows.

We are just like leaves in that wind
rustling along the edge of an old wood
and everything is insecure and how could we
know what the wise wind knows, dear?

So, because we are both lonely let
your head lie beside mine
and while the ancient wind howls in anger
let us share in silence one last dream.

Much love has been lost in the wind
though what the wind wants we shall never know;
so before we forget each other
let us be tender to each other, dear.

(*version by Desmond Egan*)

1914–1940

HET LICHT

Het licht, Gods witte licht, breekt zich in kleuren:
Kleuren zijn daden van het licht dat breekt.
Het leven breekt zich in het bont gebeuren,
En mijn ziel breekt zich als ze woorden spreekt.

Slechts die zich sterven laat, kan 't leven beuren:
O zie mijn bloed dat langs de spijkers leekt!
Mijn raam is open, open zijn mijn deuren—
Hier is mijn hart, hier is mijn lichaam: breekt!

De grond is zacht van lente. Door de boomen
Weeft zich een waas van groen, en menschen komen
Wandelen langs de vijvers in het gras—

Naakt aan een paal geslagen door de koorden,
Ziel, die zichzelve brak in liefde en woorden:
Dit zijn de daden waar ik mensch voor was.

DE LAATSTE DAG

Ze grepen hem terwijl zijn vrienden sliepen
En het verraad kuste als een vriend zijn mond.
Rumoer was in de stad, en mannen liepen
Met toortsen in de donkre straten rond.

Een menigte drong op het plein: ze riepen:
'Kruis hem! Kruis hem!' —Hij, die gebonden stond
Voor het paleis, zag in hun oogen 't diepe
Geheim, waarvoor hem God ter wereld zond.

LIGHT

Light, God's white light, breaks up into colours:
Colours, the movements of light which dissolves.
Life itself breaks into multicoloured events
And my soul dissolves when I speak words.

Only the one who lets the self die can bear life:
Oh see my blood which drips down the nails!
My windows open, my doors open
Here's my heart, here's my body: let them break!

The ground softens with spring. Through the branches
A haze of greens weaves itself and people go by
Strolling beside the ponds, along gras...

Tied naked to a beam with cord,
My soul, which broke yourself into love and words:
These are the activities for which I became man.

(version by Desmond Egan)

LAST DAY

They seized him while his friends were asleep
And the traitor kissed his mouth like a friend.
There was an outcry in town and men walked
With torches round the dark streets.

A mob crowded into the square; they shouted
"Crucify him! Crucify him!" — The one who stood manacled
In front of the palace saw in their eyes that profound
Mystery, the reason why God had sent him into the world.

En naakt werd hij gekruisigd door soldaten,
De vrouwen weenden en de priesters praatten,
Er werd gedobbeld en veel wijn vermorst.

Het voorhang scheurde, dooden werden wakker,
Een man wierp zilver ten verdoemden akker.
Het is volbracht! —Zijn hoofd viel aan zijn borst.

DE TROUBADOUR

Die 's nachts romancen floot onder de linden
En 's middags scherzo's op de markt der dorpen,
Hij heeft zijn fluit in een fontein geworpen,
En wilde een moeielijker wijsheid vinden.

Hij heeft des nachts op een rivier gevaren,
Hij zag het zonlicht dat de straten kleurde—
En wist dat hij niet leefde, maar gebeurde,
Dat daden machtloos als seizoenen waren.

Hij was een reiziger, den dag lang droomend,
Zijn doel was naar een horizon gericht,
Hij voelde 't leven uit zijn hart weg-stroomend—

En zijn gelaat was bleek, en blonk van licht,
Als van den man die, uit de bergen komend,
God zag van aangezicht tot aangezicht.

And he was crucified naked by soldiers;
Women wept; priests gossiped;
Lots were cast and plenty of wine flowed.

The veil ripped; the dead were wakened up;
Someone flung silver at a cursed plot.
It is consummated! His head slumped onto his chest.

(version by Desmond Egan)

THE MUSICIAN

The one who played tunes, nights under the limetrees
And *scherzos* by day at village markets
Has thrown away his flute into a fountain
Wanting to discover some more profound wisdom.

He had gone sailing at night along the river,
Had noticed sunlight colouring the streets...
But knew that he was not living, only existing,
That his actions were as uncontrolled as the seasons.

A wanderer, dreaming all day long,
He had taken aim at the horizon
— But he felt life trickling from his heart

And his face looked pale, it shone with light
Like that of someone coming down from the mountain
Having seen God face to face.

(version by Desmond Egan)

DE SOLDAAT DIE JEZUS KRUISIGDE

Wij sloegen hem aan 't kruis. Zijn vingers grepen
Wild om den spijker toen 'k den hamer hief—
Maar hij zei zacht mijn naam en: 'Heb mij lief— '
En 't groot geheim had ik voorgoed begrepen.

Ik wrong een lach weg dat mijn tanden knarsten,
En werd een gek die bloed van liefde vroeg:
Ik had hem lief—en sloeg en sloeg en sloeg
Den spijker door zijn hand in 't hout dat barstte.

Nu, als een dwaas, een spijker door mijn hand,
Trek ik een visch—zijn naam, zijn monogram—
In ied'ren muur, in ied'ren balk of stam,
Of in mijn borst of, hurkend, in het zand,

En antwoord als de menschen mij wat vragen:
'Hij heeft een spijker door mijn hand geslagen.'

THE SOLDIER WHO CRUCIFIED JESUS

We hammered him to the cross. His fingers grabbed
Wildly at the nail as I lifted the hammer
His voice spoke my name gently then: "You have my love—"
And his deep secret struck me forever.

I wear a grin until my teeth clench
And have gone mad—I looked for blood from Love
I had loved him but struck and struck and struck
Through his hand a nail which split the timber.

Now like a madman, a nail in my own palm,
I trace a fish—his name, his sign—
On every wall, on every door, each tree
Or on my chest or, kneeling, on the sand,

Explaining to everyone who asks
"He has driven a nail through my hand."

(version by Desmond Egan)

DE DANSER

Onder mijn huid leeft een gevangen dier
Dat wild beweegt en zich naar buiten bijt,
Zijn donker bloed bonst, zijn gedrongen spier
Trilt in krampachtige gebondenheid.

Totdat zijn pijn als warmte door mij glijdt
En dwingt naar 't worden van gebaren wier
Beheerschte haast en vastgehouden zwier
Zijn vaart nog spannen eer hij zich bevrijdt.

Men moet gepoederd zijn, dat in 't gelaat
Alleen het zwart der openschroeiene oogen
Den waanzin van 't inwendig dier verraadt.

De mond moet, roodgeverfd en opgebogen,
Zoo god'lijk trots zijn, dat hij weten laat
Dat zich zijn breede lach heeft volgezogen.

DANCER

Under my skin there lives a caged beast
Which pads untamed within me, gnawing to get out
Its dark blood courses, its coiled muscle
Curbed, shivers in spasm

Until his anguish flows through me like something warm
and forces out those words which were held back
by frustrated haste and gesturing
—they hinder his speed further before he frees himself.

My face must be powdered that the violence,
the existence of the beast inside, be intimated
only by the blackness of its burnt-out eyes.

My mouth must be rouged and shaped
to show god-like pride, not revealing the disguise
or that the broad smile is sucked inwards by an animal.

(version by Desmond Egan)

AAN EEN GRAF

Vliegen en vlinders, kinderen en bijen,
al wat als stipjes vonkt door de natuur,
warm, blij en snel, moedertje, schoot van vuur,
daar hield je van, en zie, die bleven bij je.

Want als ik hier de diepe stilte intuur,
stijgt het zo glinsterend op, dat ik moet schreien,
en duizend lachjes, liedjes, mijmerijen,
tintelen uit het gras naar het azuur.

'k Sta aan je graf als jij eens aan mijn wieg.
Moeder, vrees niet dat ik bij dit verzonken
handjevol as mij om het vuur bedrieg.

Ik ween, als jij toen, om de vrije vonken,
de bij, het kind, de vlinder en de vlieg,
die in het licht van puur geluk verblonken.

AT A GRAVE

Flies and butterflies, children, bees,
all that glitters like a spark through nature
dear mother, womb of fire, warm and joyful and swift,
those whom you loved, whom you see have stayed with you.

For when I stare into the deep silence here
it swells, it dazzles so that I have to cry out
and a thousand laughs, songs, dreams
are shining from the grass here up into the sky.

I stand at your grave as you did once by my cot.
Mother, have no fear that because of this buried
handful of ashes I would reject the flame.

So I weep, like you, for the free sparks,
the bee, that child, butterfly and fly
who dissolved in the light of pure happiness.

(version by Desmond Egan)

NOCTURNE

De maan roeit brandend
langs 't wolkenrif,
en 't bosch is paars:
vergiftigd.—

Poel en half open pad
vol heete bramen,
fel en rond
in geur.

De vlakte, een fletse ruiker
en de lippen droog;
sterren vallen
als dauw.

Gestalten jagen woest:
saters in horden;
en hun grijze adem
is zichtbaar.

Nimfen, bloemwit
met groene haren,
vluchten in 't bosch,
hijgend.

In den nevel de syrinx
en op onzen mond,
week en dartel:
Pan's fluit.—

(voor Maurice van Yzer)

NOCTURN

The moon rows burning
  along the reef of clouds,
and the wood is purple:
        poisoned.—

Pool and half open path
  full of hot blackberries,
vivid and round
        in scent.

The plain, a faded bouquet
  and the lips dry;
stars fall
        like dew.

Shapes wildly chase:
  satyrs in hordes;
and their grey breath
        is visible.

Nymphs, flour-white
  with green hairs,
escape into the wood,
        panting.

In the mist the syrinx
  and on our mouths,
weak and skittish:
        Pan's pipes.—

            (for Maurice van Yzer)

DE TUSSENKOMST

Bij mijn tafel, toen de kamer donker werd, kwamen
uit de voortijden twee gedaanten staan, en zij
wezen op een kristal, roepende mij bij namen
van wind en licht: de dood rees als een maan in mij.

Maar ruisend kwam een derde en wees naar de rand wolken,
die in het gouden westerraam lagen gedoofd:
ik zag, en weedom om de puinen van de volken
zonk in mijn hart toen hij zijn hand legde op mijn hoofd.

KWATRIJN

aan sommige kunstminnaars,
om uit het hoofd te leren

In een warm huis het knus en goed te hebben;
den vloed der kunst tot vijver laten ebben,
waar men graag spelevaart... De kunstenaars?
vliegenplaag, goed voor armoes spinnewebben.

VISITATION

The room grew dark and at my work desk stood two spirits
come back from a time before words were written down.
They pointed to my crystal, their old voices uttered
my real name, made of wind, of light. The shining moon

waxed in me like death. A third spirit came then rustling,
pointed to clouds that would rob my window of gold.
And I knew: grief at the fate of nations, our suffering,
waned in my heart when she laid her hand on my head.

(version by Paula Meehan)

QUATRAIN

For certain art-lovers to learn off...

We're snug as a bug in a heated house.
Floods of art ebb towards a pond
Where one goes boating y'know. Artists?
Kiss-my-arse locusts. Webs poverty weaves.

(version by Sean Dunne)

KOUD LANDSCHAP.

Een late najaarsdag, sneeuw in de lucht,
belofte van veel sneeuw. Een lage wei
waar 't water blank om korte wilgen stond
tot aan de zwarte koppen. Vlokken vlogen
neer, neer, al sneller langs de naakte twijgen
en tegen 't witte water, wit en weg.
Zoo, wit en weg, zoo, schuinsaf door de takken
weinige, ruige vlokken op de vlucht,
als vagebonden in een wintersch bosch
't spoor bijster.

OUDE HUIZEN AAN DE KADE.

Zoo staren lichtschuwe uilen in de zon,
Zooals die grauwe huizengevels staren
en suffen door den dag als oude vogels.
Maar met den avond staan zij scherp van bek
en scherp van klauwen op de winterlucht,
die gelig vlakt in 't Westen, effen, koud.
Zeearenden, zoo zien zij over 't water
heel donkere, groote beesten.

COLD LANDSCAPE

Almost Winter, snow in the air,
The promise of more to come.
The low fields are flooded, water laps
Around willows touching their black heads.
Snow thickens along bare twigs,
Covering the white river, white and away.
White and away, slanting through deserted
Branches, flakes, put to flight,
Like vagabonds in a wintry forest
Who've lost their way.

(version by Tony Curtis)

OLD HOUSES ON THE QUAYS

As light-shy owls stare into the sun,
so these gray housefronts stare,
drowsing through the day like old birds.
But come the night, sharp of beak and claw,
they cleave the winter sky
which shrinks above the icy saffron plain.
Thus ospreys overshadow water,
dark, hulking beasts.

(version by Anne Kennedy)

VOORJAARSLANDSCHAP.

Nog stonden alle boomen zonder blad,
de eiken en de iepen en de beuken,
als grijze bossen op de grijze lucht
zoo waren, dicht en ruig hun breede kruinen
en leken op een rij van leege kooien,
uit warrig traliewerk gevlochten kooien,
in de effen grijzig-blanke voorjaarslucht
toen daar een vogel langsvloog, donkerzwart,
heel in de verte vloog hij traag en recht
langs al die boomen, als van kooi tot kooi.

SPRING LANDSCAPE

They stood so still the leafless trees,
The oak, the elm and the beech,
A grey forest against a grey sky —
Trees, wood webbed and twisted,
Appeared like rows of empty cages
Wrought from this tangle of branches —
And the pale sky only changes
When a blackbird flies by
Moving off into the distance
Past trees, as if past cages.

(version by Tony Curtis)

IK GROET U

Ik groet u, buurman, kameraad,
Ik groet u, orgelman, soldaat,
Besteller, boer en bedelaar,
Ik groet u, blinde vedelaar!

Ik groet de honden op de straat
En 't paard dat voor de broodkar gaat.

Ik ben als gij,—ook ik bemin
Een vrouw, een kind, wat aards gewin—
Gejaagd, gedeukt en toch nog even
Gebrand op dit onzalig leven.

DE VRIENDSCHAP VOOR EEN UITGELEZEN VROUW

De vriendschap voor een uitgelezen vrouw,
De vriendschap voor het eigen kind
En voor de makkers die te goeder trouw
Vereelte voeten warmen bij mijn schouw

De vriendschap voor mijn siamees die spint
Omdat ik zachtjes op zijn kopje krauw
En voor de verzen waar ik troost bij vind.

Een zoen, een hand, een perzik waar we in bijten,
Hoezeer bemin ik die realiteiten
Boven de heilsbeloften in de wind!

I GREET YOU

I greet you, friend and neighbour,
I greet you, organ-grinder, Major,
Postman, farmer and drifter,
I greet you, blind fiddler!

I greet the dogs in the road
And the breadman's horse dragging its load.

I am just like you—I also love
A woman, child, some worldly goods—
Flustered, dented, yet for a while
Still hell-bent on this woeful life.

(*version by Dennis O'Driscoll*)

FRIENDSHIP FOR A WOMAN OF GRACE

Friendship for a woman of grace,
Friendship for one's own young child
And for the pals who in good faith
Warm calloused feet at my fireplace

Friendship for my cat which purrs
Because I softly stroke its face
And for the solace brought by words

A kiss, a hand, a peach to squeeze,
How much I value such realities
Above airy promises of other worlds.

(*version by Dennis O'Driscoll*)

'K BEN BRAHMAN. MAAR WE ZITTEN ZONDER MEID

'k Ben Brahman. Maar we ziten zonder meid.
Ik doe in huis het een'ge, dat ik kan:
'k gooi mijn vuilwater weg en vul de kan;
maar 'k heb geen droogdoek; en ik mors altijd.

Zíj zegt, dat dat geen werk is voor een man.
En 'k voel me hulploos en vol zelfverwijt,
als zij mijn lang verwende onpraktischheid
verwent met wat ze toverde in de pan.

En steeds vereerde ik Hem, die zich ontvouwt
tot feeërie van wereld, kunst en weten:

als zij me geeft mijn bordje havermout,
en 'k zie, haar vingertoppen zijn gespleten,

dan voel ik éénzelfde adoratie branden
voor Zon, Bach, Kant, en haar vereelte handen.

NOG HOORBAAR, HEEL HEEL VER, IS DE AVONDTREIN

Nog hoorbaar, heel heel ver, is de avondtrein.—
Blauw naast groen korenveld een boer aan 't werk.
Hei. Boven bos de toren van een kerk.
Rust, overal; 't diepst op de spoorweglijn.

't Is of de vijf telegraafdraden zijn
een notenbalk; de sleutel—ginds, die berk;
de noten zwaluwen, zwart op 't rode zwerk;
de vlaggetjes hun staarten, lang en fijn.

I AM BRAHMAN

I am Brahman. But we're stuck for a maid.
I do the only housework that I can:
I throw out the dishwater, fill the can;
But I've no towel, and I spill always.

She says that this is no job for a man
And I feel helpless and full of remorse
When she indulges with her magic pan
My helplessness as par for the course.

And I for ever honoured Him, so great,
Enchanter of the world and art and wit:

When she pours the oatmeal on my plate
and I see that her fingertips are split

I feel the same adoration lingers
In me for Sun, Bach, Kant, and her callous fingers.

(version by Peter van de Kamp)

AUDIBLE STILL

Audible still, very very distant, is the night train—
Blue beside green cornfield, a farmer at work.
Heather. Above the wood the spire of a church.
Rest everywhere, deepest on the railway-track.

It's as if the five telegraph-wires are
A musical staff; the clef—yonder, that birch;
The notes swallows, black against the red welkin;
The flags their tails, long and delicate.

En Mendelssohnse melodieën zingen
op 't beukenpodium de gietelingen;
de nachtegaal vangt zijn nocturnes aan:

dat hij bij 't hoogtepunt van zijn gezangen
goed uit zal halen, komt herinn'rend hangen,
als scheef point-d'orgue, 't boogje van de maan.

KENT IEMAND DAT GEVOEL: 'T IS GEEN VERDRIET

Kent iemand dat gevoel: 't is geen verdriet,
't is geen geluk, geen menging van die beiden;
't hangt over je, om je, als wolken over heiden,
stil, hoog, licht, ernstig; ze bewegen niet.

Je voelt je kind en oud; je denken ziet
door alles, wat scheen je van God te scheiden.
't Is, of een punt tot cirkel gaat verwijden;
't is, of een cirkel punt wordt en verschiet.

Je denkt: Nooit was het anders; tot mijn Wezen
ben 'k al zo lang van sterflijkheid genezen.
Je weet: Niets kan mij deren; ik ben Hij.

Tot zekerheid je twijfel opgeheven,
zo hang je als eeuwig boven je eigen leven:
je ben de wolken en je bent de hei.

And Mendelssohn melodies are sung
On the beech-podium by the blackbirds;
The nightingale sets in his nocturns:

To ensure that at the climax of his songs
He will hit the high note, the arrow of the moon
Nestles itself as a reminder, a slanting organ point.

(version by Peter van de Kamp)

DOES ANYONE KNOW THIS FEELING

Does anyone know this feeling: it's not the blues,
It isn't bliss, no mixture of the two;
As clouds surround the heath, it just hangs over you,
High, quiet, light, sincere; they do not move.

You feel old and yet a child; your thoughts look through
To God from Whom all had always seemed to sever you.
It's as if a point is widening to a sphere;
As if a sphere becomes a point, then disappears.

You think: It was always thus; for my Essence
I've so long been cured from my mortality.
You know: Nothing can harm me; I am He.

You hang, your doubts stripped to certainty,
Above your own life, as in eternity:
You are the clouds and you are the heath.

(version by Peter van de Kamp)

MIJN BROER

Mijn broer, gij leedt
Een einde, waar geen mens van weet.
Vaak ligt gij naast mij, vaag, en ik
Begrijp het slecht, en tast en schrik.

De weg met iepen liept gij langs.
De vogels riepen laat. Iets bangs
Vervolgde ons beiden. Toch woudt gij
Alleen gaan door de woestenij.

Wij sliepen deze nacht weer saam.
Uw hart sloeg naast mij. 'k Sprak uw naam
En vroeg, waarheen gij gingt.
Het antwoord was:

'Te vreselijk om zich in te verdiepen.
Zie: 't gras
Ligt weder dicht met iepen
Omkringd'.

MY BROTHER

My brother, you suffered
An end, which is not known to any man.
Often you lie beside me, vaguely, and I
Can't understand, and touch and flinch.

You walked along the road with elms.
The birds cried late. Some fright
Pursued us both. Yet you would go
Alone through the wasteland.

This night we slept together again.
Your heart beat next to mine. I spoke your name
And asked where you had gone.
The answer was:

'Too awful to be engrossed in.
See: the grass
Lies once more close
Against encircling elms.'

(version by Peter van de Kamp)

X-BEELDEN

DOOR I. K. BONSET.

'k word doordrongen van de kamer waar de tram doorglijdt
ik heb 'n pet op
orgelklanken
van buitendoormijheen
vallen achter mij kapot
kleine scherven
BLIK BLIK BLIK
en glas
kleine zwarte fietsers
glijden en verdwijnen in mijn beeltenis
+ LICHT"
de ritsigzieke trilkruin van den boom
versnippert het buitenmij
tot bontgekleurd stof
de zwartewitte waterpalen
4 x HORIZONTAAL
ontelbare verticale palen
en ook de hooge
gekromde blauwe
RUIMTE
BEN IK

X-RAYS

BY I. K. BONSET.

I am irradiated by the room through which a tram runs
I have a cap on
organnotes
from outsideandthroughme
break behind me
minute splinters
BLIK BLIK BLIK
glass also
tiny black cyclists
cut through they disappear in my form
+ LIGHT^n
the quivering trembletop of tree
diffuse all outsideme
into coloured dust
blackwhite waterposts
HORIZONTAL x 4
innumerable standing poles
and along with that the high
curving blue
SPACE
IS ME

(version by Desmond Egan)

HERINNERING DER NACHTFONTEINEN

1.

in kleine metalen platen valt de maan op mijn gezicht
ranke morbide zwarte hoer danst de fox-trott der wiebelende
achterhoofden
Bloednaakt halflokaal met lijffragmenten
Ik   Gij   Groen-bruin
Wij   wit
Niets
de witte servetten snijden mij U alles in twee
electrische lampen branden schaamteloos in lichaamsdeelen
kijk kijk kijk
losse armen steken
losse handen grijpen
losse vingers kletteren
klitteren schitteren en verlichten
lol
paradijs der avondpadden
gedrongen-uitelkaar zijn deze figuren
phénomeen van pers en druk
Enorme Padde
„Welnu?"

gulzig en gemeenschappelijk eten wij deze dingen op
Vreten wij elkander
vreten messen schalen borden
vreten lampen tafels stoelen
vreten vrouwen mannen dingen
op.
vraatzucht der nachtfonteinen
ik groet u kleine blinde eeuwigheid

en drink met vasten kaken het groene bloed van god

REMEMBERING THE NIGHT FOUNTAINS

1.

in light metal coverings the moon falls on my face
a fat and morbid black whore dances the fox-trot of wobbling
heads
A halfroom naked as blood with bits of bodies

    I   **You**   **Green-brown**
      We   **white**
        Nothingness

the white serviettes dissect me you everyone and everything
electric bulbs light up shamelessly in parts of a body
watch watch watch

loose arms protrude
loose hands grip
loose fingers pitter
patter glitter and light-up

pleasure

paradise of the toads of evening
those figures are dragged out of one another
manifestations of pulling and dragging

An Enormous Toad

„What next?"

voracious and together we devour these things
Gobble-up one another
gobble-up knives dishes plates
gobble-up lamps tables chairs
gobble-up women men things
up.

       voraciousness of night fountains
small blind eternity I salute you

and drink with set jaws the green blood of god

(version by Desmond Egan)

DE SCHONE WERELD

Iedre morgen na het nachtlijk slapen
Ligt mijn wereld nieuw door mij geschapen.

Iedre dag heb ik haar weggegeven,
Telkens één dag meer van 't eigen leven.

Telkens een kortstondiger bewoner
Zie ik haar belanglozer, dus schoner.

Schoonst zal ze eenmaal zijn als ik ga scheiden
En de grenslijn wegvalt van ons beiden.

DE ZIEL EN DE LIEFDE

Zult gij mij ooit verlaten,
Duld dan dat ik mij wend—

"Mijn kind, er gaan geen straten
Die ge niet als mijne kent."

Gij zijt de dag, mijn koning!
Achter mij ligt de nacht.

"Ik ben de deur tot de woning,
Liefste! die u wacht."

THE BEAUTIFUL WORLD

Every morning after sleep
My world lies created anew.

Every day I give away,
Is another day of my own life.

And each time I shorten it,
I see it more giving, more beautiful.

It will be most beautiful once I die
And the threshold between us falls away.

(version by Tony Curtis)

THE SOUL AND LOVE

Should you ever forsake me,
Leave me then to change —

"My child, there are no ways
Familiar to you as mine."

You are the day, my king!
Behind me lies the night.

"I am the door to your dwelling,
My love! Which waits for you."

(version by Tony Curtis)

TRISTITIA ANTE

Op de besneeuwde hei:
de hoeve en de houtmijt zwart
en de donkre spar, sterk en geëtst
onder een ster, bewaaid en strak.

In het stalen maangeplas
ken ik de planten zonderling,
de stompe bijl en de gebroken pot
door het doorzichtig-helle ijs.

Eéns knaagt de kou tot op het been
en mijn eenzaamheid zoekt het schot
dat plots de horizon tot eeuwigheid rekt
op mijn rampzalige zwerftocht.

Tot wanneer ik het bos intreed
en de haas gemarteld vind,
onbewust en stijf
in zijn bloed op de sneeuw.

Er is niets dan hevig wit
in mij, en ik raak dat licht niet kwijt;
en er is niets zo smal en nauw
als het eigen lijf.

TRISTITIA ANTE

The farm and black wood-stack stand
With the hazy fir that's fixed
And etched beneath stars that shine
On moorland draped in snow.

I know strange plants that sprout
In the steel splash of the moon,
The damaged pot and blunt axe
Clarified in the glare of ice.

When cold cuts to the bone
On my doomed journey,
My solitude seeks the sight
Of horizons stretched to eternity

Until, in the forest, I find
A tortured hare
Out cold, stiff
Among bloodstains in the snow.

Nothing's in me only white,
This light there's no getting rid of,
And nothing is as small and narrow
As your own body.

(version by Sean Dunne)

HERFST

Het is een land van grijsaards na de zomer,
hier geeuwt de heide in haar gal van zonde;
het bruin der eiken heeft de geur der honden,
het dorp gloeit in zijn klokken van october.

De honig druipt vermoeid in aarden potten
waaraan de handen zich getroost verenen;
en eenzaam duurt 't gemaal der molenstenen,
't kasteel staat in zijn grachten te verrotten.

Sterfbedden blinken van het goud der vaderen,
't is avond en de zonen zien het wonder:
't geboortehuis dompelt in nevel onder
en jeugd en lief en 't àl zijn niet te naderen.

AUTUMN

A land of old codgers after the summer
Where heather yawns in its bile of sin.
Dog-scent lingers on the brown of oaks,
The village glows in October bells.

Jaded honey drips into fired pots
On which resigned hands join.
The lonely grind of millstones lasts,
The castle rots in its moat.

Deathbeds blink in the gold flash of parents,
Sons see the miracle at evening:
A birthplace immersed in mist
and everything—youth, love—out of reach.

(version by Sean Dunne)

LANDSCHAP

Kristalwegen schept de volle maan
in vorstnacht
In donkerte drijven straten wiggen van harde klaarten
hoeken scheiden steenkantscherp
kluisduisternis van duizellicht
Maanbomen vergaren en dragen
schaduwmythos
Begerend alle klaarte
verlangend alle maanstraalstraten
is de vijver
glad en eenzaam
heldere drager van het veelvoudig éne
        van het éne veelvoudige
licht

LANDSCAPE

The full moon creates a crystalpath
In frostnight
In darkness streets drive wedges of harsh clarity
Corners cut brick shapes
Secure the darkness from dazzling light
Moontrees gather and carry
Shadowmyth
Yearning for clarity
Wanting all paths of moonlight
Is the pond
Smooth and lonely
Carrier of many forms
   of the one form
Light.

(version by Tony Curtis)

ALPEJAGERSLIED

Voor E. du Perron

Een heer die de straat afdaalt
een heer die de straat opklimt
twee heren die dalen en klimmen
dat is de ene heer daalt
en de andere heer klimt
vlak vóór de winkel van Hinderickx en Winderickx
vlak vóór de winkel van Hinderickx en Winderickx van de beroemde
    hoedemakers
treffen zij elkaar
de ene heer neemt zijn hoge hoed in de rechterhand
de andere heer neemt zijn hoge hoed in de linkerhand
dan gaan de ene en de andere heer
de rechtse en de linkse de klimmende en de dalende
de rechtse die daalt
de linkse die klimt
dan gaan beide heren
elk met zijn hoge hoed zijn eigen hoge hoed zijn bloedeigen hoge hoed
elkaar voorbij
vlak vóór de deur
van de winkel
van Hinderickx en Winderickx
van de beroemde hoedemakers
dan zetten beide heren
de rechtse en de linkse de klimmende en de dalende
eenmaal elkaar voorbij
hun hoge hoeden weer op het hoofd
men versta mij wel
elk zet zijn eigen hoed op het eigen hoofd
dat is hun recht
dat is het recht van deze beide heren

SONG OF THE ALPINE HUNTER

to E. du Perron

A man goes down the street
a man goes up the street
two men strutting down and up
which is to say
one man is going down
and the other is going up
just at the shop of Hinderickx & Winderickx
just at the famous shop of Hinderickx & Winderickx gentlemen's
   hatters
one takes his high hat in his right hand
the other his high hat in his left hand
& first one & then the other
the right and the left one going down one going up
the right going down
the left going up
both of these gentlemen
each with his high hat his own his very own
stalks past the other
just at the door
of the shop
of Hinderickx & Winderickx
gentlemen's hatters
then both these gentlemen
the right and the left one going up one going down
once safely past each other
replaces high hat on head
don't get me wrong
each puts his hat on his own head
as is right and proper
as is the right of a proper gentleman

(version by Theo Dorgan)

HULDEGEDICHT AAN SINGER

Slinger
        Singer
                naaimasjien
Hoort
        Hoort
                Floris Jespers heeft een Singernaaimasjien gekocht
Wat
        Wat
jawel
        Jespers Singer naaimasjien
hoe zo
        jawel
                ik zeg het u
                Floris Jespers heeft een Singernaaimasjien gekocht
Waarom
        waardoor
                wat wil hij
Jawel
        hij zal
                hoe zo
                        Circulez
                                want
        SINGERS NAAIMASJIEN IS DE BESTE

de beste
        waarom
                hoe kan dat
                        wie weet
                                alles is schijn
Singer en Sint Augustinus
Genoveva van Brabant
                        bezit ook een Singer
                                die Jungfrau von Orleans

        Een Singer?
jawel

ODE TO SINGER

Swing
　　　Singer
　　　　　Sewingmachine
Hear
　　Hear
　　　　Floris Jespers has bought a Singersewingmachine
What
　　What
oh yes
　　　Jespers Singer sewing-machine
how come
　　　oh yes
　　　　　I'm tellling you
　　　　　Floris Jespers has bought a singersewingmachine
Wherefore
　　　whereby
　　　　　what does he want
Oh yes
　　　he will
　　　　　how come
　　　　　　　Circulez
　　　　　　　　'cause
SINGER'S SEWINGMACHINE IS THE BEST

the best
　　　wherefore
　　　　　how's that
　　　　　　who knows
　　　　　　　　nothing is real
Singer and Saint Augustine
Genoveva of Brabant
　　　　　also owns a Singer
　　　　　　　die Jungfrau von Orleans

A Singer?
oh yes

jawel jawel jawel ik zeg het u een Singer
versta-je geen nederlands mijnheer
Circulez
     Bitte auf Garderobe selbst zu achten
ik wil een naaimasjien
iedereen heeft recht op een naaimasjien
ik wil een Singer
iedereen een Singer
Singer
       zanger
             meesterzangers
                       Hans Sachs
heeft Hans Sachs geen Singernaaimasjien
waarom heeft Hans Sachs geen Singer
Hans Sachs heeft recht op een Singer
Hans Sachs moet een Singer hebben
Jawel
       dat is zijn recht
          Recht door zee
             Leve Hans Sachs
                Hans Sachs heeft gelijk
hij heeft recht op

SINGERS NAAIMASJIEN IS DE BESTE

alle mensen zijn gelijk voor Singer
Circulez
een Singer
Panem et Singerem

Panem et Singerem *Panem et Singerem* *Panem et Singerem*

et Singerem et Singerem

ik wil een Singer
wij willen een Singer
wij eisen een Singer
wat wij willen is ons recht
         ein fester Burg ist unser Gott

oh yes oh yes oh yes I'm telling you a Singer
don't you speak English Mister
Circulez
    Bitte auf Garderobe selbst zu achten
I want a sewingmachine
everyone has a right to a sewingmachine
I want a Singer
everyone a Singer
Singer
      singer
           mastersingers
                Hans Sachs
has Hans Sachs no Singermachine
why has Hans Sachs no Singer
Hans Sachs has a right to a Singer
Hans Sachs must have a Singer
Oh yes
      that is his right
      Right on
          Long live Hans Sachs
            Hans Sachs is right
he has a right to

SINGER'S SEWING MACHINE IS THE BEST

all men are equal to Singer
Circulez
a Singer
Panem et Singerem

Panem et Singerem   **Panem et Singerem**   *Panem et Singerem*

    et Singerem et Singerem

I want a Singer
we want a Singer
we demand a Singer
what we want is our right
      ein fester Burg ist unser Gott

Panem et Singerem *Panem et Singerem* *Panem et Singerem*

et Singerem et Singerem

Waarom
hoe zo
wat wil hij
wat zal hij
Salvation army
Bananas atque Panama
de man heeft gelijk
hij heeft gelijk
gelijk heeft hij jawel
jawel
jawel
waarom
wie zegt dat
waar is het bewijs
jawel *hij heeft gelijk*

Panem et Singerem *Panem et Singerem* *Panem et Singerem*

Singerem Singerem

SINGERS NAAIMASJIEN IS DE BESTE

Panem et Singerem   *Panem et Singerem*   *Panem et Singerem*

et Singerem et Singerem

Wherefore
        how come
                what does he want
                        what will he do
Salvation Army
Bananas atque Panama
        the man is right
        he is right
right he is oh yes
                oh yes
                        oh yes
                                wherefore
                                who says
                                where is the proof
                oh yes *he is right*

Panem et Singerem   *Panem et Singerem*   *Panem et Singerem*

Singerem et Singerem

SINGER'S SEWING MACHINE IS THE BEST

(version by Peter van de Kamp)

SOUVENIR

Schoon d'avond valt en tussen de beide grijze gevelrijen
het donker zwaar hangt als een klos en overdadig
ontsteekt geen hand het licht aan de lantaarnen

Zo wentelt plots aan d'ogen u het wonder van een vreemde stad
de grijze huizen van u dees' anders zo bekende stede

De zonnestralen sloegen hard aan d'aarde over dag
en uit het vuur van 't rosse loof persten zij die geur der aarde
daarop ons dulle zinnen de herrefst toewaarts matelik glijden

Dees' overdaad van zinnelike wondren van lichten en van geuren
is zó lauw en vol dat gij niet kunt begrijpen waarom
aan 't eind van deze dag
geen lach zich legt over uw brede mond
zoals een ree languit en lui zich aan een rotswand legt

SOUVENIR

It's nightfall and between two grey facades
A sumptuous darkness hangs heavy as a mill stone
But no hand kindles the flame in the street lights.

And so the marvel of a strange city rolls before you;
The dark houses of my city now unfamiliar to you....

All day the sun beat down upon the earth,
Its red leaves of flame squeezing from the land the scent
Which our numbed senses will carry into Autumn.

This abundance of sensuous marvels, fragrance and light,
So taken for granted. I can't gather why,
When the day draws to a close,
No smile lies upon your lips
As beautiful as a deer upon a rock.

(version by Tony Curtis)

IK BEN DE HAZEL-NOOT

Ik ben de hazel-noot.—Een bleeke, weeke made
bewoont mijn kamer, en die blind is, en die knaagt.
Ik ben die van mijn zaad een duisternis verzade.
En 'k word een leêgt', die klaagt noch vraagt.

'k Verlaat me-zelf; 'k lijd aan me-zelven ijle schade.
Ik ben 't aanhoudend maal, in een gesloten kring,
van eene domme, duldelooze, ondankb're made.
Maar raak' de vinger van een kind me, dat me rade:
hij hoort mijn holte; ik luid; ik zing.

I AM THE HAZEL-NUT

I am the hazel-nut. An anaemic worm
Inhabits my chamber, and blindly gnaws away.
I whose seed has digested the darkness of loam
Am turned into emptiness uncomplainingly.

I vacate my self, the victim of brain-damage,
The inexhaustible dinner—in a spellbound ring—
Of one gormless, ungrateful, tormenting maggot.
But the finger of a child who figures me out
Fathoms my hollowness. I resonate. I sing.

(version by Michael Longley)

DE ZIEKE MAN

Nadat de zieke man,
zowat vier jaren door,
door iedereen was verwend geweest,
door iedereen zacht behandeld
en zacht was aangesproken, en
gewassen en in bed gelegd,
gekrabd, in bed gelegd, geraden,
gestreeld, gelakseerd, in bed gelegd,
en iedereens zachte wil, vier jaren,
tot eigen heil had ondergaan—
daar sloot hij opééns
zijn kasten, laden, ramen, deuren;
en op de buitenkant van iedere deur
plakte hij een papier,
waarop hij had geschreven:
Iedereen kan verdampen.
Ik ook.

THE SICK MAN

After the worst part of four years
during which the sick man
had been pampered by everyone,
spoken to gently,
washed, put to bed,
scratched, put to bed,
counselled, stroked, purged
and tucked in tight,
and had, for his own good,
undergone—almost four years!—
all that gentleness—from everyone—
he suddenly shut them up,
his cupboards, drawers and doors,
and on the outside of all the doors
stuck a note on which he'd written:
Everyone can now get lost.
Myself included.

(*version by Pat Boran*)

COLUMBUS

Als een drieëenheid dreef zijn kleine vloot
Over het wijde, nooit bevaren water
Naar 't land dat hij verwachtte, aldoor later,
Maar vast, als aan 't eind van 't bestaan de dood.

Hij wist, zonder berichten en bewijzen,
Het nieuwe werelddeel te liggen aan
Een verre kim, en anders zou 't verrijzen
Tijdens zijn naadring, diep uit de oceaan.

Met door geen wrevel aangetast geduld
Werd iedren dag de afstand uitgerekend,
Op de nog leege kaarten aangeteekend,
En geen verwachting door de ruimt' vervuld.

Een enkel maal stond zijn gelaat verstoord,
Wanneer de kleine *Pinta* achterbleef
En hij des avonds in zijn dagboek schreef:
"Wind vast, 't volk ontevrêe, van land geen spoor."

Wanneer hij eenzaam zat in de kampanje
Kwamen soms oproerkreten doorgedrongen;
Hij vreesde dood noch leegte, alleen gedwongen
Terug te keeren naar 't gehate Spanje.

Toen eindlijk—op een ijle grijze lijn—
Vreemd slank geboomte als met pluimen wuifde,
En 't volk na lang bedwongen doodsangst juichte,
Stond hij gebukt door diep verborgen pijn.

't Wondend besef van wat hem had gedreven:
Niet het begeeren van schatrijke ontdekking,
't Verlangen voort te zeilen steeds; zijn leven
Wist hij nu doelloos, eindeloos van strekking.

COLUMBUS

His little fleet floated in a trio
Across the wide, unexplored waters,
After the country he was watching-for—always receding
But inevitable as death is at the end of life.

Without report or evidence, he knew
That the new world lay stretched along
Some far horizon and would emerge unexpectedly
At his approach, out of the profound ocean.

Patiently and without resentment
Distance was calculated by each day,
Recorded on a map still blank:
Hope unfulfilled in that emptiness.

Sometimes his face showed annoyance
When the little *Pinta* fell behind;
Evenings, he entered in his dairy:
'Wind favourable; crew uneasy; no sight of land.'

As he sat on his own in the stern
Cries of mutiny would sometimes seep out...
But it was not death nor the empty space that he dreaded,
It was going back to hateful Spain.

When at last—in a thin grey line—
Slender, alien trees tossed as if with plumes
And the men cheered out of a dread they had long hidden,
He was oppressed for a while by a deep-seated anguish

—The wounding discovery of what had been driving him on:
Not any greed to come upon riches
But a craving to keep sailing forever. Now he realised
His life was meaningless, aimless of any purpose.

Hij droeg een voorgevoel van ballingschap:
Na ongenade een lange kerkerstraf,
Bevlekte glorie en gebroken staf,
't Oud hoofd gebannen in een monnikskap;

Reeds vastbesloten, in dien eersten stond,
Op een klein schip met weinigen te vluchten;
Reddend in 't eeuwig wijken van de luchten
Een waan van ruim: *de wereld is niet rond.*

IN MIJN LEVEN...

In mijn leven, steeds uiteengerukt
Door de vlagen waar 'k aan blootsta,
Daar 'k niet kan hechten aan liefde en geluk
Die mij zullen drijven tot ik doodga,
Ontstaan soms plotsling enkle plekken
Van een stilte zoo onaangedaan,
Dat ik geloof in slaap te zijn gekomen
Bij de diepten waar geen onderstroomen
Meer door 't eeuwig stilstaand water gaan.

He had a premonition of exile,
Of a long term in jail after disgrace,
His reputation ruined, his staff broken
And his old head banished into a monk's hood...

And now he was determined—after that first moment—
To escape with some few on a little ship
And preserve through the endless recession of sky
An impression of space, a sense that *the earth is not round.*

(version by Desmond Egan)

WITHIN MY LIFE...

Within my life, which is continually torn
Because of those gusts to which I'm susceptible
(Since I can never achieve love and happiness)
And which will drive me on until I die—
At times there suddenly emerge traces
Of a silence so undisturbed
That I imagine I have moved into a sleep
In depths where there are no undercurrents
To move any more in water eternally still.

(version by Desmond Egan)

'PARADISE REGAINED'

De zon en de zee springen bliksemend open:
waaiers van vuur en zij;
langs blauwe bergen van den morgen
scheert de wind als een antilope
voorbij.

zwervende tussen fonteinen van licht
en langs de stralende pleinen van 't water,
voer ik een blonde vrouw aan mijn zij,
die zorgeloos zingt langs het eeuwige water

een held're, verruk'lijk-meeslepende wijs:

'het schip van den wind ligt gereed voor de reis,
de zon en de maan zijn sneeuwwitte rozen,
de morgen en nacht twee blauwe matrozen—
wij gaan terug naar 't Paradijs'.

HOLLAND

De hemel groots en grauw.
daaronder het geweldig laagland met de plassen;
bomen en molens, kerktorens en kassen,
verkaveld door de sloten, zilvergrauw.

dit is mijn land, mijn volk;
dit is de ruimte waarin ik wil klinken.
laat mij één avond in de plassen blinken
daarna mag ik verdampen als een wolk.

'PARADISE REGAINED'

The sun and the sea have erupted, sheet-lightning,
fans of fire and silk;
along the blue mountains of morning
the wind grazes like a gazelle.

I stroll between fountains of light,
around watery, radiant piazzas
with a fair-haired woman who is singing
in clear tones to the everlasting ocean

this lighthearted air that beguiles me:

'The ship of the wind lies ready for our journey,
the sun and the moon are snow-white roses,
morning and night are two blue sailors—
we shall return to Paradise'.

                        (*version by Michael Longley*)

HOLLAND

The sky overpowering, grey; beneath it
limitless lowland, a scattering of pools;
trees, windmills, greenhouses, steeples
mapped out by ditches that mirror the sky.

This is my land, these my people; this
the space I want to echo with my voice;
let me glimmer in pools for one evening,
then evaporate like mist or a cloud.

                        (*version by Michael Longley*)

HERINNERING AAN HOLLAND

Denkend aan Holland
zie ik brede rivieren
traag door oneindig
laagland gaan,
rijen ondenkbaar
ijle populieren
als hoge pluimen
aan den einder staan;
en in de geweldige
ruimte verzonken
de boerderijen
verspreid door het land,
boomgroepen, dorpen,
geknotte torens,
kerken en olmen
in een groots verband.

de lucht hangt er laag
en de zon wordt er langzaam
in grijze veelkleurige
dampen gesmoord,
en in alle gewesten
wordt de stem van het water
met zijn eeuwige rampen
gevreesd en gehoord.

MEMORY OF HOLLAND

Thinking of Holland
I picture broad rivers
meandering through
unending lowland:
rows of incredibly
lanky poplars, huge
plumes that linger
at the edge of the world;
in the astounding
distance smallholdings
that recede into space
throughout the country;
clumps of trees, townlands,
stumpy towers, churches
and elms that contribute
to the grand design;
a low sky, and the sun
smothering slowly
in mists, pearl-grey,
mother-of-pearl;
and in every county
the water's warning
of more catastrophes
heard and heeded.

(version by Michael Longley)

LANDSCHAP

In de weiden grazen
de vreedzame dieren;
de reigers zeilen
over blinkende meren,
de roerdompen staan
bij een donkere plas;
en in de uiterwaarden
galopperen de paarden
met golvende staarten
over golvend gras.

POLDERLAND

Ik loop door 't polderland
onder den hellen regen;
oneindig is het land,
oneindig zijn de wegen,

die naar de kimmen gaan;
in lage hemelstreken
heerst tussen zwarte kreken
het mistig licht der maan.

o, dertigstromenland,
het volk dat u bewoont
versombert in krakelen
die geld en God verdelen,
purper en doornenkroon.

oneindig is het land,
oneindig zijn de wegen
die naar de kimmen gaan;
ik loop den morgen tegen
in 't mistig licht der maan.

LANDSCAPE

Animals in the pastures
are grazing peacefully;
the herons hang-glide
above lakes that glisten;
the bitterns stand still
by a shadowy pool;
and in water-meadows
the horses are galloping
with wavy tails
over wavy grass.

(version by Michael Longley)

POLDERLAND

Brightness of rain wavering
Over the polderland.
Roads endlessly unravelling
To a painted horizon.
Polished streams blackening
Under a hesitant moon.

Ah, land streaming with waters
And disputes, your sombre people
Living between God and Mammon,
Suffering luxury,
Luxuriously suffering,
Saved and damned.

The rain-bright and endless
Roads that scar the polderland
Draw me into the horizon
That is moon-vague now
As I cross the threshold
Into the far morning.

(version by Seamus Deane)

POLDERLAND

Ik loop door 't polderland
onder den hellen regen;
oneindig is het land,
oneindig zijn de wegen,

die naar de kimmen gaan;
in lage hemelstreken
heerst tussen zwarte kreken
het mistig licht der maan.

o, dertigstromenland,
het volk dat u bewoont
versombert in krakelen
die geld en God verdelen,
purper en doornenkroon.

oneindig is het land,
oneindig zijn de wegen
die naar de kimmen gaan;
ik loop den morgen tegen
in 't mistig licht der maan.

POLDERLAND

I walk through the polders
beneath infernal showers,
a landscape without end,
without end the roadways

that reach the horizon;
against banks of darkness
the watery moonlight
daubs heaven's backdrop.

O land of thirty streams,
benighted sects have split
hairs about God, Mammon,
power, the crown of thorns.

A landscape without end,
without end the roadways
that reach the horizon;
I walk towards morning
in watery moonlight.

(*version by Michael Longley*)

AFVAART

Aan het roer dien avond stond het hart
en scheepte maan en bossen bij zich in
en zeilend over spiegeling
van al wat het geleden had
voer het met wind en schemering
om boeg en tuig voorbij de laatste stad.

OVER DE JABBOK

Toen ik het einde had bereikt
van mijn verdorvenheden,
stond God op uit het slijk,
en weende;
en ik stond naast Hem, ziende neder
op een verloren eeuwigheid.

En Hij zei: je had geen gelijk;
maar dat is nu voorbij, van heden
tot aan die andere eeuwigheid,
is maar één schrede.

DEPARTURE

The heart stood at the helm that night
And boarded moon and woods
And sailed across a mirroring
Of all that it had suffered
Cruising with wind and twilight
Round bow and rigging past the final town.

(version by Peter van de Kamp)

ACROSS THE JABBOK

When I had reached the base
of my depravities,
God rose up from the filth
in tears;
and I stood beside Him to survey
a lost eternity.

And He said: you were not right.
But that is past, from the present
to the next eternity
is one short stride.

(version by Dennis O'Driscoll)

GRAFSCHRIFT

Een naamloze in den drom der namelozen,
Aan de gelijken schijnbaar zeer gelijk,
Door geen vervoering stralend uitverkozen
Tot heersen in een onaantastbaar rijk—

Wie van die hem vergaten of verdroegen
Ontwaarden uit hun veilige bestek
De schaduw van twee vleugels, die hem joegen,
Den fellen klauw in zijn gebogen nek?

En nu, na het begeerde, het ontbeerde,
Na de onrust en het levenslang geduld:
Een steen, door 't groen gebarsten, en verweerde
Letters en cijfers, die de regen vult.

ZONDAG

De stilte, nu de klokken doven,
Wordt hoorbaar over zondags land
En dorpse woningen, waarboven
Een schelpenkleurge hemel spant.

De jeugd keert weer voor de' in gedachten
Verzonkene, die zich hervindt
Een warm van onbestemd verwachten,
In zondagsstilte eenzelvig kind.

En tussen toen en nu: 't verwarde
Bestaan, dat steeds zijn heil verdreef;
De scherpe dagen, waar de flarde
Van 't wonde hart aan hangen bleef.

WRITING ON A TOMBSTONE

Someone anonymous in the anonymous throng,
To those like himself he obviously had much in common;
Was never, through inspiration, transported into the light
To preside in unassailable authority.

And of those who forgot him or forgave, who
Could make out from a secure retreat
The shadow of these two wings which drove him on
Or the terrible claw in his bowed neck?

So now, after the longed-for, the lost,
After the unease, the patience of a lifetime:
One stone cracked by the overgrowth, and weathered
Letters, numbers which the rain fills.

(version by Desmond Egan)

SUNDAY

Silence, now the bells are still,
Can be heard over Sunday-country
And rural homes, over which
A shell-coloured heaven tightens.

One's youth comes back again to someone deep
In thought and he finds within
That warm feeling of a longing unspecified
In the lonely child of Sunday-silences.

And between then and today: that mixed-up
Existence which did away with his peace of mind;
Those thorny days to which the flitters
Of a wounded heart had clung.

Niet te verzoenen is het leven.
Ten einde is dit wellicht nog 't meest:
Te kunnen zeggen: het is even
Tussen twee stilten luid geweest.

KAMPERFOELIE

Ik had niet vaak meer aan dat huis gedacht,
Noch aan dien tuin. Dit alles is verleden.
Eindlijk raakt ieder ieder leed ontgleden
Al is het hart ook bijna omgebracht.

Vanwaar dan dat, terwijl 't ontembaar hart
Al lang naar andre, verdre dingen haakte,
Ik mij weer in 't voormalige wist verward,
Omdat ik aan den geur dacht, zwoel en lauw,
Die van de kamperfoelie zich losmaakte
Bij 't stijgen van den zomeravonddauw?

Life cannot be comprehended.
Maybe one's purpose is no more than this:
To be able to say it has for a while
Been noisy between the two silences.

(*version by Desmond Egan*)

HONEYSUCKLE

I didn't think about the house much,
Nor about the garden. All that is over.
Grief runs off, finally, this way and that
Even if the heart is nearly finished-off as well...
So although the resilient heart was now longing
For other unattainable things, why was it
That I discovered I was once again caught-up in the past—

Was it because I remembered the scent, heavy and warm,
That comes from honeysuckle around
Dewfall on a summer evening?

(*version by Desmond Egan*)

DE IDIOOT IN HET BAD

Met opgetrokken schouders, toegeknepen ogen,
haast dravend en vaak hakend in de mat,
lelijk en onbeholpen aan zusters arm gebogen,
gaat elke week de idioot naar 't bad.

De damp, die van het warme water slaat
maakt hem geruster: witte stoom...
en bij elk kledingstuk, dat van hem afgaat,
bevangt hem meer en meer een oud vertrouwde droom.

De zuster laat hem in het water glijden,
hij vouwt zijn dunne armen op zijn borst,
hij zucht, als bij het lessen van zijn eerste dorst
en om zijn mond gloort langzaamaan een groot verblijden.

Zijn zorgelijk gezicht is leeg en mooi geworden,
zijn dunne voeten staan rechtop als bleke bloemen,
zijn lange, bleke benen, die reeds licht verdorden
komen als berkenstammen door het groen opdoemen.

Hij is in dit groen water nog als ongeboren,
hij weet nog niet, dat sommige vruchten nimmer rijpen,
hij heeft de wijsheid van het lichaam niet verloren
en hoeft de dingen van de geest niet te begrijpen.

En elke keer, dat hij uit 't bad gehaald wordt,
en stevig met een handdoek drooggewreven
en in zijn stijve, harde kleren wordt gesjord
stribbelt hij tegen en dan huilt hij even.

En elke week wordt hij opnieuw geboren
en wreed gescheiden van het veilig water-leven,
en elke week is hem het lot beschoren
opnieuw een bange idioot te zijn gebleven.

THE IDIOT IN THE BATH

With hunched-up shoulders, eyes shut tight,
trotting almost and frequently entangled in the rug,
ugly and awkward, dangling from nurse's arm,
every week the idiot goes to the bath.

The vapour that exudes from the water
makes him more restful: white steam...
And with every garment that is taken from him,
he is seized more and more by an old familiar dream.

Nurse lets him glide in the water,
he folds his thin arms on his chest,
he sighs, as with the quenching of his first thirst
and round his mouth a great joy slowly gleams.

His worrisome face has become empty and beautiful
his thin feet stand upright like pale flowers,
his long, pale legs, which are already slightly withered
are looming up like birch trunks through the green.

He is in this green water still as if unborn,
he knows not yet that some fruits never ripen,
he hasn't lost the wisdom of the body
and doesn't need to understand the things of the mind.

And every time that he is taken out of the bath,
and rubbed dry hard with a towel
and is dragged into his stiff, hard clothes
he struggles and then he weeps a little.

And every week he is born again
and cruelly separated from the safe water-life,
and every week he is destined
once more to remain a frightened idiot.

(version by Peter van de Kamp)

POGROM

Is dat de maan, die naar het laatst kwartier gaat,
of een gelaat, omspeeld door walm en vlam?
Waar is Berlijn en waar de Grenadierstraat? *
—Wat deed de jongen, toen de bende kwam?

Is dat zijn schim, die daar voor de rivier staat,
is dit het water, dat hem tot zich nam,
is hier de Spree, en daar de Grenadierstraat?
—Het is de Amstel, het is Amsterdam.

Op 't Rembrandtplein gaan de lantarens branden.
Over de daken sproeit een lichtfontein.
—Ik druk mijn nagels dieper in mijn handen.

De Jodenbreestraat is een diep ravijn.
Een korte schreeuw weerkaatst tussen de wanden.
—Het is maar tien uur sporen naar Berlijn.

*De Grenadierstraat is een joodse winkelstraat in het
oosten van Berlijn.

POGROM

Is that the moon, nearing its final quarter,
or a face, surrounded by smoke and flame?
Where is Berlin and where Grenadierstreet?*
— What did the boy do, when the gang came?

Is this, by the river, his steadfast shadow?
is that the water, that took him,
is this the Spree, and that there Grenadierstreet?
— It is the Amstel, it is Amsterdam.

On Rembrandtplein the lanterns burn.
A fountain of light sprays over the rooftops.
— I sink my nails deeper in my hands.

Jodenbreestraat is a deep ravine.
A short scream resounds between the walls.
— It's but ten hours by train to Berlin.

(*Grenadierstreet is a Jewish shopping street in the
Eastern part of Berlin.)

(version by Mary O'Donnell)

1940–1960

DE LAATSTE BRIEF

De wereld scheen vol lichtere geluiden
en een soldaat sliep op zijn overjas.
Hij droomde lachend dat het vrede was
omdat er in zijn droom een klok ging luiden.

Er viel een vogel die geen vogel was
niet ver van hem tussen de warme kruiden.
En hij werd niet meer wakker want het gras
Werd rood, een ieder weet wat dat beduidde.

Het regende en woei. Toen herbegon
Achter de grijze lijn der horizon
Het bulderen—goedmoedig—der kanonnen.

Maar uit zijn jas, terwijl hij liggen bleef,
Bevrijdde zich het laatste wat hij schreef:
Liefste, de oorlog is nog niet begonnen.

THE LAST LETTER

The world was full of peaceful sounds,
As a soldier slept on his overcoat.
Smiling, he dreamt there was no war,
And in his dream a bell began to toll.

A bird flew down that was no bird,
Landed, not far from him, amongst
The herbs. He would never wake again,
The grass turned red with blood.

It rained. It blew. It began once more,
From behind grey lines on the horizon:
The kind-hearted thunder of cannons.

And while the soldier was lying there,
A letter fell from his coat, the last words
he wrote: My love, this war has not yet begun.

(*version by Tony Curtis*)

PINKSTEREN

Ontvang den vlam des Heren:
Hij heeft u rijp bevonden
om midden uit uw zonden
van Hem te profeteren.

En voel het blinde wonder
op uw tong preluderen:
gij kunt de taal schakeren
naar alle spraak en monden.

Onder het samenkomen
van klank en wezen moeten
zin en begrip verdwijnen;

onder het hete schijnen
van dit vuur Zijner dromen,
laat God Zich door u groeten.

PENTECOST

Eat the fire of the Lord:
He has deemed you ripe
in the midst of sin
to prophecy of Him.

And feel on your tongue
the blind wonder play;
your language can be harmonised
with any word of mouth.

When sound and being
blend together,
sense and meaning disappear:

under the scorching rays
of His visionary flame
God greets Himself through you.

(version by Dennis O'Driscoll)

TRINITEIT

God scherpt Zijn wet op deze steen,
die mijn bestaan geworden is.
Maar Jezus Christus geeft ons vis
en wijn tot Zijn gedachtenis.

Heeft Een van Beiden Zich vergist?
Wij zijn een duister fenomeen,
zolang niet in ons leven rijst
het licht van den Heiligen Geest.

Heilige Geest, kom in het vers,
waarin Gij Drieën, Een voor Een,
hetzelfde zijt en ik alleen
zingend van U de woorden ben.

Heilige Geest, vervul het vers
zo gans, dat er geen vezel is,
die niet van Uw belevenis
vibreert, als van de liefde vlees.

Moeder van Jezus is het vlees.
Zuster van Christus is het vers.
Vader, die in de hemelen zijt,
kome Uw koninkrijk.

TRINITY

The stone that God whets laws with
has become my own foundation.
But Jesus Christ bequeathes us fish
and wine to serve as testimony.

Has One of Either erred?
We are shady creatures
unless our lives can open out
to admit the Holy Spirit's light.

Holy Spirit, enter this verse
in which Ye Three, One by One,
are identical and—a solo voice—
I join with Thy words as I sing.

Holy Spirit, imbue this verse
so fully that every cell
throbs with your experience
the way flesh senses love.

Mother of Jesus is the flesh.
Sister of Christ is the verse.
Father, who art in Heaven,
may Thy Kingdom come.

(version by Dennis O'Driscoll)

INSTRUMENT

Die nacht stonden machines in het donker:
woorden werkten nooit ontgonnen taal,
en beelden bloeiden magistraal
op uit het suizelend ontvonken
van heel het neergelegde materiaal
der ziel, alles wat ging verloren:
haar naam, haar lichaam uitverkoren,
een kind, nog voor het was geboren,
verneveld, het werd allemaal
lied—ik bleef grondeloos en licht
liggen tegen het morgenlicht.

INSTRUMENT

That night machines stood in the dark:
Words worked language never reclaimed
And images flowered masterly
Out of the dizzying spark
Of all the material stretched down
In the soul, all that had gone:
Her body elect, her name,
A child that had faded
Before its birth, it all became
Song—I remained, lying down light
And bottomless against the morning-light.

(version by Peter van de Kamp)

DE CEDER

Ik heb een ceder in mijn tuin geplant,
gij kunt hem zien, gij schijnt het niet te willen.
Een binnenplaats, meesmuilt ge, sintels, schillen,
en schimmel die een blinde muur aanrandt,
er is geen boom, alleen een grauwe wand.
Hij is er, zeg ik, en mijn stem gaat trillen,
ik heb een ceder in mijn tuin geplant,
gij kunt hem zien, gij schijnt het niet te willen.

Ik wijs naar buiten, waar zijn ranke, prille
stam in het herfstlicht staat, onaangerand,
niet te benaderen voor noodlots grillen,
geen macht ter wereld kan het droombeeld drillen.
Ik heb een ceder in mijn tuin geplant.

THE CEDAR

I have planted a cedar in my garden;
you can see it, but you do not seem to want to.
A backyard, you snigger, cinders, peelings,
and fungus assaulting a blind wall;
there is no tree, just a grey partition.
It is there, I say, and my voice is trembling;
I have planted a cedar in my garden;
you can see it, but you don't seem to want to.

I point outside where its slender, young stem
stands in the autumn light, unassaulted,
not approachable by fancies of fate;
no power in the world can drill this dream vision.
I have planted a cedar in my garden.

(version by Peter van de Kamp)

DE ACHTTIEN DODEN

Een cel is maar twee meter lang
en nauw twee meter breed,
wat kleiner nog is het stuk grond,
dat ik nu nog niet weet,
maar waar ik naamloos rusten zal,
mijn makkers bovendien,
wij waren achttien in getal,
geen zal de avond zien.

O lieflijkheid van lucht en land
van Hollands vrije kust—
ééns door de vijand overmand
vond ik geen uur meer rust;
wat kan een man, oprecht en trouw
nog doen in zulk een tijd?
Hij kust zijn kind, hij kust zijn vrouw
en strijdt de ijdele strijd.

Ik wist de taak die ik begon
een taak van moeiten zwaar,
maar 't hart dat het niet laten kon
schuwt nimmer het gevaar;
het weet hoe eenmaal in dit land
de vrijheid werd geëerd,
voordat een vloekb're schennershand
het anders heeft begeerd,

voordat die eden breekt en bralt
het misselijk stuk bestond
en Hollands landen binnenvalt
en brandschat zijne grond,
voordat die aanspraak maakt op eer
en zulk germaans gerief,
ons land dwong onder zijn beheer
en plunderde als een dief.

THE EIGHTEEN DEAD

A cell is but two metres long
and scarce two metres wide,
but smaller still is the plot of ground
that I have yet to know,
but where I yet shall nameless rest,
my comrades too,
eighteen men were we in all,
and none shall see the evening.

O loveliness of light and land,
of Netherlands' free coast,
once ravished by the enemy,
I knew no hour of rest.
What can a man, upright and true,
still do in such a time?
He kisses his child, he kisses his wife
and fights a futile fight.

I knew the task that I had begun,
a task of cursed strife,
but a heart that never could resist,
has never shied from danger;
knowing how once in this land,
freedom was applauded,
before a cursed rapist's hand
secured it otherwise.

Before he who blusters and breaks oaths
had the gall to do this deed,
and captured Holland's territories,
and violated his soil;
before he who claims such honour,
such German expedience,
forced our people within his thrall,
and plundered like a thief.

De rattenvanger van Berlijn
pijpt nu zijn melodie;
zo waar als ik straks dood zal zijn,
de liefste niet meer zie
en niet meer breken zal het brood
noch slapen mag met haar—
verwerp al wat hij biedt of bood,
de sluwe vogelaar.

Gedenkt, die deze woorden leest,
mijn makkers in de nood
en die hen nastaan 't allermeest
in hunne rampspoed groot,
zoals ook wij hebben gedacht
aan eigen land en volk,
er komt een dag na elke nacht,
voorbij trekt ied're wolk.

Ik zie hoe 't eerste morgenlicht
door 't hoge venster draalt—
mijn God, maak mij het sterven licht,
en zo ik heb gefaald,
gelijk een elk wel falen kan,
schenk mij dan Uw genâ,
opdat ik heenga als een man
als ik voor de lopen sta.

The vermin-catcher of Berlin
now pipes his melody,—
and certain as I will soon be dead,
my dearest no more will see,
and will not break bread
nor sleep with her—
reject all that he proposes—
that legerdemain encroacher.

Commemorate, who reads these words,
my comrades in such need,
and those dearest ones remember most,
in great adversity,
as we have done
of our own land and folk—
day dawns in the wake of night,
and every cloud drifts by.

I see how the early morning light
cuts through the lofty grid.
My God, that my dying may be slight—
for finally I have fallen
just as anyone can fall.
Confer on me your mercy,
that I go hither as a man,
when I stand before the guns.

(version by Mary O'Donnell)

NA DE BEVRIJDING

I

Schoon en stralend is, gelijk toen, het voorjaar,
Koud des morgens, maar als de dagen verder
Opengaan, is de eeuwige lucht een wonder
Voor de geredden.

In 't doorzichtig waas over al de brake
Landen ploegen weder de trage paarden
Als altijd, wijl nog de nabije verten
Dreunen van oorlog.

Dit beleefd te hebben, dit heellijfs uit te
Mogen spreken, ieder ontwaken weer te
Weten: heen is, en nu voorgoed, de welhaast
Duldloze knechtschap—

Waard is het, vijf jaren gesmacht te hebben,
Nu opstandig, dan weer gelaten, en niet
Eén van de ongeborenen zal de vrijheid
Ooit zo beseffen.

II

Regelmaat der kerende getijden!
Wat is 't hart, dat het ooit heeft gevreesd,
Schoon het wist, dat lente 't kwam bevrijden,
Stralend als zij altijd is geweest.

Alomtegenwoordig, onverstoorbaar
Is het leven, dat den dood ontbloeit,
En de kleinste klacht schijnt nauwlijks oorbaar,
Waar de rogge om de ruïnes groeit.

AFTER LIBERATION

I

Sheer, bright-shining spring, spring as it used to be,
Cold in the morning, but as broad daylight
Swings open, the everlasting sky
Is a marvel to survivors.

In a pearly clarity that bathes the fields
Things as they were come back; slow horses
Plough the fallow, war rumbles away
In the near distance.

To have lived it through and now be free to give
Utterance, body and soul—to wake and know
Every time that it's gone and gone for good, the thing
That nearly broke you—

Is worth it all, the five years on the rack,
The fighting back, the being resigned, and not
One of the unborn will appreciate
Freedom like this ever.

II

Turning tides, their regularities!
What is the heart, that it ever was afraid,
Knowing as it must know spring's release,
Shining heart, heart constant as a tide.

Omnipresent, imperturbable
Is life that death springs from.
And complaint is wrong, the slightest complaint at all,
Now that the waving rye crop skirts the ruins.

(version by Seamus Heaney)

DE DAPPERSTRAAT

Natuur is voor tevredenen of legen.
En dan: wat is natuur nog in dit land?
Een stukje bos, ter grootte van een krant,
Een heuvel met wat villaatjes ertegen.

Geef mij de grauwe, stedelijke wegen,
De' in kaden vastgeklonken waterkant,
De wolken, nooit zo schoon dan als ze, omrand
Door zolderramen, langs de lucht bewegen.

Alles is veel voor wie niet veel verwacht.
Het leven houdt zijn wonderen verborgen
Tot het ze, opeens, toont in hun hogen staat.

Dit heb ik bij mijzelven overdacht,
Verregend, op een miezerigen morgen,
Domweg gelukkig, in de Dapperstraat.

DAPPER STREET

Nature is only for the smug or the empty.
And anyway: what *is* nature any longer in this country?
A little wood the size of a newspaper,
A hill with cottages on it.

Give me a grey, city road,
A waterfront riveted with quays,
Clouds, never so beautiful as when, framed
Through attic windows, they move along the sky.

Everything is rich for the one who doesn't expect richness.
Life keeps hidden her wonders
Until suddenly she reveals them at their very best.

I realized this by myself,
Rainsoaked, one drizzly morning,
Utterly happy in Dapper Street.

(version by Desmond Egan)

VERWACHTING

Weet gij het ook de ganse nacht?
De vogels komen. Aan een geuren
—van wind, van water?—valt te speuren
hoe 't lage land een komst verwacht.

Mórgen het teken aan de lucht
—een frons, een lijn, een krimpend wolken—
en dan, bui van geluid, een vlucht
die dalen gaat: de vogelvolken.

En wéér staan in verwondering
wij tussen dit gevleugeld sneeuwen;
morgen—dan zijn wij, lieveling,
het eerste paar van duizend eeuwen.

THE BURIED BIRDS

Are the cliffs of your dream the colour of dawn?
Birds cluster. From the day the waves
tip back their heads, the sea can smell
how the flat road shapes to re-see them.

The sky gives no impression of height,
but a finger half-points, a private cloud
bleaches out, then loudspeakers, engines snarl
back into the feel of weather: the lives of birds.

We are whipped from our own hardened bodies
to breathe all the moments of the past,
brought together like two baptismal words,
the millenium clinging to our feet.

(version by Medbh McGuckian)

EXPECTATION

Did you know it too all night long?
The birds are coming. From the scent
—of wind, of water—one can sense
how the low lands expect an advent.

Tomorrow the sign against the sky
—a frown, a line, a shrinking of clouds—
and then, shower of sound, a flight
beginning its descent: the bird-crowds.

And once more in amazement
we stand among this winged snowing;
tomorrow—then we will be, darling,
the first couple of a thousand ages.

(version by Peter van de Kamp)

BLOEMEN

Als alle mensen eensklaps bloemen waren
zouden zij grote bloemen zijn met lange snorren.
Vermagerde vliegen, dode torren
zouden blijven haken in hun haren.
Tandestokers, steelsgewijs ontsproten,
zouden zwellen tot gedraaide tafelpoten,
katoenen knoppen zouden openscheuren
tot pluchen harten die naar franje geuren,

en op de bergen zouden gipsen zuilen staan
die gipsen druiven huilen.

Op het water dreven bordkartonnen blaren,
de vlinders vielen uit elkaar tot losse vlerken
en van geur verdorden alle perken
als alle mensen eensklaps bloemen waren.

REGENRATIE

Ieder gedicht
dat ik schrijf
is het laatste
is mijn dood.

Dan smelt mijn gezicht
bijzonder groot
uit in mijn lijf
in mijn schoot.

Als ik wegloop
mors ik een hoop
dode manen
en kruip-organen,

FLOWERS

If everyone decided to be flowers
they'd be big ones with long moustaches.
Expiring flies, already dead beetles,
would be snatched into their hair.
Toothpicks, stalks gone to seed,
would rumble into twisted table legs,
cotton buds would quake open
into velvet hearts smelling of fringes,

and up there on the mountain plaster columns
would be weeping with plaster grapes.

On the stream cardboard leaves would float,
the butterflies would plunge apart into loose wings
and with the perfume all flowerbeds would wilt
if people, say, wake up to being flowers.

(version by James Liddy)

REGENERATION

Every poem
that comes
is the end
is the last.

Then my face
melts down out of scale
into my body
on my lap.

When I drift off
I spill a mound
of dead mane
and crawling organs.

en ikzelf dool,
zo dun dan
zo fijn van vrees
als een Chinees
symbool
voor 'man',

(één lijn
voor gebaar,
en één voor voet,
waaruit bij mij
nog wat inkt bloedt)

heen.

Schaamte: het oor
groeit het eerst weer aan,
spitst, st: leest iemand dit voor
Dan zwelgt een oogbal,
ontluikt en tuurt: weent iemand al?
En dan spruit bang mijn ellendige
bonzende inwendige uit.

Om zich te bevredigen
staat daar dan
vlak achter de lezende
een geheel volledige
dodelijk vrezende
Vroman.

As I drift
slender now
fear-refined
a Chinese
symbol
of "man".

(A line
for gesture
another for foot
from which
ink bleeds)

Shame: the ear

grows back first
cocks: sh: maybe somebody is reciting this.
Then an eyeball swells
looks out checks:
are there tears?
And then miserably
my scratching inside
squirts out.

To placate himself:
behind the reader
looms a fully complete
worried paranoid
Vroman

(version by James Liddy)

EEN KLEIN DRAADJE

Met dat hoofd gebeurt nog eens wat.
Het gelaat ligt me al te plat
op de vette hersenkast.
Er gebeurt vast wat.

O, als ooit dit peinskistje splijt
als een vrij eetbare brij
verschijnt dan dit brein van mij
en bevlekt met gedachten de grond
maar de dood verzegelt mijn mond,
en minder dood dan wel veilig
sterft het schijnheilig.

Door de dood word ik graag overmand.
Ik vrees meer mijn gezond verstand.

Ik vrees dat leger van spinnen-
-de zenuwcellen daarbinnen.

Dat vreselijk web vol webben
kan ik eigenlijk niet goed hebben.

Wat zou er b.v. gebeuren
als twee draadjes zouden scheuren
en contact maken met elkaar
onzichtbaar, diep onder mijn haar,
terwijl ik uitwendig zo
maar in een winkel bezig ben
groenten en vlees te ko-
-pen...

Er knetteren geen vlammen en vonken.
Iemand zegt: is hij dronken?

Opeens zit ik voor ons huis op de stoep
met zesduizend blikken soep.
En zegt mijn tedere vrouw:

THIN WIRE

Something is bound to happen yet to my head.
The face lies all too flat on me
on its fat brainbox.
Something will happen for certain.

If ever, O, this thought-box should split
it's as quite edible stuff
that this brain of mine will appear
and splatter to the ground with thought
—but no, death will close my mouth
and not so much dead as innocuous
it will pass-away in mock-holiness!

I'm resigned to being bested by death—
it's my sanity I fear-for.

I'm afraid of this host of spiders
—the nerve-cells inside...

No, I just can't face
the terrifying web of webs.

What, e.g., might happen
if two of the wires should split
and make contact with each other
unseen, deep under my hair
even as I appear
to be in some shop buying
meat and vege-
tables...?

(No flames crackle, no sparks.)
Someone wonders: Is he drunk?

And suddenly I'm on the doorstep in front of our house
with six thousand cans of soup.

lieverd, wat doe je nou?
dan zeg ik: nu gaan we eten,
o nee, ik ben de soep vergeten.

Gebeurt het onder het dichten,
wie purp publiek dan inlichten
dat dit geen genialiteit
maar een purpje los is, of kwijt?

Een draadje dat de stroom opslurpt
van murp gedachtengurpt.

En kurpsluiting leidt tot brurp—
Brarp! Hurp! Hurp!

While my dear wife asks:
What are you up-to now, darling?
And I reply: Now we're going to eat...
—Oh no! I've forgotten the soup.

Or it might happen while I'm writing poetry
—who *purp* enlighten the public
that no this is not genius
but only loose or stray *purpage*?

So a wire which carries the current
of murpy gurps of thought...

And what if shurp circuit should lead to brurp—
Brarp! Hurp! Hurp!

(*version by Desmond Egan*)

SAMEN RIMPELEN

Dom de liefde die de huid bespiedt
en de veelbronnigheid eronder niet,
die taal der welvingen, wier warm verlangen
stom als van monden door glad vel vervangen
door de ontledingskunstenaar krom wordt geuit
welke bang binnentuurt, door een omvleesde ruit.

En wel de man, zijn schat in liefde tellend,
haar binnen zijn gedachten zacht ontvellend;
wel de man wiens hand met kennis ligt
op haar serratus, haar quitaalgewricht.

Tot zijn schier slapende, verwarmde oor
klinkt haar inwendig weerbare veelstemmig door.

Het bloed, van dicht- en van dichtbijheid zwart
wervelend om de taaie witte kleppen van haar hart;
lucht stoeiend in haar zachte alveolen,
ja, witte cellen die van wee tot weefsel dolen;

haar voor haar die uit haar schedel rijst
buigt voor hem, geurt en vergrijst.

Hem is het schrompelen van haar opperhuid
lief als een leren zak waaruit
voor heerlijkheden is betaald
met haar volgroeide buit.
Als laatste wat hij te voorschijn haalt
vindt hij de huiver die haar eens ontlook.
want plooien is ontplooien ook.

En hij—zijn spiegel vult zich met blij, droog
land van wratten, rimpels en een wittig oog.

Zijn lijf, doorkolkt met cellenmist,
nu troebel tot aan de mond,
wil tot één slok aaneengewist
weg in de grond.

WRINKLING TOGETHER

Love is foolish which studies the skin
and not the fecundity within,
that language of curves, whose warm issue
is dumb as mouths replaced by seamless tissue
clumsily rendered with artistic legerdemaine
viewed anxiously, through a fleshed-in pane.

Who but the man, counting love's treasure,
softly denuding her in his thoughts;
the man whose hand knowingly takes her measure
limning her quittal joint, her serratus.

In his dream-snug ear repeatedly
he hears her resolute polyphony.

The clabbered blood, viscous, dark
whirling through the tough white valves of her heart;
air romping in her pliant alveoli,
yes, white cells wandering from sac to sigh;

every single hair which rises from her skull
bows to him, allures him and goes dull.

However unsightly the shriveling of her skin
he loves it like a leather purse
out of which he has been deeply reimbursed
for pleasures dearly bought yet still delicious.
The last thing he unearths
is the first quiver of her bud,
for folding is unfolding too.

And he, his mirror fills up with the easy dry
land of warts, wrinkles and a bleary eye.

His body, swirling with cell-mist,
clouded up to the mouth,
wants to be swallowed up in one big sip
and spewed into the ground.

(version by Anne Kennedy)

SOTTO VOCE

Zoveel soorten van verdriet,
ik noem ze niet.
Maar één, het afstand doen en scheiden.
En niet het snijden doet zo'n pijn,
maar het afgesneden zijn.

Nog is het mooi, 't geraamte van een blad,
vlinderlicht rustend op de aarde,
alleen nog maar zijn wezen waard.
Maar tussen de aderen van het lijden
niets meer om u mee te verblijden:
mazen van uw afwezigheid,
bijeengehouden door wat pijn
en groter wordend met de tijd.

Arm en beschaamd zo arm te zijn.

SOTTO VOCE

So many kinds of sadness
I won't name them.
But one, the parting and separating.
And it's not the cutting that hurts
but to be cut off.

Still it is pretty, the skeleton of a leaf,
butterfly-light resting on the earth,
only worth its being.
But between the veins of suffering
nothing more to please you with:
meshes of your absence
kept together through some pain
and growing bigger with time.

Poor and ashamed to be so poor.

(version by Peter van de Kamp)

OP EEN PAAR UREN

om wat muziek
te maken heb ik
zoveel gedaan
gedaan en vergeten—

om mijn verlangen
te bevruchten heb ik
zoveel steden gemaakt
gemaakt en gebroken—

om mijn dagen in
een vuur van wanhoop
te verbranden ben
ik ziek geweest

er is een smaak
van herfst in de bomen
zeggen de oude
dichters

er hangt een kleur
van honger boven
de huizen klagen
de dames

in een bouwdoos woon
ik als een kind overal
vingers vermoedend,
duister en kussen.

ODE: IN A FEW HOURS

To make a bit of music
I've done so much
done and forgotten —

to make pregnant my desire
I've built city after city
raised up and razed —

to scorch my days
at the flames of despair
I've fallen sick

the trees
smack of autumn
say the old poets

hanging over the houses
the colour of hunger
complain the ladies

I live like a child
in a kit
for building

everywhere suspecting
fingers
darkness and kisses.

(version by Eamon Grennan)

DE BUIGZAAMHEID VAN

HET VERDRIET

hoe liefelijk is de russische dame
en luister naar wat zij zegt:

ik ben maar een gewone dame
geen dame van het russische hof

ik heb lang aan slapeloosheid geleden
maar gelukkig dat is nu voorbij

mijn geliefkoosde voedsel is slakken
mijn geliefkoosde man een matroos

's nachts kijk ik graag naar de sterren
en gelukkig gaan we nog dood

als de wereld één enkel bed was
dan bleef ik er altijd in

hoe liefelijk is de russische dame
en luister naar wat zij zegt.

DISTRESS,

ITS PLIANCY

How lovely the Russian lady
And listen, listen to what she says:

I'm only a common or garden lady
Nothing like a Russian duchess

Never a wink of sleep for ages
But praises be that's in the past

The food I love most of all is snails
The man I love most of all's a sailor

At night I love to watch the stars
And praises be there's death in store

If all the world were a single bed
I'd stay in it forever

How lovely the Russian lady
And listen, listen to what she says.

(*version by Eamon Grennan*)

BOMMEN

De stad is stil.
De straten
hebben zich verbreed.
Kangeroes kijken door de venstergaten.
Een vrouw passeert.
De echo raapt gehaast
haar stappen op.

De stad is stil.
Een kat rolt stijf van het kozijn.
Het licht is als een blok verplaatst.
Geruisloos vallen drie vier bommen op het plein
en drie vier huizen hijsen traag
hun rode vlag.

FEBRUARIZON

Weer gaat de wereld als een meisjeskamer open
het straatgebeuren zeilt uit witte verten aan
arbeiders bouwen met aluinen handen aan
een raamloos huis van trappen en piano's.
De populieren werpen met een schoolse nijging
elkaar een bal vol vogelstemmen toe
en héél hoog schildert een onzichtbaar vliegtuig
helblauwe bloemen op helblauwe zijde.

De zon speelt aan mijn voeten als een ernstig kind.
Ik draag het donzen masker van
de eerste lentewind.

BOMBING

The town is still.
The streets
have expanded.
Kangaroos peek through the windows.
A woman passes.
The echo hastily
picks up her footsteps.

The town is still.
A cat rolls stiffly from the sill.
Light is replaced like a block.
Three four bombs fall soundlessly on the square
and three four houses slowly
hoist their red flag.

(version by Mary O'Donnell)

FEBRUARY SUN

Again the world opens up like a girl's room
street happenings drift in from white expanses
workers with alum hands
build a windowless house of stairs and pianos.
With schoolish inclination the poplars throw
a ball full of bird voices to one another
and way up an invisible plane draws
bright blue flowers on bright blue silk.

Like a serious child the sun plays at my feet.
I bear the fluffed mask
of the first spring wind.

(version by Mary O'Donnell)

VERS PER 7 JUNI '51

Bedoel je Josje met de kleine ogen?
Nee, met de grote.
Bedoel je Josje met de schelle stem?
Nee, met de mooie.
Bedoel je Josje met het haar dat naar niets ruikt?
Nee, met dat fijn ruikt.
Bedoel je Josje aan wie je nooit denkt?
Nee, aan wie ik altijd denk.
Bedoel je Josje die nooit graag Engelse woorden wil
                                 opschrijven?
Nee, die dat juist wel graag doet.
Maar die dan met schrijfletters schrijft?
Nee, die met grote drukletters schrijft.
Maar die de woorden van een zin altijd van elkaar schrijft?
Nee, die veel woorden van de zin aan elkaar schrijft.
Bedoel je Josje die voor een scheepje spaart?
Nee, die voor een zaklantaarn spaart.
Bedoel je Josje die niets om je geeft?
Nee, ik bedoel Josje die graag bij mij is.

NEW VERSES FOR JUNE 7, 1951

You mean Josie with the small eyes?
No, the big ones.
You mean Josie with the shrill tongue?
No, the sweet one.
You mean Josie whose hair smells of nothing?
No, smells good.
You mean Josie who never crosses your mind?
No, who's always on my mind.
You mean Josie who hates to write English words?
No, who loves to.
But the one who scribbles script?
No, who writes block capitals.
But the one whose sentences are all stops and starts?
No, they run long and smooth.
You mean Josie who's saving for a little boat?
No, for a torch.
You mean Josie who doesn't care for you at all?
No, Josie, that Josie, who loves to be with me.

(version by Eamon Grennan)

IK DRAAI EEN KLEINE REVOLUTIE AF

ik draai een kleine revolutie af
ik draai een kleine mooie revolutie af
ik ben niet langer van land
ik ben weer water
ik draag schuimende koppen op mijn hoofd
ik draag schietende schimmen in mijn hoofd
op mijn rug rust een zeemeermin
op mijn rug rust de wind
de wind en de zeemeermin zingen
de schuimende koppen ruisen
de schietende schimmen vallen

ik draai een kleine mooie ritselende revolutie af
en ik val en ik ruis en ik zing

VISSER VAN MA YUAN

onder wolken vogels varen
onder golven vliegen vissen
maar daartussen rust de visser

golven worden hoge wolken
wolken worden hoge golven
maar intussen rust de visser

I REEL OFF...

i reel off a little revolution
i reel off a pretty little revolution
i am no longer of land
i am water again
i bear foaming caps on my head
i bear fleeting chimeras in my head
on my back a mermaid rests
on my back the wind rests
the wind and the mermaid sing
the foaming caps murmur
the fleeting chimeras fall

i reel off a pretty little rustling revolution
and i fall and i rustle and i sing

(version by Mary O'Donnell)

FISHERMAN FROM MA YUAN

under clouds birds sail
under waves fly fish
but in between rests the fisherman

waves become high clouds
clouds become high waves
but in the meantime rests the fisherman

(version by Peter van de Kamp)

LIEDJE

Alle roekoemeisjes
van vanavond
alle toedoemeisjes
van vannacht
wat zeggen we daar nu wel van?
Niets.
We laten ze maar zitten
maar zitten maar liggen maar slapen
maar dromen van jajaja.

VOOR EEN DAG VAN MORGEN

Wanneer ik morgen doodga,
vertel dan aan de bomen
hoeveel ik van je hield.
Vertel het aan de wind,
die in de bomen klimt
of uit de takken valt,
hoeveel ik van je hield.
Vertel het aan een kind,
dat jong genoeg is om het te begrijpen.
Vertel het aan een dier,
misschien alleen door het aan te kijken.
Vertel het aan de huizen van steen,
vertel het aan de stad,
hoe lief ik je had.

Maar zeg het aan geen mens.
Ze zouden je niet geloven.
Ze zouden niet willen geloven dat
alleen maar een man alleen maar een vrouw,
dat een mens een mens zo liefhad
als ik jou.

SONG

All roocoogirls
of this evening
all oodogirls
of tonight
what should we say about that?

Nothing.
We just let them sit
just sit just lie just sleep
just dream of yesyesyes.

(version by Peter van de Kamp)

FOR SOME FUTURE DAY

When I die tomorrow,
just tell the trees
how much I loved you.
Tell it to the wind
which clambers up the trees
or falls down from the branches,
how much I loved you.
Tell it to a child,
young enough to understand.
Tell it to a pet
just by looking at it.
Tell it to the houses of stone,
tell it to the town,
how I loved you.

But don't tell a person.
They wouldn't believe you.
They wouldn't want to believe that
only just a man only just a woman,
that a human loved a human
as I you.

(version by Peter van de Kamp)

ZILVER PRATEN

Zilver praten in parken
de gele knapenzon
toont zijn gespannen lijf aan
de meisjes op de kiezelpaden
zij draaien hun zinnen
als parasollen om en om.

EEN VERGEEFS GEDICHT

Zoals je loopt,
door de kamer uit het bed
naar de tafel met de kam,
zal geen regel ooit lopen.

Zoals je praat,
met je tanden in mijn mond
en je oren om mijn tong,
zal geen pen ooit praten.

Zoals je zwijgt,
met je bloed in mijn rug
door je ogen in mijn hals,
zal geen poëzie ooit zwijgen.

SILVER TALK

Silver chatter in parks;
the yellow rent boy sun
displays his tense body
to the girls on the pebbled walks.
Their senses are spinning,
sentences twirling like parasols.

(version by Theo Dorgan)

A FUTILE POEM

The way you move,
Rising from bed to cross over
To the table with your comb,
No line of mine will ever move.

The way you speak,
Your teeth in my mouth
And your ear brushing my tongue,
No pen will ever speak.

And how you fall silent,
Your blood warm in my back
& your eyes fixed on my neck,
No poetry will ever fall silent.

(version by Theo Dorgan)

EEN VROUW BEMINNEN...

Een vrouw beminnen is de dood ontkomen,
weggerukt worden uit dit aards bestaan,
als bliksems in elkanders zielen slaan,
te zamen liggen, luisteren en dromen,
meewiegen met de nachtelijke bomen,
elkander kussen en elkander slaan,
elkaar een oogwenk naar het leven staan,
ondergaan en verwonderd bovenkomen.

'Slaap je al?' vraag ik, maar zij antwoordt niet;
woordeloos liggen we aan elkaar te denken:
twee zielen tot de rand toe vol verdriet.

Ver weg de wereld, die ons niet kan krenken,
vlak bij de sterren, die betoovrend wenken.
't Is of ik dood ben en haar achterliet.

TO LOVE A WOMAN...

To love a woman is to escape from death,
to be torn away from this earthly state,
thunder-struck in each other's souls,
to lie together, listen and dream,
to rock with the night trees,
kiss each other and strike each other,
to want to kill for the flicker of an eye,
go under and come up, amazed.

'Are you asleep?' I probe, but you do not respond;
wordless we lie, conceiving each another:
two souls brimming with grief.

Far away the world, which cannot injure us,
nearby the stars, signalling sorcery.
It's like I'm dead and have left her behind.

(version by Mary O'Donnell)

WILLEN

Ik neem mijn buik op en wandel,
ik heb mijn ogen open,
ik heb mijn borst als kennisgeving aangeslagen,
ik zou die pijnboomhouten paal in mij
vertikaal willen treffen met licht:
een lang lemmet licht om de dagen te turven.
Ik zou een rood totem willen snijden
waarom mijn hartstocht zich als wingerd slingert,
een beeld voor alledag, waaraan de vingers leven.
Ik heb het te nemen.

Ik zou een mens willen maken uit wrok
en afgeslagen splinters: een winterman
met een gezicht van louter ellebogen.
En bomen zouden stampen bij zijn langsgaan
en had hij één minuut te leven,
rood zou hij zijn en rood van kindertranen
en rood.

Ik pak mijzelf als altijd weer tezamen,
ik zie het water aan,
ik neem mijn hongerige maag en wandel,
ik zie een eetsalon voor twintig standen:
wanden zijn er genoeg; hij vloekt
van een doorvoeld gemis aan ramen.

Luister toch wat ik zeggen wou:
in Florida schildert men negers zwart,
in Florida schilt men negers
en Spanje stinkt van het bloed.
Ik wou van mijn lijf een Korea maken,
ik wou mijzelf zijn beneden mijn middenrif,
ik wou een vlag zien kiemen uit een zaadje.
Ik zal het kiemen zien.

WANTING TO

I take up my belly and go,
I have my eyes open,
I have beaten my breast in notification,
I should like to strike vertically with light
that pine-tree pole in me:
a long blade of light to tally the days.
I should like to carve a red totem
round which my passion winds like grapevine,
an everyday image, upon which the fingers live.
I have to take it.

I should like to create a man out of spite
and struck-off splinters: a winterman
with a face of sheer elbows.
And trees would stamp as he passes
and should he live for one minute,
he would be red and red from children's tears
and red.

I put myself as ever together again,
I look at the water,
I take my hungry stomach and go,
I see an eating-salon for twenty ranks:
there are enough partitions; he curses
from an intense lack of windows.

Do listen to what I wanted to say:
in Florida they paint the negroes black,
in Florida they skin negroes
and Spain reeks of blood.
I wanted to make a Korea of my body,
I wanted to be myself below my midriff,
I wanted to see a flag sprout from a seed.
I shall see the sprouting.

(version by Peter van de Kamp)

NIETS VAN DAT ALLES

Zoals matrozen zingen...
maar matrozen zingen niet:
zij spugen in de zee,
zij kennen de achterkant van steden
en de voorkant van de koude wind;
matrozen zingen niet.

zoals de vogels vrolijk...
maar hun vrolijkheid is vluchten:
zij zijn beschoten,
hun jong is dood.
(zij kennen geen droefheid ook).

zoals de zon...
maar zie het rode stof rond boekarest.
wolken? zijn koude mist.
de klaproos? onkruid.
zand: zand.
water: water.

een mens weet nauwlijks wat de mens is.
de dichter weet alles van niets.

NOTHING OF ALL THAT

The way sailors sing...
But sailors don't sing! Sailors
spit in the sea, know
only the arse-end of cities,
the cold fronts of wind.
Sailors don't sing.

The way birds gaily...
But gaiety doesn't last
when you're being shot at
and your young are dead.
(The same is true for sadness.)

The way the sun...
But look, see the dust choke the city,
the clouds shrouding everything,
flowers that might as well be weeds...
Sand is sand,
water water.

Man can hardly speak of man.
I'm afraid the poet knows nothing.

(version by Pat Boran)

EEN VROUW *12*

Haar mond: de tijger, de sprong, de tol
Om en om naar zeven maanden zomer.
Haar lijf: de liane die te laaien lag,
Korenschelp.

Vlak is mijn wit,
En wit als een stenen vis.
Onthuisd is mijn vel.
Ontvolkt ben ik.

Zij is een andere geworden. Mijn oog ontwend,
Die hoog als de zee en stollend in mijn nekvel woonde.

A WOMAN 12

Her mouth: the tiger, the leap, the toll
Round and round towards seven months of Summer.
Her body: the liana which lay blazing,
Cornshell.

My white is flat,
And white like a stone fish.
My skin is evicted.
I am de-populated.

She has become another. Cured from my eye,
Who lived high as the sea and curdling in the scruff of my neck.

(version by Peter van de Kamp)

DE ZON OP MIJN HAND

Schrijvend met de zon op mijn hand
ademend tussen blote woorden
op de strandwei van het papier
zie ik een kind door de regels lopen,
zorgeloos, met ogen die alles
drinken tot op de bodem. Alles.

Als ik het roep bij mijn eigen naam
blijft het even tussen twee zinnen
wachten, kijkt mij verwachtend aan,
ledigt mij en laat mij achter:
dorstend boven een zee van taal.

THE SUN ON MY HAND

Writing with the sun on my hand
Breathing between the bare words
On the white-strand of the paper
I see a child walk through the lines,
Carefree, with eyes that drink it all in
Down to the bottom of the page. All.

When I call to him by my own name
He stays fleetingly between two lines,
Then looks at me expectantly,
Empties me, then leaves me behind;
Thirsting above a sea of language.

(version by Tony Curtis)

THE SUN ON MY HAND

The sun lights my hand writing
hairs are trees maybe that slope
to the white beach of paper. Sunbathers
are words in lines my child walks among
untroubled taking it all in. Everything.

I summon what is surely mine
his eyes are on me expecting something
more than I know to give. No word
from him empties the shore
returns everything to the sea of language.

(version by James Simmons)

GIJ STAAT GELEUND OP UWE SPAAD' EN RUST.

Gij staat geleund op uwe spaad' en rust.
Er ligt een gele made in de voor,
En onverklaarbre vreze groeit in u
En houdt uw handen in: gij laat ze leven.

Gij herkent het toeval:
Hoe zon in modder leven schiep,
Een cel, een bleke made, een worm.
Gij keert u om. Gij ziet den avond komen
En vreest het toeval dat zal naderen
Gelijk een avond, gelijk een ziekte,
Gelijk het stil bezoek van onze dood.

Wat is er, dan dit vreemd gebeuren:
Dat in ons het leven eenzaam staat
Vóór zijn geheim, dat in ons het leven
Vraag werd.
Nergens is er voor een antwoord plaats of tijd.

En als gij eenzaam zijt of angstig
Vóór de harteloze eeuwigheid,
Weiger alle troost:
Mens, vlees geworden vraag.

YOU STAND

You stand, leaning on your spade, and rest.
A yellow maggot wriggles in the furrow.
A fear you cannot voice wells up
to stay your hand: *Let it live.*

Yours now is the hand of chance,
like the sun that created life
in mud—a cell, a worm, this sallow maggot.
You turn to see the evening
fall, and fear that which comes
like evening, an illness,
the unheralded visit of a death.

What else is there but strangeness?
That in us life stands alone
before its secret, that in us
life becomes a question
without place or time for answers.

And when you're alone or afraid
before heartless eternity,
reject all consolation:
man, questioning incarnate.

(version by Pat Boran)

ENKELE BIOGRAFISCHE GEGEVENS

soms stapt hij mee met de klas
en zingt met de joelende kinderen
dag meester dag lieve meester
hak je hoofd niet af met het bord

soms stapt hij in de film
en kust de bête-ogige blonde
dag mollige malvezijzoete
maak je buik nog maar dikwijls bloot

soms stapt hij op een hart
een hoofd een paar zere tenen
sorry partner volgende keer beter
het spijt me 't was harder bedoeld

soms stapt hij achter een vlag
en soms voor een bokkenwagen
naast pascal eluard wilfred owen
nooit tout sage maar ook niet tout fol

en eenmaal stapt hij eruit
als een kind uit de schemerige
                                    zandbak
dag leven dag lieve leven
nu zien wij elkaar nooit weerom

SOME BIOGRAPHICAL DATA

sometimes he steps out with the class
and sings with the mocking children
bye teacher bye dearest teacher
don't hack your head off with the board.

sometimes he steps into a movie
and kisses the blank-eyed blonde
bye buxom sugar-cup
keep on baring your belly.

sometimes he steps on a heart
a head a few tender toes
sorry mate better luck next time
I apologise; it should have hurt more.

sometimes he steps out behind a flag
and sometimes before a goat-cart
next to pascal eluard wilfred owen
never tout sage but never tout fol

and once he'll step out
as a child from the powdery sandbox
bye life bye precious life
now we'll never meet again.

(version by Mary O'Donnell)

HERFSTWEER

Hier nog te staan bij de oude ramen waar zij lag
lenig en welig als een dier... dat te verdragen
al zoveel lange jaren, en nooit meer een dag,
die als een dag werd van die langvervlogen dagen...

Zij vond haar weg naar dit verloren erf nooit weer,
en de terugweg naar haar graf ging mij verloren;
dit dak bleef, en die steen ook ergens, en oud zeer —
herftsweer verwaait de rest — niet meer om aan te horen.

AUTUMN WIND

Always to stand here by the old windows where she lay
soft and large as an animal... enduring that too
for so many long years and not a day ever
that was a day to be counted among the lost...

She never found her way to that lost yard again
and the way back to her grave got lost on me;
that roof and that stone remained somewhere, and old pain—
autumn wind blows away the rest—hearing it is unbearable.

(version by Desmond Egan)

1960 – 1980

REQUIESCAT

Terwijl een lauwe wind de jonge populieren liefkoosde
en de zomer, een puffende dikke dame, echt steeds
op het terras van américain verkoeling zocht,
trok ik mijn zwarte pak aan om je te begraven

daar ging dan je beeltenis voorgoed in de schrijn
van mijn fotoalbum en ik
was zo moe, doodmoe, van je hofdichter en nar
te spelen, ik heb niet gehuild

integendeel, toen ik wist dat deze liefde er weer opzat,
verkleedde ik mij snel en ben aan het tafeltje
van de zomer gaan zitten en heb gedichten gemaakt
als rose bloesems, dwarrelend in de blauwe wind.

REQUIESCAT

As a warm gust strokes young poplars
And summer—a fat, panting woman—really townish,
Hassles for an outside drink at the Américain,
I put on my black suit to bury you.

Your image was set forever in my album
As in a shrine. I was sick to the teeth
Of playing your poet and fool. No way did I cry.

Instead, when I knew our number was up
I changed fast and sat at summer's table,
Making poems that flutter
Like pink blossom in a blue breeze.

(version by Sean Dunne)

REQUIESCAT

While sweet breezes were stroking the young poplars
and Summer—a fat woman short of breath—was desperate
for a cool spot on the Hotel terrace,
I put my black suit on to bury you.

I locked your image forever away in the shrine
of my photograph album. I was so tired, dead tired,
of playing your little laureate and jester
that I didn't cry at all, not a single tear.

But knowing love had had it at last
I changed quickly and went to Summer's table
where I have sat making poem after poem—
pink blossoms twisting in the blue wind.

(version by Eamon Grennan)

DE EIKEL SPREEKT

Waar mijn ontbladerde vader
zijn harige takken laat ruisen,
en de bast van mijn moeder
met welgevallen beziet,
wordt de mier op de grond
door mijn val invalide.
Wellicht word ik woudreus,
en schud met de vuist naar
mijn vader die kromgroeit.

PARK

Papieren arken op een vijver van beton.
Spreeuwen harken pieren in een grijs gazon.
Bomen met roos: uit hun kruin vallen duiven
als Noach seniel met de broodzak gaat wuiven.

THE ACORN SPEAKS

Now that father's leaves are falling,
hear his hairy branches murmur,
see him look with belching pleasure
at my mother's husk beneath him;
on the ground the ant is crippled
by the impact of my falling.
I will grow to be a giant
shake my splendid fist of branches
at my father when he is crooked.

(version by Theo Dorgan)

A PARK

Paper arks drift on a concrete lake.
Birds rake for worms on a lawn of slate.
Trees blossom dandruff: doves spill from their heads
As a homeless Noah starts breaking bread.

(version by Ruth Hooley)

NO, NO NANETTE

Tea for two heeft voor de oorlog
iets voor mijn vader gedaan.
En ook voor mij.
Hij liep langzaam om
het langer uit een huis
te kunnen horen
en miste zo lijn 2.
In de volgende zat mijn moeder.

NO, NO, NANETTE

Tea for Two, before the War,
did something for my dad.
Also for me.
He slowed down
to hear it wafting
from a house
and so he missed the number 2.
The next one brought my mum.

(*version by Dennis O'Driscoll*)

OCHTEND

De nevels trekken op, het water
staat rechtop in het land.
Jij, die een voorsprong hebt in ongeluk,
waar denk je aan?
De vogels barsten los in luid kabaal
vrolijk voor mij omdat ik vrolijk ben.
'Laten we niet sentimenteel zijn
over vogels' zeg jij 'ze maken tenslotte
een hels lawaai, ook je onsterfelijke nachtegaal'.

SLIJTAGE

Bovenop de berg stopt het kamermeisje
een munt in de panoramakijker
en richt hem op de overkant waar zij nu
een minuut haar vriendje hout ziet hakken.

Forceer het oog terug, maar nooit
staat wie dan ook daar in zo'n ronde lijst
zoiets begrijpelijks te doen.

Zelfs heel exact, twee kanten blouses
uit Beiroet, worden vaag
omdat de lucht trilt.
Of zijn de ogen zelf beslagen?

Het is de regen die voortdurend regent
in versleten films
en ruisend valt op oude schellak platen.

MORNING

The mists disappear, the water
stands upright in the land.
You, who are ahead in unhappiness,
what are you thinking of?
The birds break loose in loud turmoil
joyful for me as I am joyful.
"Let's not be sentimental
about birds" you say "after all they make
a hellish noise, even your eternal nightingale".

(version by Joan McBreen)

LOSS

Up on the mountaintop the chambermaid puts
a coin in the view-finder
and points it to the other side where she now
for one minute sees her boyfriend cutting
wood.

Force the eye back but never
is whoever stands there in such a round frame
doing something perfectly understandable.

Even quite exact, two lace blouses
from Beirut, become vague
because the air trembles.
Or are the eyes themselves misty?

It is the rain that perpetually rains
in worn-out films
and falls, rustling on old shellac records.

(version by Joan McBreen)

OOM KAREL: EEN FAMILIEFILMPJE

Vanmiddag een familiefilmpje gezien. Oom Karel
niets vermoedend in een bootje bij Loosdrecht.
Drie weken later was hij dood, niet meer vatbaar voor celluloid.

Hoe goed zou het zijn een filmpje van zijn sterven te bezitten
als operateur zijn laatste adem af te draaien
vertraagd het stollen van zijn blik, het vallen van die hand
langs de ijzeren bedkant nog eens en nog eens te vertonen.

Of op topsnelheid, zodat het doodgaan van oom Karel
iets vrolijks krijgt, een uitgelaten dans op een krakend bed,
de omhelzing van een onzichtbare vrouw

die teruggedraaid hem wakker kust; de ogen
worden weer blik, kijken in de lens, de hand wijst
Oom Karel leeft, oom Karel is dood.

UNCLE CHARLES: A HOME MOVIE

Saw a home movie this afternoon. Uncle Charles
unsuspecting in a small boat near Loosdrecht.
Three weeks later he was dead, no longer susceptible for celluloid.

How good it would be to possess a movie of his dying
to reel off as operator his final breath
to show in slow motion again and again his sight
coagulate, that hand drop past the iron bedside.

Or in top speed, so that there's some fun in Uncle Charles'
last moments, an elated dance on a creaking bed,
the embrace of an invisible woman

who in reverse kisses him awake; the eyes
regain sight, look into the lens, the hand points.
Uncle Charles lives, Uncle Charles is dead.

(version by Peter van de Kamp)

DE HYENA

Empirische wetenschap laat van reputaties
dikwijls weinig heel: de oude Egyptenaren
vereerden hem hoog, en nog Plinius hield vol dat de steen
die hij meedragen zou in zijn oog, de hyaenia,
als hij onder de tong werd gelegd in de toekomst deed schouwen.
Helaas,

wat hij in zijn oog meedraagt is enkel een loensende blik
van vraatzucht en achterbakse opdringerigheid;
geel glanst zijn iris, ja: wanneer hij zich volschrokt
met wat luipaard of wat leeuw aan aas voor hem achterliet.
Een gluiperige bietser is hij, een lijkenopgraver,
          meer niet,

Meer niet? in het eerste circus dat ik ooit zag,
(Amar), was ook een hyena-nummer, wat
het inhield weet ik niet meer: maar een man of een vrouw
moet met ze zijn opgetrokken, ze hebben verzorgd,
toegesproken, te eten gegeven, geaaid, liefgehad zelfs
          misschien.

Het lijkt me een vreemde hobby, rond te reizen
met een troep gedresseerde kadaveropruimers: zo iets
als een kamer verhuren aan een begrafenisdienaar,
terwijl tientallen mooie meisjes om onderdak vragen.
En daarbij: zelfs de ergste beul koos zijn beeltenis niet graag
          tot embleem.

Zijn foto ligt voor me: een kruiperig-inkennige kop,
de staart slaafs tussen de poten, half gekromd
om te vluchten of toe te sluipen, een houding gespeend
van iedere fierheid of gratie—en toch, als zijn blik
zich zalvend aan de mijne vastzuigt, grom ik:
          'Zo, neef!'

THE HYENA

Modern Science has destroyed his reputation:
the Ancient Egyptians held him in high regard.
Plinius said that the stone he kept in his eye
would, if placed under the tongue,
show what the future held.

But if the truth be told,
his eye is the eye of a sly glutton;
his yellow iris glitters like Dutch gold
when he gorges himself
on a leopard's or a lion's discarded prey.
He's nothing more than a scrounger.
And that's all there's to be said about him.

But is that all?
The first circus I ever went to
had a troupe of performing hyenas.
I forget how their act went: but I remember thinking
that someone must have looked after them,
fed, groomed, and perhaps made love to them.

To my mind it seems a strange way of life—
travelling the length and breadth of the country
with a bunch of trained scavengers:
like renting your spare room to an undertaker
when the woman you love is looking for digs.
And besides, we're judged by the company we keep.

It happens I've got his photo in front of me:
head down as if preparing himself
to run away or sneak up on me.
When he catches my eye with that slavish look of his,
I laugh hyenaically and growl,
"How's life abusing you, coz."

(version by John Hughes)

EEN POOLS MEISJE STAANDE OP EEN STOEL

voor dr. Hans Joseph Maria Globke,
dertien jaar medewerker van Hitler,
veertien jaar medewerker van Adenauer

Stel u voor een meisje uit Polen:
zij is naakt en zij staat op een stoel,
daar staat zij al bijna een uur.

En die stoel staat voor de appèlplaats
en op de appèlplaats aangetreden
staan de gevangenen van Neuengamme.

Voor het front van de stinkende
voor de hel opgeschreven mannen
uit alle delen van Europa

loopt een krachtiggevoede officier
op en neer als een god
met glimmend gepoetste laarzen.

Nou stel u dus voor: één keer dat hij langs
de stoel komt mikt hij een knipoog
naar het meisje dat naakt op de stoel staat

en het ongelooflijke gebeurt:
het meisje, de polsen gebonden op de rug,
spuugt de officier in zijn gezicht!

En deze, razend, trapt de kruk
onder het kind weg en het koord spant;
zij hangt: en duizenden zien haar sterven.

En nu komt het. Deze officier is vandaag
rechter in Bielefeld, Würzburg,
Aachen, Mannheim of Münster.

A POLISH GIRL STANDING ON A CHAIR

for Dr. Hans Joseph Maria Globke
for thirteen years Assistant to Hitler
for fourteen years Assistant to Adenauer

Imagine a girl from Poland
naked and standing on a chair,
she's been there nearly an hour.

The chair stands on the parade ground
and there the prisoners
of Neuengamme are lined up.

Before the fetid men
from all the corners of Europe,
men stamped for hell,

a well-fed officer struts
up and down like a god
with a gleam on his polished boots.

Imagine, as he passes the chair,
he once cocks a wink
at the girl standing there naked

and the incredible happens,
she—wrists behind her back—
spits in the officer's face.

And he, frothing, kicks the chair
from under her; the rope tautens,
she hangs: thousands watch her die.

Now, a guess: this officer is
judge today in Bielefeld, Würzburg,
Aachen, Mannheim or Münster.

'Dit is infaam!' roept hier iemand,
'die ss-officier was een ander! Die heeft
nu in Bremen een net restaurant.

De rechtsgeleerde die jij bedoelt
heeft alleen de wetjes gemaakt
of de vonnissen getekend!'

'Verontschuldig dan mijn fout; maar
dan spuwde ook het meisje op de stoel
de verkeerde duitse meneer in zijn gezicht.'

Someone cries: "This is shameful!
the SS-officer was someone else
who now owns a decent restaurant

"in Bremen—the lawyer you mean
only framed the legislation
or signed the sentences."

"Pardon my error—then,
the girl on the chair spat in the face
of the wrong German gentleman."

(*version by Gregory O'Donoghue*)

DE TERUGGEWEZEN GAVE

't Was winter en al schemerig in de stad.
Ik wilde het Janskerkhof over gaan,
eigenlijk om bij Anne Frank te leggen
een bosje bloemen dat ik bij mij had.
Ik had ze al van het papier ontdaan,
maar week terug. Het beeldje op het plein
in deze schemering leefde en zag mij aan
en stille lippen wilden mij iets zeggen,
terwijl ik onbewegelijk bleef staan.
Niets stoorde dit ontijdelijk samenzijn.
Tot hoorbaar werd haar woordenloos vermaan,
zij, een Joods kind dat weet van eeuwen heeft:
'Gij waart daarbij. Ook nu zij niet meer leeft.'

THE REJECTED GIFT

In winter, with dusk enshrouding the town,
I passed through Janskerkhof in Amsterdam
With flowers for Anne Frank held close in my arms.
I stripped off the paper, was laying them down,
Then froze—in the square, in the half-light, aware
That this stone child was alive, was watching me,
Wanting some word from her unmoving lips
To be uttered and heard as I stood there stock-still.
Nothing disturbed this moment we shared
'Till the silent rebuke of this innocent girl
With all of her people's history to bear
Came across loud and clear: 'You were there.
For Anne Frank in Janskerkhof in Amsterdam
As much life now as she lived through then.'

(*version by Ruth Hooley*)

THE REJECTED GIFT

It was winter and already dusky in town.
I wanted to cross the *Janskerkhof*,
actually to lay by Anne Frank
a bunch of flowers I had with me.
I had already removed the paper,
but shunned back. The statue on the square
was alive in this dusk and looked at me
and quiet lips wanted to tell me something
while I remained motionless.
Nothing disturbed this timeless meeting.
Until her wordless reproach became audible,
she, a Jewish child that knows of ages:
'You were there too. Even now that she lives no more.'

(*version by Peter van de Kamp*)

DODENHERDENKING

De namen der gevallenen
die wij zo snel vergaten
worden soms nog gezongen
bij monde van de stormwind.

Dan: luister aan de palen.

Ik hoorde het eens vervaarlijk
onder Zalk en Veecaten—
te zwaar haast voor de masten
en de metalen draden.

REMEMBRANCE DAY

The names of the dead
that we forgot so soon
are sometimes sung
in the storm-wind's fury.

Then: listen at the poles.

I once heard its raving
below Zalk and Veecaten—
too heavy almost for the masts
and the metal wires.

(version by Robert Greacen)

REMEMBRANCE DAY

The names of the fallen,
names we forgot so soon,
are sometimes lamented
by the howling stormwind.

Put your ear to the poles.

That din overwhelmed me
below Zalk and Veecaten—
too much for poles to bear
almost, and metal wires.

(version by Michael Longley)

ONTOLOGIE

Als ik bedenk wat van mij
geworden is geen glazenwasser
geen playboy geen dropverkoper
vind ik mij wel eens terug op
de vreemdste plaatsen
duizelend in een dakgoot
deinend op de geparfumeerde
schoot van een dame
op de tenen voor de ramen
van een snoepgoed-etalage.

ONTOLOGY

When I think of me
And what I have
And have not become,
Not a window-cleaner,
Not a playboy, not
A seller of licorice,
Then I find me
In the oddest places—
Lying dazed in a gutter,
Cradled in the perfume
Of a woman's embrace,
Stretched on tiptoe
For the blaze of colour
In a sweetshop window.

(version by Seamus Deane)

AFSCHEID

Zul je voorzichtig zijn?

Ik weet wel dat je maar een
boodschap doet
hier om de hoek
en dat je niet gekleed bent voor
een lange reis.

Je kus is licht,
je blik gerust
en vredig zijn je hand en voet.

Maar achter deze hoek
een werelddeel,
achter dit ogenblik
een zee van tijd.

Zul je voorzichtig zijn?

FAREWELL

Will you take care?

I know you're only going to the shop
Round the corner
and that you aren't dressed for a
journey.

Your kiss is light,
your gaze quiet,
and peace of mind is in your hand and
foot.

But beyond this corner
A continent,
beyond this moment
a sea of time.

Will you take care?

(version by Peter van de Kamp)

DODENPARK

We wandelden des avonds door de tuinen
Van het crematorium; achter heg en hazelaar
Stond laag de vroege maan; ik at wat kruimels
Van mijn vest en jij genoot van een sigaar.

Je dacht wellicht aan zeer bezwete negers
Op hete plantages in de weer. Ook aan
Je gezicht meende ik zoiets af te lezen.
Ikzelf keek door de heg naar de maan.

We spraken niet. Wat viel er ook te zeggen?
We dachten maar aan een maan en aan zweet.
O, nergens heerste er ooit zo'n rust. Slechts
Af en toe klonk uit een urn een kreet.

DE DICHTER

Toen het letterkundig tijdschrift
Hem een briefje toe deed komen,
Waarin stond: 'Mijnheer, uw verzen
Waren lang niet slecht, we zullen
Er eerdaags een paar van plaatsen,'
Zwol zijn borst tot slagschiphoogte.
Heel zijn leven werd nu anders.
Hij ging doen alsof hij grote
Mensen hoogstpersoonlijk kende.
Hij zei stad wanneer jij blad zei.
Hij zei held wanneer jij speld zei.
Hij zei ach wanneer jij dag zei.
En daarvan wilde hij leven!

PARK OF THE DEAD

We strolled at night through the gardens
Of the crematorium; behind hedge and hazel
Stood, low, the early moon; I ate some crumbs
Off my wastecoat and you enjoyed a cigar.

You thought perhaps of very sweaty negroes
Up and at it in hot plantations. In your face
Too I thought I could detect something like that.
I myself looked through the hedge at the moon.

We did not speak. For what was there to say?
We only thought of a moon and sweat.
Oh, nowhere ever reigned such peace. Only
now and then there was a cry from an urn.

(version by Peter van de Kamp)

THE POET

When the literary journal
Sent to him a letter saying:
'Sir your verse is not at all bad,
'We will publish extracts shortly,'
His breast swelled up to warship stature.
His whole life had now been altered.
He began to act as if he
Knew great men most intimately.
He'd say 'bin' when you would 'pin' say.
He'd say 'oh' when you would 'go' say.
And from that wished to make a living!

(version by Michael Hartnett)

WAT DOET MEN ANDERS

wat doet men anders
dan kijken in een
gedicht naar wat er
daarbuiten gebeurt

EEN DORP

een dorp is een cirkel
met de hand rond een
kerk getrokken;

een duif is een zeer
eenvoudige luchtledige
lijn op een dak;

een voorjaar maakt natte
vlekken op het papier
van de lucht;

en kijk, dit is pas
werkelijkheid: straks
laat ik het regenen
op mijn gedicht
zodat het uitvloeit
tot een akwarel
van doordrenkte,
onleesbare woorden.

WHAT DOES ONE DO

What does one do
but look in a
poem to what
goes on out there.

(version by Peter van de Kamp)

A VILLAGE

A village is a circle
Drawn by hand round
A church;

A dove is a very
Simple vacuous
Line on a roof;

A Spring makes wet
Stains on the paper
Of the sky;

And look, now *this* is
Reality; soon
I will make it rain
On my poem
So that it flows out
Into a water-colour
Of drenched,
Illegible words.

(version by Peter van de Kamp)

NAAR BUITEN

Hij sloeg de deur in 't slot. Vanonder bomen
buiten klonk nog zijn vloek: toen werd het stil.
Waren zij dat woest hart te na gekomen?
Hun tam spel, somwijl door een zweem onwil
vertraagd, het kon weer doorgaan, knechten schoven
gordijnen dicht, de lampen gingen aan,
om hun haard schoven zij in goed geloven
aaneen: men wist er amper nog zijn naam.

OUTSIDE IN THE OPEN

He slammed the door shut. From under trees
outside, his cursing echoed: then fell silent.
Had they come too close to that wild heart?

Their cosy game, which earlier a hint of reluctance
might occasionally delay, could continue now; servants drew
the curtains across; lights went on...
they pushed close to the fire in soothing complicity
together; they hardly remembered his name.

(version by Desmond Egan)

HOOGSTE TIJD

De kroeg loopt leeg, de maan is onder.
Doodstil kijken de sterren naar het gehucht
dat slapen gaat, niet langer afgezonderd
van de omtrek. Zijn oud onderdak ontvlucht,
strompelt hij mompelend en stombeschonken
naar waar het dreunen van de zee doorkomt,
donker en zalig. In zijn ogen vonken
hoop en wanhoop om waaraan geen ontkomt.

TIME, PLEASE

The pub empties, the moon is down.
The stars in deadly silence stare
At the village settling into sleep,
Its outline one with the landscape.
Pissed, he stumbles from his shelter,
Muttering at the graceful wave's roar.
In his eyes, hope and despair are sparks
Kindled within the inescapable dark.

(*version by Sean Dunne*)

TIME NOW PLEASE

The pub empties out, the moon sets. The stars
in deadly silence regard the village: how it prepares
for bed, how it merges back to the land's contour
with the dousing of the lights. One creature staggers,
stumbles muttering drunken curses from his old lair;
he's reeled to where the sea shouts him down: her rude
darkness, her restless bliss. His eyes glitter
with hope, with despair — common fate none can elude.

(*version by Paula Meehan*)

IK

Ik
schrijf gedichten
als dunne bomen.

Wie
kan zo mager
praten
met de taal
als ik?

Misschien
is mijn vader
gierig geweest
met het zaad.

Ik heb
hem nooit
gekend
die man.

Ik heb
nooit
een echt woord gehoord
of het deed pijn.

Om pijn
te schrijven
heb je
weinig woorden
nodig.

I

I
write poems
like thin trees.

Who
can talk
in such
lean words
as I?

Maybe
my dad was
stingy
with seed.

I never
knew
the man.

I never
heard
a real word
that did not hurt.

To write
hurt
you need
few
words.

(version by Peter van de Kamp)

IK HEB

Ik heb
een huis.

Het huis
dat ik heb
is mijn leven.

Wat ik gedaan heb.

Wat ik ben.

Ik vraag
geen mensen
bij mij thuis.

Ik weet
dat wie koffie
bij mij drinkt
zich later ophangt.

I HAVE

I have
a house.

The house
that I have
is my life.

What I have done.

What I am.

I invite
no people
to my house.

I know
that whoever drinks
coffee at my place
will hang himself later.

(version by Peter van de Kamp)

DE MAN VAN TOLLUND

Als een verwante
die men zelden ziet in het gezin,
en die plots in een hoek van de kamer zit,
een verbeten koning vol tweedracht en stilte,
slaapt hij niet, maar rust in stilte.

Geen worm heeft zich aan hem gevoed,
Het ongedierte zijn wij nu,
met onze happige blik.

In zijn tijd vol goden, en zangen,
oorlogen en schepen en
vergelding
werd hij met een touw van leder gewurgd
en gestort in zijn eigendom: de grond, en in
een tijd van ijs en ijzer.

Sporen van vlaszaad, gerstekoek en varkensgras
in het darmkanaal:
het was winter toen hij stierf, hikkend naar lucht
en gevangen in de klei van het laagveen zonder kalk.

De mannen van het dorp stonden rond hem,
duwden een gaffel tegen zijn keel en knikten
toen hij geofferd werd aan de jaarlijkse vruchten.
Of was hij een moordenaar? Een ketter? Een deserteur?

Knielend in het luchtledig ruim
zocht zijn lijf naar zijn eigendom: de aarde en vond takken noch boom;
wraak beroerde hem niet,
want hij glimlacht in het moeras dat hem bewaart.

Een kist rot, stenen verpoederen, gras wordt hooi en drek;
hij ligt, voor eeuwen verwant aan de mensen,
gevat in het touw, met een oor geplet en tandeloos.

TOLLUND MAN

Like a relative
whom one seldom sees in the family,
and who sits suddenly in a corner of the room,
a grim-faced king full of discord and silence,
he does not sleep, but rests in peace.

No worm has fed off him,
The vermin, that's us now,
with our eager glances.

In his time full of gods, and chants,
wars and ships and
retribution
he was strangled with a rope made of leather
and dumped in his property: the ground, and in
a time of ice and iron.

Traces of flaxseed, barley cake and knotgrass
in the intestinal canal:
it was winter when he died, gasping for breath
and emprisoned in the clay of the limeless peat moor.

The men of the village stood round him,
pressed a pitchfork against his throat and nodded
as he was sacrificed to the annual fruit.
Or was he a murderer? A heretic? A deserter?

Kneeling in the vacuous hold
his body sought its property: the earth and found branches nor tree;
revenge did not touch him,
for he smiles in the bog that preserves him.

A coffin rots, stones pulverize, grass becomes hay and dung;
he lies, for ages related to people,
set in the rope, with an ear crushed and toothless.

('Toen ik machtig op je zat,
vond ik de wereld prachtig

tot ik gloeide van de spijt
om het verzinken van de dingen.

Je schreeuwde als hond en ree en geit
toen ik je zoon heb verwekt.

Een dolk van lindehout was ik
in je vel, dat eindeloos moeras.')

Het zuur dat hem heeft bewaard
groeit in het gras.
Gebogen wacht hij op de gerechtigheid
van wat hij was.

Als er bloed is: geronnen.
Als er een man is: aangetast door
het geweldig tijdloos gas en door de handafdrukken van de jaren.
Als er blauw is: weggeveegd
als het blauw van je ogen, na jaren.

('Het is een man van klei
die tot je spreekt.
Ik heb gedood en werd gedood.
De vogels dalen in het westen.')

In ammoniak en mest,
in zwarte stekels,
onder een hoed van lood:
mijn dood.

Heb ik verkracht?
Ben ik het gevecht ontlopen?

Mijn moeder wist dit
toen zij mij in de wereld bracht
van bramen, adders en seringen,
in de val en in de veendamp
van haar leven.

('When I was astride you in full might,
I found the world radiant'

till I glowed with regret
for the sinking of things

You cried like a dog and roe and goat
when I conceived your son.

A dagger of limewood was I
in your skin, that endless bog.')

The acid that has preserved him
grows in the grass.
Arched he waits for justice
of what he was.

If there is blood: curdled.
If there is a man: affected by
the powerful timeless gas and by the hand-prints of the years.
If there is blue: swept away
like the blue of your eyes, after years.

('It is a man of clay
that speaks to you.
I killed and was killed.
The birds descend in the west.')

In ammonia and dung,
in black prickles,
under a hat of lead:
my death.

Did I rape?
Did I shun the fight?

My mother knew as much
when she bore me into the world
of blackberries, adders and lilacs,
in the trap and in the bog mist
of her life.

Ik wist het nooit,
daarom gllimlach ik thans
en zak als het hoornvee
met balgpijn in de polder.

Misschien roepen de kinderen terecht dat ik
lachwekkend want beschimmeld ben.

Zij kennen gerechtigheid,
al begeren zij haar niet.

Mijn hangen is voorbij
al krimpt mijn nekvel voor eeuwen nog ineen
en ben jij tot op het gebinte gekweld
door wat mij werd aangedaan.

Mijn tong steekt uit, ik spreek niet meer,
ik zit van nu af in uw kleren
en hinnik in je glimlach
met mijn bloed en mijn snot en mijn zaad.

Ben ik dit maar
dat zijt gij dit ook.

Op zoek naar een gebaar zit gij in mijn misbaar
gewrikt en dagenlang vervormd.

Hou oud ben je nu?

Wordt vuur je straf
of zwel je tot je barst?

Het slachtoffer heeft recht gesproken.

Je beweegt naar gelang ik verander,
en je bent ook bewaard; je raapt, terwijl het afschuwelijk licht
nog in je brandt, al onze flarden samen.

I never knew;
that's why I smile now
and sink like the horned cattle
with stomach-ache in the polder.

Maybe the kids are right to cry that I
am ludicrous, being mildewed.

They know justice,
though they do not covet it.

My hanging is past
though the scruff of my neck still will shrink for ages
and you are tormented to the truss
by what was done unto me.

My tongue sticks out; I speak no more;
I sit from now on in your clothes
and neigh in your smile
with my blood and my snot and my seed.

Be I but this
that this thou art too.

In search of a sign you are firmly wrenched
in my dissent and distorted for days.

How old are you now?

Will fire be your punishment?
Or will you swell till you burst?

The victim has administered justice.

You move as I change,
and you too are preserved; you gather, while the horrific light
still burns in you, all our shreds together.

(version by Peter van de Kamp)

BRILJANT FILOSOFEREND

Briljant filosoferend
over het leven liet ik
de aardappels verbranden.
Een onmiskenbaar bewijs
van emancipatie.

DRIE JAAR WAS IK ONGEVEER

Drie jaar was ik ongeveer
toen ik op een najaarsavond
door het raam stond te kijken
met mijn neus voor het eerst
boven de vensterbank uit
zodat ik toen pas ontdekte
dat er een huis werd gebouwd
tegenover het onze. Met grote
beslistheid verkondigde ik:
dat halen ze 's zomers weer weg.
Mijn moeder die het ook niet helpen kon
moest erom lachen. Tegen het einde van
de tweede wereldoorlog toen mijn ouders
al waren vergast, staken de Duitsers
het huis in brand. Na de bevrijding
werd het weer opgebouwd. Het staat er
nog en ook ik droom nog herhaaldelijk
van betonnen en bakstenen gebouwen
die een veelbelovend uitzicht
drastisch te niet doen.

BRILLIANTLY PHILOSOPHISING...

Brilliantly philosophising
about life I let
the potatoes burn.
Unmistakable proof
of emancipation.

(version by Peter van de Kamp)

I WAS ABOUT THREE YEARS OF AGE

I was about three years of age
when one autumn evening I
stood looking out of the window
with my nose for the first time
above the window-sill
so that I only then discovered
that a house was being built
across the road from ours. With great
certainty I proclaimed:
they'll take that away in the summer.
My mother, who couldn't help it either
had to laugh. Close to the end of
the second world war, when my parents
had already been gassed, the Germans put
the house on fire. After liberation
it was rebuilt. It still stands
and I too still dream repeatedly
of concrete and brick buildings
which destroy drastically
a promising view.

(version by Peter van de Kamp)

MIJN MOEDER IS MIJN NAAM VERGETEN

Mijn moeder is mijn naam vergeten,
mijn kind weet nog niet hoe ik heet.
Hoe moet ik mij geborgen weten?

Noem mij, bevestig mijn bestaan,
laat mijn naam zijn als een keten.
Noem mij, noem mij, spreek mij aan,
o, noem mij bij mijn diepste naam.

Voor wie ik liefheb, wil ik heten.

DIEP IN DE PUT WAAR HAAR GEBEENTE LIGT

Diep in de put waar haar gebeente ligt,
verschijnt hij elke avond als haar slaaf
en maakt haar uit elkaar gevallen lichaam gaaf
en brengt weer trekken aan op haar gezicht.

Wanneer zij op haar voetstuk zich verheft,
kracht, aan zijn spijt ontleend, haar schouders schraagt
en hij—van schuld vervulde dwerg—vergeving vraagt
voor wat zijn hand haar aangedaan heeft, treft

hem van haar stalen mond het snijdend spreken.
Hij voelt van zijn geduld de vliezen breken
en steekt zijn mes ver in haar trotse rug.

Een held is hij. Hij heeft het kwaad bestreden.
Hij legt devoot en met zichzelf tevreden
het zware deksel op de put terug.

MY MOTHER HAS FORGOTTEN MY NAME

My mother has forgotten my name
my child knows not yet what I'm called.
How can I feel secure at all?

Name me, assert my existence,
let my name be like a chain.
Call me, call me, address me,
oh, call me by my deepest name.

For those I love, I want to be named.

(version by Peter van de Kamp)

DEEP IN THE PIT

Deep in the pit where her bones lie
he appears every night as her slave
and makes her disjointed body whole
and brings back features on her face.

When she lifts herself up on her pedestal,
force, drawn from his remorse, supports her shoulders
and he—dwarfed with guilt—asks forgiveness
for what his hand has done to her, is hit

by the piercing mouth of her steel speech.
He feels the waters of his patience break
and sticks his knife deep into her proud back.

He is a hero. He has fought the evil.
Devout and pleased with himself he
places the heavy lid back on the pit.

(version by Joan McBreen)

JE TRUITJES EN JE WITTE EN RODE

je truitjes en je witte en rode
sjerpen en je kousen en je directoirtjes
(met liefde gemaakt, zei de reklame)
en je brassières (er steekt poëzie in
die dingen, vooral als jij ze draagt)—
ze slingeren rond in dit gedicht
als op je kamer.

kom er maar in, lezer, maak het je
gemakkelijk, struikel niet over de
zinsbouw en over de uitgeschopte schoenen,
gaat u zitten

(intussen zoenen wij even in deze
zin tussen haakjes, zo ziet de lezer
ons niet) hoe vindt u het,
dit is een raam om naar de werkelijkheid
te kijken, alles wat u daar ziet
bestaat. is het niet helemaal
als in een gedicht?

YOUR SWEATERS

your sweaters
your stockings
your red and white sashes
your bras
your "made with love" panties
(there's poetry there
especially if you're in them)
lie strewn about this poem
as about your bedroom.

Dear Reader do come in
and make yourself comfy:
don't trip over syntax
and kicked-off shoes.
Take a seat please
(in the meantime
we'll kiss a bit
in brackets
so the reader won't see):

how do you like it:
This window in front of you
overlooks reality; whatever
you see out there
exists. Isn't that exactly
how it is in a poem?

(version by Eamon Grennan)

BALLADE VAN DE TRAAGHEID

Ik hou van de traagheid van liggen in gras, als een vorst:
ik, uitkijkend over mijn aanhangers,
mijn ledematen, zeggend tot mijn linkerarm:
jij daar, breng mijn hand eens voor
mijn mond, dat ik geeuw, in orde,
ga maar weer liggen, goed zo,
tucht moet ik hier hebben.

Ik hou van de traagheid van zijn,
zen, zegt men in het oosten, ik geloof dat het
hetzelfde is.
Ik hou van de traagheid van liggen in bed,
jij naast mij, je knieën in mijn knie-
holtes, als twee s'en, de traagheid waarmee je me
niet gezegd hebt dat je al wakker was,
je uit lippen bestaande ontvankelijkheid,
de traagheid waarmee ik sneller en sneller kom,
de kalmte waarmee ik wilder en wilder word,
de traagheid van jouw diplomatisch lichaam
dat geeft en neemt, jouw corps diplomatique,

en de traagheid van een sigaar nadien,
de traagheid van grandeur, de traagheid van wie
zich te pletter rijdt tegen een boom in vertraagde
film, het majestuoso van een ontploffing, plechtig,
plechtig eindigt dit leven.

BALLAD OF INDOLENCE

I love the indolence of lying on the grass
like a king: I survey my subjects
and say to my left arm—You there, bring
that hand to mouth. I've a yen
to yawn. Well done. Lie down. I must have order here.

I love the indolence of sin
—'sen' say our easterners, as if
all sense and sins were the same. I love
the indolence of lying in bed beside you,
your two knees tucked
into the hollows behind my knees, the pair of us
folded over one another
like two esses. I love the lazy way
you didn't say
you were awake, the way you are all lips
receiving me, taking me in, the indolence
I come with faster faster, my composure
growing wilder, the indolence of your
diplomatic body, your *corps diplomatique*
that gives and takes, and afterwards

the indolent cigar, indolence of grandeur,
the indolence of one who crashes into
a tree in slow motion
and slowly goes to pieces in
one massive majestic explosive blow-up:
solemnly, solemnly this life ends.

(version by Eamon Grennan)

BOODSCHAP OVER DE TIJDEN

Die taal spreek ik niet
dus hou op met dat boek
onder mijn ogen te bewegen

En dat land wantrouw ik
het voert iets in zijn schild
het is mij te rustig

Trouwens, wat doen de kinderen
ik hoor ze al uren niet meer
staan ze in brand?

MESSAGE ABOUT THE TIMES

Look, I don't speak the language,
It's useless shoving that book
Under my eyes.

And that country I distrust
Is up to something,
They're too quiet for my liking

And here, what're the children up to,
Not a peep out of them for hours,
Are they on fire?

(*version by Theo Dorgan*)

SIGN OF THE TIMES

Look, I don't speak the language
so you needn't bother with your book—
waving it under my nose

and as for this country: I don't trust it
it's up to something, it's much
too quiet for my liking

besides which, what are the children at?
—it's *hours* since they made a sound
are they on fire or what?

(*version by Desmond Egan*)

WANDELING NAAR PARFONDEVAL

voor H.R.S. en C. Postma

De wind wuift over mijn gezicht
schaduw van wat blad.

Het pad gaat hoger straks
de heuvel op, daarachter schuilt gevaar

of veiligheid? In elk geval
vervolg van weg, een bocht

en dan de trage afloop naar het dal
waar water smiespelt

om het badend gras. Gelukkig
was ik op die dag, geen kwaad

bericht in krant uit stad
kon maken dat ik dit vergat.

THEATER

Ik neem je mee
achter het toneel
waar de spelers kontknijpen
kaarten
beursberichten lezen
in het stof staren
yoga doen
hoesten achter hun hand.

A STROLL TO PARFONDEVAL

for H.R.S. and C. Postma

The wind sways over my face
shadow of some leaf.

Shortly the path will climb
into the hill—is it danger behind,

or safety? In any case
the unfolding road, a bend

and then the slow fall to the glen
where water sussurates

in the bathing grass. Happy
to be abroad that day, no evil

news in the papers from town
could strike my mood down.

(version by Theo Dorgan)

THEATRE

I take you with me
behind the scenes
where actors clench their buttocks
play cards
read stock market reports
stare into dust
practise their yoga
cough into their fists.

Waar ze tussen twee levens staan
geen enkele rol vervullen
en toch op hun plaats zijn.

Op die plek
tussen opkomen en afschminken
tussen dollen en douchen
horen ook wij thuis.

Lichamen klaar om te verroeren
monden open om te spreken
maar nog niet...

Where they are between lives
playing no part at all
and yet perfectly in place.

In this territory
between entrances and taking-off makeup
between horseplay and homegoing
we too belong.

Bodies ready to stir
mouths open to speak
but not yet...

(version by Theo Dorgan)

THE THEATRE

I bring you along with me
backstage to where actors
feel their tailend grow tight
play games of cards
glance-over stockmarket reports
stare at the dust
practise yoga
cough into their hands

—where between two lives they wait
playing no role whatever
though they are in readiness.

To that very spot between
making an entrance and taking the makeup off
between having a laugh and having a shower
have the two of us come

bodies ready to make a move
mouths open to say something
but not quite yet...

(version by Desmond Egan)

KRONIEK VAN AMSTERDAM

Er wordt een weduwe van in de zeventig
gevonden met een afgesneden keel.

Haar meid, die vele jaren bij haar diende,
is spoorloos—alleen dat stukje van haar jurk...

De odds en ends van de geschiedenis
liggen in het water van de stad.

Enige dagen later immers vindt men
in de Lindengracht een vrouwenromp.

Later nog de benen in de Prinsengracht;
een litteken wijst uit: het is de meid.

Tenslotte, een week later weer, vist men
uit de Brouwersgracht een hoofd: het klopt...

Whodunnit—een nuchtere kalfsslager,
zijn vrouw en een ongelukkige kruier?

Welnee-het is Hermina Wouters oud 28 jaar,
zij heeft de weduwe en haar meid vermoord.

Dus wordt zij van onderen levendig geradbraakt,
het linkerbeen even onder de knie afgehakt.

Daarna het rechter-en de rechterhand,
een snee in de strot, de kop in twee slagen.

De stukken worden naar de overkant
van het IJ gebracht en daar tentoongesteld.

AMSTERDAM CHRONICLE

A widow in her late seventies
Is discovered with her throat cut.

Her long-serving maid has disappeared—
Leaving behind only a thread of her uniform.

The loose ends of this case
Are to be found floating in water.

Two days later a woman's torso
Is retrieved from the Linden Canal.

Then the legs are found in the Prince's Canal;
A scar identifies them as the maid's.

A week later her shaven head is recovered
From the Brewer's Canal.

Whodunnit—a master-butcher,
With too much time on his hands?

No—Hermina Wouters (28)
Is accused of the murders.

So she's broken on the wheel,
Her legs hacked off below the knees,

Her right hand is severed,
Her throat is slit, she's beheaded.

Only then is she shipped across the Het IJ
To be put on public display.

(version by John Hughes)

NIEUWE TRUI

In de schaduw van een muur
bekeek ik mijn nieuwe trui
en nieuwe bloes en pantalon, alles nieuw.
Mijn hand beefde licht, mijn hart
zwol van geluk, ik wilde ook nog
tranen in mijn ogen hebben maar
ik hield mij in, de zon steeg op, wat
er ook gebeuren mocht, ik had een
nieuwe trui en bloes en pantalon.

Daar kwam een dunne jongen
met een bril en haar zo blond als brood,
hij droeg een smalle jas, hij zwaaide
met een zwarte paraplu, nu
was het plotseling nacht, ik
vergeleek mijn trui met de zijne en
met zijn bloes, die hij niet aan had,
zijn pantalon verwees naar de maan,
die rees en rees en wat er gebeurde,
ik weet het niet, de jongen werd zo dun
en teer en zijn bril tien maal te groot
en ook zijn schoenen en zijn toch al
smalle jas en ik zat daar maar en
de zon rees en ik wist niet wat mij
overkwam en mijn trui glom en nu
stond ik maar op en overzag de aarde,
ik spoedde mij naar huis, haastig
haastig, wolken joegen langs de hemel,
overwoekerd door het beven van mijn
hand struikelde ik keer op keer, ik kende
mijzelf niet, wie was ik, dat ik bang
was en radeloos, ik had spieren en
magere armen als stokken, ik was voor
niemand bang maar spoedde mij heen
met nieuwe trui en bloes en pantalon

NEW SWEATER

In the shade of a wall
I looked at my new sweater
and new shirt and trousers, all new.
My hand trembled slightly, my heart
swelled with joy, I also wanted
to have tears in my eyes but
I contained myself, the sun rose, whatever
might happen, I had a
new sweater and shirt and trousers.

A thin boy appeared
with spectacles and hair as blond as bread,
he wore a tight coat, he waved
a black umbrella, now
it suddenly was night, I
compared my sweater to his and
to his shirt, which he didn't have on,
his trousers referred to the moon,
which rose and rose and what happened,
I don't know, the boy grew so thin
and brittle and his spectacles ten times too big
and his shoes too and his coat, which was
tight anyway, and I just sat there and
the sun rose and I didn't know what
was happening to me and my shirt shone and then
I just stood up and surveyed the earth,
I rushed home, in haste
in haste, clouds raced along the sky,
overgrown by the trembling of my
hand I stumbled time and again, I didn't
know myself, who was I, to be afraid
and at my wit's end, I had muscles and
thin arms like sticks, I was afraid of
no one but rushed off
with new sweater and shirt and trousers

en mijn pantalon fladderde in de
angstaanjagende wind als een jonge vogel,
o, dunne jongen, waarom vertoonde jij je nutteloze
verschijning aan mij, hele moerassen
kwamen sindsdien in mijn leven voor, ik moest zo
nadenken maar het ondoordachte in mijn trui
benauwde mij.

ENIGE TRANEN

Toen ik aan u dacht, schoten mij enige tranen te binnen.
Buiten hing een grijs daglicht.
De radio stond zachtjes aan.
Ik staarde voor mij uit; er viel niet veel te zien,
dus zag ik niets.
Wel ontdekte ik een gevoel van ontreddering, dat gepaard
ging aan een gevoel van eenzaamheid.
Beide kwamen goed van pas, want
nu ging ik mij in hen verlustigen,
waarna ik mij in de keuken begaf, vervolgens
alle kamers in het huis betrad, de trap nogmaals
afdaalde, mij enige tijd roerloos ophield
in de w.c. en tenslote nam ik weer plaats in
mijn stoel.
In zekere zin wist ik mij geen raad.
De avond viel en weldra ook de nacht.
Zacht jankend begaf ik mij naar buiten.
De deur sloot ik zorgvuldig achter me, alsof
wat ik ging doen eindelijk gebeuren ging.

and my trousers were flapping in the
terrifying wind like a young bird,
oh, thin boy, why did you show your useless
appearance to me, entire swamps
have occurred in my life since, I had to
think so much but the thoughtlessness in my sweater
oppressed me.

(version by Peter van de Kamp)

SOME TEARS

When I thought about you, some tears came to mind.
Outside there was a grey daylight.
The radio was on softly.
I stared in front of me; there wasn't much to see,
so I saw nothing.
I did discover a sense of confusion, coupled
with a sense of loneliness.
Both came in very handy, for
now I went on to wallow in them,
after which I proceeded to the kitchen, next
entered all the rooms in the house, once more descended
the stairs, for some time stayed motionless
in the toilet and finally again sat down in
my chair.
In a sense I was at my wit's end.
The evening fell and before long the night too.
Softly bawling I went outside.
I carefully closed the door behind me, as if
what I was going to do was at last going to happen.

(version by Peter van de Kamp)

DE BOER

Het was dag. Ik voelde, dat ik het dorp moest verlaten. Dat deed ik. Weldra
was daar een boerderij, waarvan de muren geel bepleisterd waren, en waar ik
vroeger, in alle vroegte kastanjes zocht om te verkopen. Het was einde
september. Gehaast kwam ik het erf op om aan de deur te rammelen.
Achter mij verloor zich het landschap in wit zonlicht. Een vogel viel
bijna op de grond, wist ik. Dorre boomgaarden hingen scheef.
Niemand deed open. Ik begaf mij zijwaarts, om de stal heen, tot waar
mest lag. Er heerste een lege stilte, waarin alles verzonk, maar alles bleef
overeind. Oude beuken stonden in dubbele rij langs een pad.
Niets voegde zich bij me. Mijn hand bleef hangen waar ik hem stil
hield, mijn lichaam stond recht. Geen wind waaide er. Weilanden
gingen schuil achter geboomte. Het gebeurde dat ik op mijn schreden
terugkeerde. Ik zag opnieuw geen leven, dat moest zo zijn. Geleidelijk
voelde ik mij vereenzamen. Het was alsof ik om die reden in het verwilderde
gazon voor het huis ging liggen, waar een met gaas bespannen planken
hek aan de grond doorrotte. Er stond geen blauwe lucht meer aan de
hemel. Het wekte misschien de indruk dat ik uitrustte, maar ik was
springlevend. Daarom stond ik op en verliet fluitend het erf. Achter mij
denderde plotseling een lawaai, dat mij als het ware besprong. Ik
weende, want nu was ik verloren. De boer stond uitdrukkingsloos buiten met z
gezin aan de hand. Ik zag niets. Er heerste diepste
stilte, waarin de dingen op de juiste plaats gelaten en roerloos recht overeind
stonden. Maar toch was het alsof ik een stem hoorde, ver weg, maar ook dicht
bij, zelfs in mij, dwars door dit zwijgen der dingen heen, maar zonder het
te verbreken, waarvan ik de taal niet verstond, maar die mij in tranen
bracht.

HE FARMER

It was day. I felt I had to leave the village. I did. Before long
there was a farm, whose walls were plastered yellow, and where,
in the past, at the crack of dawn I looked for chestnuts to sell. It was the end
of September. I hurried into the yard to rattle at the door.
Behind me the landscape lost itself in white sunlight. A bird nearly
fell down on the ground, I knew. Barren orchards hung askew.
No one answered the door. I went sideways, around the stable, to where
the dung lay. An empty silence reigned, into which all had sunk, but all remained
erect. Old beeches stood in a double row along a path.
Nothing joined me. My hand remained hanging where I kept it
still, my body stood erect. No wind blew. Pastures
were hidden behind trees. It came about that I retraced my
steps. I again saw no life, it had to be thus. Gradually
I felt lonely. It was as if for that reason I lay down in the weed-grown
lawn in front of the house, where the planks of the fence covered with gauze
were rotting at ground level. There was no blue sky left in the
heavens. This may have created the impression that I was resting, but I was
alive and kicking. That's why I jumped up and left the yard whistling. Behind me
a din suddenly rumbled, which as it were leapt upon me. I
wept, for now I was lost. The farmer was standing expressionless outside with his
family by his side. I saw nothing. There reigned deepest
silence, in which the things, left in their proper place and motionless, stood
erect. But yet it was as if I heard a voice, far away, but also close
by, even inside me, straight through this silence of the things, but without
breaking it, the language of which I didn't understand, but which brought me to
tears.

(version by Peter van de Kamp)

SCHOONMAAK

heel voorzichtig
met haar ragebol
veegt de huisvrouw
in de oksel van het plafond

giechelend
lacht het gebouw zich in puin

RÉGIME

in a flurry of zeal
with her feather duster
she cleans under the armpits
of the ceiling

cracking up, hysterical
the structure falls apart

(version by Ruth Hooley)

CLEANING

very cautiously
with her duster
the housewife wipes
in the armpit of the ceiling

giggling
the building splits itself laughing

(version by Peter van de Kamp)

SED NON FRUSTRA

Teneinde een mannelijk voorkomen
te bekomen,
streefde ik een baard na.

Ik schoor me niet
en
ik schoor me niet.

En ja hoor,
na vier dagen kon je al wat zien.

Het leek net of ik me
vier dagen niet geschoren had.

SED NON FRUSTRA

You may have heard
How I adhered
To my desire
For a beard
That, had it appeared,
Would not require
Me to proclaim
My sex was male.

So for four days
I did not shave.
I did not shave
For four whole days.
Something appeared.
No. Not a beard.
You may have heard.
For all I'd slaved.

For four whole days
At not being shaved
That's how I appeared,
unshaved, no beard.

(*version by Seamus Deane*)

DE LEGE KAMER BLIJFT DE LEGE KAMER

De lege kamer blijft de lege kamer.
Alleen ikzelf er in en niemand opent
de deur, geen vrouw of vriend, geen vreemde.
Ik heb dit eerder meegemaakt maar nu
ben ik al zoveel jaren ouder
en valt het zoveel moeilijker te geloven
dat dit weer overgaat, dat ik zal lopen
misschien niet vrij van deze zieke man maar toch
weer in het licht waarvan ik heb gehouden.

THE EMPTY ROOM

The empty room is still the empty room.
There's only me inside and no one
opens the door; no woman, no friend, no caller.
I've been through it all before, nevertheless
I'm a lot older now
And find it a lot harder to believe
That this will change and that I'll walk
—Not freed from my sick body, but once more
In that light I loved.

(version by Desmond Egan)

THE EMPTY ROOM

The empty room is still the empty room.
Only myself within and no one opens
the door, no woman or friend, no stranger.
I've been here before but
I am much older now and
it is so much harder to believe
that this will pass, that I shall walk,
perhaps not delivered of this sick man but yet
once more in the light which I have loved.

(version by Joan McBreen)

WAD

Kraste het water enige uren geleden
met zijn hoeven nog tegen de dijk:
nu ligt het wad voldaan en zwetend
voor zich uit. Vogels pikken ongedierte
uit zijn plooien. Hier en daar een rilling
door zijn huid, waar wind het water raakt.

MUD-FLAT

Where are all the fussy waders
when the water is laughing and lapping
at the embankment, and the coxswain
is being hauled by all eight
of the crew, under the city's bridges?

And where is all this,
when the ebbing is so grey and distant
at the far side of the mud,
and the godwits go nicely
among the smaller crustacea?

Some parts of this morning's flood
are now these small, shivering ponds.

(version by Seán Lysaght)

MUD-FLAT

Only a few hours ago the water with its hooves
still scraped against the dyke:
now the mud-flat lies contented and sweating
stretched out. Birds pick vermin
from its folds. Here and there a tremble
through its skin, where wind touches the water.

(version by Peter van de Kamp)

ALLERZIELEN

Een vlieg, dáár alleen op zijn gemak
waar alles vlak is, wit en strak,
bemerkt hoe plotseling zijn firmament
beweegt en schudt; dit niet gewend
(nooit van zijn leven was hij oogge-
tuige van een schoonmaak) sterft hij,
vaart ten hemel en wordt opgezogen.

DE DICHTER DUIKT

Voorbij. Geen vorm zo uitgebalanceerd
of hij verdwijnt, geen plons zo elegant
of hij vergaat, in kringen, onbestemd.
Een salto telt zolang de plank nog trilt,
zolang het meisje op de rand van het bassin
me ziet, hoe ik mijn haren schud.

ALL SOULS' DAY

A solitary fly, nice and content,
there where it's smooth, white and tense
observes how all of a sudden its firmament
moves and quakes. Unused to this
(never in its life before eyewitness
to such a clean-up) he dies
and sailing heavenwards is hoovered up.

(*version by Micheal O'Siadhail*)

THE POET DIVES

past. No matter how poised the shape
it will vanish, or how elegant that splash
it will die into circles, uncertain.
Somersaults count as long as the board trembles,
as long as the girl at the edge of the pool
watches me, look! how I toss my hair.

(*version by Micheal O'Siadhail*)

DIE OCHTEND IN APRIL

Die ochtend in april
waarop mijn vader doodging,
enige tijd nadat het eerste licht gekropen kwam
onder het ongestreken en te kort gordijn
van de speciale kamer voor de stervenden,
die ochtend heb ik voor het eerst
de dood van heel dichtbij gezien.
Hij was niet speciaal gruwelijk,
ook niet een zorgzame verlosser
maar traag en efficiënt.
Hij zat verborgen in de gummi slang
waarmee het doodsgereutel pijnlijk
werd verminderd
en in de zakdoek die niet hielp
tegen het koude zweet
en in de blauwe glans die plotseling
op het gelaat lag,
in de adem die de kamer vulde, waar
geen reukwater meer hielp.
Hij gaf mijn vaders hand de kracht
nog voor een laatste groet
en deed een beetje ouderwets aan
in de plechtige gedaante van een non
die het laken hoger trok
en het dode gezicht nog doder maakte.

THAT APRIL MORNING

That April morning
when my father died,
the first light having sneaked
beneath the skimpy, crumpled curtain
of the room reserved for dying,
that morning for the first time
I had a close-up view of death.
He was not particularly horrific
nor a tender saviour
but slow and quietly efficient.
He lay trapped in the rubber tubing
which muffled painfully
the death-rattle
and in the futile handkerchief
he raised against cold sweat
and in the blue wash suddenly
enveloping his face,
in the breath that saturated the room,
where perfume had no impact.
He gave my father's hand the strength
to show a last farewell
and seemed a mite old-fashioned
in the solemn presence of a nun
who drew the sheet up higher,
made the dead face deader still.

(version by Dennis O'Driscoll)

EEN FATA MORGANA IN VLAANDEREN

De vogels vielen plots dood neer.
De vissen verdorden in het water.
De bomen trokken hun wortels uit de aarde.
Hun bladeren stortten loodzwaar neer.
Jan van Ruusbroec glimlachte.
Op het strand hield de branding op.
De bergen zakten in elkaar.
De bloemen hielden hun geur in.
Woorden vielen uiteen in lettergrepen.
Pieter Bruegel glimlachte.
De aarde hield op met draaien.
De eeuwigheid begon.
Hadewych glimlachte.
De mieren bleven staan in lange rijen.
De pauwen trokken hun veren uit.
Het gras begon een blauwe droom.
Jeroen Bosch glimlachte.
De steden versteenden.
De rozen begonnen te bloeden.
De stilte brak los.
De eindeloze slapeloosheid begon.
En ik, ik keek naar jou.
De zon scheen in mijn gezicht.
Ik knipperde met de ogen.

FATA MORGANA IN FLANDERS

Birds suddenly dropped dead.
Fish dried up in water.
Trees uprooted themselves from the earth.
Their leaves falling heavy as lead.
Jan van Ruusbroec smiled.
Waves ceased to beat on the strand.
Mountains crumbled.
Flowers kept their fragrance to themselves.
Words took off in syllables.
Pieter Bruegel smiled.
The earth ceased to revolve.
Eternity began.
Hadewych smiled.
Ants stood in long queues.
Peacocks plucked their feathers.
Grass started to dream blue.
Jeroen Bosch smiled.
Cities collapsed.
Roses began to bleed.
Quietness broke loose.
Eternal sleeplessness began.
And I, I stared at you.
The sun shone on my face.
I blinked.

(version by Gabriel Rosenstock)

ALS IK EENS ÉÉN KEER ÉÉN DAG EEN NIJLPAARD ZOU KUNNEN ZIJN

Als ik eens één keer één dag een nijlpaard zou kunnen zijn
maar dan wel met mijn gewone menselijke verstand,
dan zou ik naar de Dam gaan
en een toespraak houden
over de regels der rechtvaardigheid,
en luisteren zou men,
en terwijl de telexen van de wereld zouden ratelen
zou ik alweer bij jou zijn
en jouw ranke lijf tegen mijn enorme grijze romp koesteren.

HET BEZOEK

Op een dag was het zover.
Ik besloot haar eindelijk eens op te zoeken.
Haar gieren deden mij peinzend open.
Haar honden gingen mij voor naar haar vertrekken,
de sporen van hun tanden in mijn been.
Haar slangen schonken mij een kopje thee in,
met een wolkje melk, en roerden het om met hun tongen.
Haar slakken likten mijn mondhoeken schoon.
Zij was er niet, zij was zojuist vertrokken,
zei haar hyena, huilend in mijn nek.
En zij komt nooit meer terug,
zei haar spin, de aanzet tot een web
reeds strak gespannen om mij heen.

IF JUST FOR ONCE

If just for once for just one day I could be a hippopotamus,
but then one with my plain human sense,
I would go to Dam Square
and make a speech
about the rules of justice,
how they would listen,
and while the telexes of the world were rattling away
I would already be with you
and cherish your slender body against my enormous grey trunk.

(version by Peter van de Kamp)

THE VISIT

One day the time had come.
I decided to pay her a visit at last.
Her vultures let me in pensively.
Her dogs showed me to her rooms,
the marks of their teeth in my leg.
Her snakes poured me a cup of tea,
with a drop of milk, and stirred it round with their teeth.
Her snails licked the corners of my mouth clean.
She was not there; she had just left,
said her hyena, crying in my neck.
And she will never come back,
said her spider, the onset of a web
already stretched tightly around me.

(version by Peter van de Kamp)

CHANSON

Gerafelde popdeun, stukgezongen blues
& versteende jazz of geroeste rock
en mijn eeuwenoude lied:

nooit iemand te hebben ontzien,
nooit troost te hebben geboden
dan om eigen bestwil, nooit of
nooit een gemeend gebed of offer.

Als een ziekte, onverhoeds en onnaspeurbaar.
Als hitte die in alle hoeken woedde
en waarvoor geen schuilplaats bestaat
was mijn leven dat ik zag opbranden,

een toeschouwer, niet bij machte
de verschrikkelijke zaal te verlaten.

A WORN-OUT POP-SONG

A worn-out pop song, a tattered blues,
a jazz petrified as rock—
this is my life's theme:

never to have spared anyone,
never to have offered comfort
but to please myself, never,
neither honest prayer nor sacrifice.

Like a sudden mysterious illness,
a fire that raged in every quarter—
there could have been no protection—
my life burned up

as I stood there, unable
to escape the terrible performance.

(version by Pat Boran)

DOOD, DONKERE DADER EN ZACHTE HAND

Dood, donkere dader en zachte hand
maanlicht op een werveling van bladeren,
deur naar een verzonken land,
naar slaap en eindelijke stilte in de aderen.

Ik vrees mijn laatste knik om u te groeten:
stof van zoveel doden aan mijn voeten,
dood, aanwezig in alles wat ik nader,
die zuigt aan mij, zuigt aan mijn vader,

gij zijt nog ver genoeg dat ik u bezingen kan.

DEATH, DARK AGENT

Why not simply moonlight on a swirling of leaf?
Instead, the dark agent of a hated land
comes to claim the tribute of grief
as the pulse fades in the cherished hand.

I find words for a dripping oar
and a hooded gondolier, rowing ever closer,
and words, too, as he comes ashore
to lift the hood from his boatman's face—

but no words that would discover there
my own late face.

(version by Seán Lysaght)

DEATH, DARK DOER

Death, dark doer and soft hand
moonlight on a whirling of leaves,
door to a submerged land,
to sleep and final silence in the veins.

I fear my last nod to greet you:
dust of so many deaths at my feet,
death, present in everything I approach,
that sucks on me, sucks on my father,

you are still remote enough for me to sing of you.

(version by Peter van de Kamp)

UIT DE LUSITAANSE VARIANT

I

Fortuinen in kniebroek
bewandelen de oude paden
        der politieke roulette

toen was het karlsbad
nu estoril achter sintra (steriel &
                glad als een geschoren onderbuik)

rechts staat de bank van de heilige geest &
                        de handel,

links leegt een donkere knecht
de betegelde beerput van het casino

zigeunerende kledenverkopers
spritsen een fluim in een vismand

zweet bijt in gebarsten lippen,
minimolens snorren in de wind

wie nu iets bezit
wordt morgen bezeten

Het oog dwaalt
                langs palmen en perken,
        het talmt
bij de waterpartij, bij de ijsman, de gauwdief, de duttende
                                ezelberijder

ginds, achter klimroos en bereklauw
schemeren de strooien hoeden van
stramme heren   die beverig
        en blauw
het verleden een zekere toekomst voorspellen

FROM THE LUSITANIAN VARIANT

I

Fortunes in knee breeches
tread the old paths
          of the political roulette

it was karlsbad then
now estoril beyond sintra (sterile &
                              smooth as a shaven belly)

on the right stands the bank of the holy ghost &
                              commerce,

on the left a dark servant empties
the tiled cesspool of the casino

gipsying rug vendors
squirt a phlegm in a fish basket

sweat bites into burst lips,
toy mills whirr in the wind

who owns something now
will tomorrow be possessed

the eye wanders
          past palms and flowerbeds,
      it tarries
at the water garden, at the iceman, the bag-snatcher, the snoozing
                              donkey rider

in the distance, beyond rambling rose and hogweed
shimmer the straw hats of
rigid gentlemen   who, shaky
      and blue,
predict a secure future for the past

III.I *DUEL*

We gaan op dienstreis
langs vergeten wegen

ik speel door het hoofd
en huis in het hart
      van een zeer hoog commando

ik ben de rebel
die hij steeds weer bedwingt

we zijn even ingetoomd als onbeteugeld

als ik hem uitspeel
houdt hij mij achter

wat ons verdeelt
brengt ons ook bij elkaar

we komen tot bundeling
van krachten

O mystiek van het eerste begin

het vonkje der ziel springt
al over

hij krijgt mijn zin
en ik maak mij meester
      van zijn gedachten

III.1 *DUEL*

We go on a business trip
past forgotten roads

i'm playing through the head
and am housing in the heart
            of a very high commando

i am the rebel
whom he time and again tames

we are as reined in as unbridled

when i play him out
he keeps me behind

what separates us
also brings us together

we reach a bundling
of forces

O mystique of the first begining

the spark of the soul jumps
over already

he gets things my way
and i master
    his thoughts

III.4 *DANÇA MORTAL*

Ik had nog voor de nacht
patrijzen willen jagen

het dorpsplein trilt verlaten in de zon

ik speelde hier in vroeger dagen
en loop aangeschoten door de kom

Een hinderlaag: opeens
omsloten door een haag van hoge stemmen

sta ik vastgenageld op een veld—

ik ben in een oogwenk
door kinderen ontwapend

de kring gaat zingend rond
en weerloos word ik uitgeteld:

> *Eén is je rokje van water*
> *twee is je lijfje van brood*
> *drie is ik eet je wel later*
> *vier is je handen zijn rood*
>
> *één twee drie heden,*
> *zeg je gebeden—*
> *want jij bent dood!*

De hitte beduimelt het lichaam,
de middag wordt lood op de huid
vliegen verkoperen de oogkassen
van een kadaver

het is al later dan ik dacht:

ik had nog voor de nacht
patrijzen willen jagen

III.4 *DANÇA MORTAL*

I had wanted to go hunt
partridges before nightfall

the village square quivers deserted in the sun

i used to play here in former days
and walk half-smashed through the hub

An ambush: suddenly
surrounded by a hedge of high voices

i stand nailed to a field—

in the wink of an eye i am
disarmed by children

the circle goes round singing
and defenseless I am counted out:

> *One is your kirtle of water*
> *two is your body of bread*
> *three is i will eat you later*
> *four is your hands they are red*
>
> *one two three and now*
> *make your last vow—*
> *for you are dead!*

The heat thumb-marks the body
the afternoon turns to lead on the skin
flies copper-plate the sockets
of a cadaver

it is later than i thought:

i had wanted to go hunt
partridges before nightfall

IN DIENST VAN HET WIEL.

In dienst van het wiel.
Eerst als het wiel goed
aanloopt, maak ik pas
een mooie kans om me
ooit vrij te lopen.

Maar dan ook nooit meer vluchten
hoor, zegt de waarsprekende aap
half vermanend, half verwijtend,

alvorens te zijn opgegaan
in dienst van het wiel.

VAN LIEVERLEDE; ZO

Van lieverlede; zo
komen zij nader: 8 roeiers,
steeds verder landinwaarts

groeiend in hun mytologie:
met elke slag steeds verder
van huis, uit allemacht roeiend;
groeiend tot alle water weg is,
en zij het hele landschap

vullen tot de rand. Acht—
steeds verder landinwaarts
roeiend; landschap daar al geen
water meer is: dichtgegroeid
landschap al. Landschap,
steeds verder land-

inwaarts roeiend; land
zonder roeiers; dicht-
geroeid land al.

IN THE SERVICE OF THE WHEEL.

In the service of the wheel
Only once the wheel
Really drags will I stand
A fine chance of
ever running clear.

But then it's never escape again,
says the truth-telling ape
half admonishing, half reproaching,

before being absorbed
in the service of the wheel.

(version by Peter van de Kamp)

BIT BY BIT

Bit by bit; thus
they draw near: 8 rowers
ever further inland,

growing in their mythology:
with every beat ever further
from home, rowing with might and main;
growing till all water is gone,
and they fill the whole landscape

to the brink. Eight—
ever further inland
rowing; landscape there being
no more water: grown-over
landscape all. Landscape
ever further in-

land rowing; land
without rowers; rowed-
over land all.

(version by Peter van de Kamp)

1945

De Duitsers stonden bewaakt bij elkaar
bij de uitvalsweg, een troep verrotte augurken.
Sommigen waren jongens zo oud als ik
met niets dan regenlucht om zich heen.
Eén roerde in een vierkant pannetje
op zijn hurken.

De oorlog was over, door kinderen verloren,
met veel te lange geweren getraind,
als tovenaarsleerlingen van het kwaad geboren.

Zij leren hun tafels moeiteloos,
zij laten zich doden bij Elst en Verdun,
ze kunnen meer brood aan dan je dacht.

Hun verveling grenst altijd aan boosheid,
ze schoppen tegen de dagen aan
als tegen vuilnisbakken.
Lang blijven ze op de muren schrijven
en naar de kleren en de onkwetsbaarheid
van de volwassenen snakken.

1945

The Germans stood together under guard
near the exit road, a bunch of rotten gherkins.
Some were boys as old as I
with nothing but a rain-sky around them.
One stirred in a square pot
on his hunches.

The war was over, lost by children,
trained with rifles that were far too long,
born like sorcerer's apprentices of evil.

They learn their tables effortlessly,
they get themselves killed near Elst and Verdun,
they can handle more bread than you thought.

Their boredom always borders on anger,
they kick against the days
as if against rubbish bins.
They keep on writing on the walls
and craving for the clothes
and invulnerability of the grown-ups.

(version by Peter van de Kamp)

1980 – 1994

VERONTRUSTEND VOORWERP

(Bij een tekening van Alberto Giacometti)

Hij was er al voorbij
toen iets zijn ooghoek trof
nu keert hij op zijn schreden terug
en ziet maar weet niet wat

Een voorwerp
zonder kant noch wal
een ding maar
zonder naam

Hij bukt zich
bang en blij ineen
maar pakt het niet
hij kijkt zich rijk

Dan is hij weer alleen.

DISCONCERTING OBJECT

(On a Drawing by Giacometti)

He had passed it
when something caught the corner of his eye
now he retraces his steps
and looks but knows not what

An object
neither here nor there
a thing but
without a name

He stoops
afraid and glad at once
but does not reach
the view enriches

Then he's alone again.

(version by Peter van de Kamp)

BEATRICE

In de vijftiende werd zij geschilderd
in de zestiende verloor zij een arm
in de zeventiende verdwenen haar benen
in de achttiende weg was haar buik
in de negentiende vergingen haar borsten
in de twintgste werd zij bijkans gewist.

Zo zou het gegaan kunnen zijn.

Steeds bleker werd het beeld.
En boven wat verdween zweven haar lippen
en een deel van haar kin.
En onder wat verging flappert de door de wind
opgenomen zoom van haar roestrode rok.

Zo is het.
Zuiver als een A huivert haar gestalte in terracotta na.

De schilder voorbij kan ik haar aanraken en
horen wat ze zei.

Is het al af?
Mag ik nu weg?
Mijn vriendje wacht
op de hoek van de straat.

Daar gaat ze
nu is ze de hoek om.

Op de lege muur verschijnt de hand van de schilder
zijn penselen wenken
ik kom naderbij.

Zo zal het gaan.

BEATRICE

In the fifteenth she was painted
in the sixteenth she lost an arm
in the seventeenth her legs disappeared
in the eighteenth her belly was gone
in the nineteenth her breasts perished
in the twentieth she was well-nigh erased.

Thus it could have been.

Ever fainter the image.
And above that which disappeared float her lips
and a part of her chin.
And underneath that which perished flutters
the seam of her rusty-red skirt taken in by wind.

Thus it is.
Pure like an A quivers her appearance in terracotta.

Past the painter I can touch her and
hear what she said.

Is it finished?
Can I go now?
My boyfriend's waiting
at the corner of the street.

There she goes
now she's round the corner.

On the empty wall the hand of the painter appears
his brushes beckon
I come near.

Thus it will be.

(version by Peter van de Kamp)

OVER TIJD

Die stilte aan zee, zo laat in het daglicht,
liet je op zoek naar de grenzen gaan —
schelpen verkleurden voor je voeten,
het licht gleed weg met de wind langs je schaduw
en ruimte viel neer op je hart —
hoe ongekend werd het geluk, hoe eenvoudig
ontroering, hoe tastbaar in de diepte van de dag —
in de verte lag het leven, een starre,
beweeglijke schittering, ver van de aarde,
ver van het heden, en ginds lag, gevend,
de nacht.

ABOUT TIME

At dusk the silence by the sea
enticed you to beachcomb borders —
shells darkened at your feet,
light slipped away with the wind past your shadow
and space enamoured your heart —
how remarkable your happiness — how simple
the emotion, how palpable in the depths of the day —
Far from the shore, far from the present,
life lay, a stubborn, agile glimmer
and behind you lay, bestowing,
the night.

(version by Greg Delanty)

ABOUT TIME

This silence at the sea's edge, so late in the afternoon,
sent you searching for horizons —
shells paled at your feet,
the light slipped away with the wind, effacing your shadow
and empty space consumed your heart —
how boundless your joy — how pure
the resonance, echoing in the crevices of the day —
in the distance, life glittered,
agile, literal, far from the shore,
far from the present, and beyond this,
the beacon of the night.

(version by Anne Kennedy)

ARCHEOLOGISCHE VONDST

Een archeoloog beging onlangs
een schromelijke vergissing.
In de woestijn van Nevada
haalde hij vanonder het zand
de radioactieve resten
van een gokapparaat,
waarmee hij het bewijs leverde
dat Las Vegas inderdaad heeft bestaan.
De arme man had blijkbaar
in een verkeerde richting gegraven
en was aldus op de laatste resten
van onze toekomst gestuit.

ARCHAEOLOGICAL FIND

An archaeologist recently
got it totally arse-ways.
In the Nevada wastes
he dug up
the radioactive remains
of a roulette wheel,
which conclusively proved
that Las Vegas really did exist.
The poor fucker was obviously
digging in the wrong direction
and accidentally discovered in the sand
the last remnants of the future.

(version by Gabriel Rosenstock)

AFRICAN QUEEN

voor Mariam

Niets van haar gaat voorbij.
De spiegel houdt haar beeld vast.
Het bed bewaart haar vorm
precies zoals ze heeft gelegen.
De volheid van haar mond,
de zachtheid van haar knieën,
zo iets lost nooit meer op.
Zelfs haar parfum is een deel
van mij geworden. En alles wat ze zei
is aanwezig, zij kan nooit verdwijnen,
ook al is zij nu onzichtbaar.
Haar tong proefde naar liefde.
Haar handen vertelden over tederheid.
Al wat ze streelde van mij is nu weg,
is nu bij haar, is nu van haar.
Ik weet nog hoe het was
toen zij er was. Ik kijk naar haar
ook als zij er niet meer is.

AFRICAN QUEEN

for Mariam

No part of her will fade.
The mirror holds her image.
The bed retains her form
Exactly as she has lain.
Fullness of mouth,
Tenderness of knees,
These cannot pass away.
Even her perfume
Is part of me. Everything she said
Is in the present tense; she appears everywhere
Even when out of sight.
Her tongue tasted of love.
Her hands spoke gentleness.
Any part of me that she caressed is me
No longer, is she and all of her.
I know what she was like
When she was here. When she is not
I see her always.

(version by Gabriel Rosenstock)

SOMS

Soms moet ik ruiken aan die zwavelput,
proef ik weer as en kan het kermen horen.
Wat is er toch zo zoet aan het verloren,
het bijna verloren gaan. Ik wend mij af
van het bekoorlijk dal waarin ik anders
de voren trek die goed zijn om te zien,
die ook nog vrucht voortbrengen.
Hoe is de helleveeg betoverend en
moeder aardes waarde wel constant
maar tijdlijk niet courant en het
bederf, het stinkende bederf trek-
pleister tot de buil weer openberst
in karmozijn en geel. De brand die Patinir
en Bosch altijd weer feller schilderden
dan 't vage vuur daarnaast, waaraan
geen ziel zich schroeit, geen mens zich warmt.

Om van de hemel maar te zwijgen,
waar koelte stroomt, waarnaar wij zullen
hijgen. Maar later, straks, nu niet.
Nu even niet.

SOMETIMES

Sometimes I must smell that sulphur pit,
Once more I taste the ashes and can hear the groans.
What is so sweet, then, about being lost,
Almost being lost. I turn away
From the delectable valley where I would
Draw the furrows, fair to the eye,
And also bearing fruit.
How enchanting is the hell-cat and
Mother Earth's value is constant, yes,
But not current just now and
Decay, stinking decay, a balm,
Drawing until the boil bursts yet again
In crimson and yellow. The fire which Patinir
And Bosch always painted brighter
Than neighbouring dim purgatory, which
Singes no soul, warms no man.

Not to mention heaven
Where coolness flows, for which we shall
Pant. But later, soon, not now.
Not just now.

(version by Peter van de Kamp)

ZO OUD ALS TOEN

'Jongen, bederf je ogen niet.'

Ik zat maar weer in Het Leven te lezen
in de donkere kamer vol vreemd porselein
en Delftsblauwe borden.
Ook 's zomers was het vroeg laat in dat huis.
Grootvader klutste zijn eitje
en zei toen ik opkeek:
'Je opa houdt veel van z'n eige.'

Buiten hadden de beuken
een kleur alsof brons
kon roesten als ijzer.
De vijver, nooit meer geschoond,
lag zwart te verlanden.

Zo oud als toen hoop ik nooit meer te worden.

AS OLD AS THEN

'You'll ruin your eyesight, lad.'

I was reading *Het Leven* again
in the dark room full of strange porcelain
and Delft Blue plates.
Even in summer, in that house it got late early.
Grandfather tapped his egg
and said when I looked up:
'Your granddad is his own best friend.'

Outside, the beeches
coloured as if bronze
could rust like iron.
The pond, never again cleaned
was turning to black ground.

I hope to never again become as old as then.

(version by Michael O'Loughlin)

A NOS GLORIEUX MORTS

Het schooltje is al lang gesloten,
vervallen en weer opgeknapt
door wie er in vakanties wonen.

De bakker komt nog loeiend langs,
het raadhuis gaat nog open
als er wordt zakgelopen

op 't stoffig plein voor de mairie,
wanneer een kleine tricolore
de tijd van 't jaar aangeeft.

Van een verlaten huis zakt eerst
het dak en dan een zijkant in.
Er wordt hier nooit iets afgebroken.

En de soldaat verschiet van kleur:
zijn ijzer raakt niet aangevreten,
wordt nu en dan met verf bestreken.

De laatste keer was het pauwblauw.
De nacht zag er misschien zo uit
toen hij dichtbij te velde lag

op zijn nog gave rug. Het past ook bij
de sierlijk opgeslagen panden
van zijn solide, als gegoten jas.

Hij leunt op zijn geweer als op een spa.
Onder de kolf haalt op het voetstuk
Labroche Octave de eeuwigheid

en met hem nog acht namen.
De oogst was klein, zelfs voor zo'n
nietig dorp. Toch haalt het nog de tien

met Bador Jules, victime civile.

A NOS GLORIEUX MORTS

The school is long closed down
dilapidated, done up again
as someone's holiday home.

The baker still comes roaring by,
The town hall still opens
when sack races are run

on the dusty square in front of the Mairie,
when a small tricolour
gives the time of year.

First the roof and then a wall
of a deserted house collapse.
Here nothing is ever demolished.

And the soldier gets discoloured:
his iron is not corroded
gets the occasional lick of paint.

The last time was peacock blue.
Maybe that's how the sky looked
when he lay close to the ground

on his still-in-one-piece back. It also
goes with the neatly folded skirts
of his solid coat, a perfect fit.

He leans on his rifle as on a spade.
Under the butt on the pedestal
Labroche Octave has become immortal.

And another eight names with him.
The harvest was small, even for such
a hamlet. Still, it makes the ten

with Bador Jules, victime civile.

(version by Michael O'Loughlin)

DE STAD EEN VOGELRESERVAAT

Ik zag een meeuw die uitgleed op het ijs
en hoorde eens bij ondergaande zon
twee hanen kraaien in een boom.

Ook zag ik op een stille zondagmorgen
een sperwer op de stoep van een kantoor;
hij had een muisje in zijn klauwen
en keek mij zo woest aan
dat ik maar liever verder liep.

Voorts heb ik waargenomen
dat vogels 's morgens vroeg
graag op de rijweg lopen
en later als met tegenzin
de lucht in gaan.

Ik heb het allemaal gezien, gehoord.
Gelukkig maakt wie niets verzinnen kan
veel mee.

THE TOWN A BIRD SANCTUARY

I saw a gull that slipped on the ice
and heard once at sunset
two cocks crow in a tree.

I also saw, on a quiet Sunday morn
a sparrow hawk on the pavement of an office;
it had a little mouse in its claws
and looked at me so ferociously
that I preferred to walk on.

Furthermore I observed
that birds early in the morning
like to walk on the roadway
and later as if reluctantly
take to the air.

I saw it all, heard it all.
Fortunately he who can't invent
experiences a lot.

(version by Peter van de Kamp)

BEURTELINGS

Vannacht was ik uit de dood opgestaan.
De kamer hield zich stil maar het glasgordijn
woei op en bewoog mij tot tranen toe.

Ik riep je want ik wou je zeggen hoe
gewoon het voelde om levend te zijn.
Ik vond je in bed, de leeslamp was nog aan,

je lag wit naast mij met je ogen dicht.
Slaap je, vroeg ik. Het trok in je gezicht.

TURN AND TURN ABOUT

Tonight I resurrected from the dead.
The room lay very still but the lace curtains
kept wavering, moving me to tears.

I called out to you, wanting you to hear
how normal it felt to be alive, no strain.
I found you — reading lamp still on — in bed

beside me, your eyes screwed shut, face white.
You asleep, I asked. Your face flickered like a light.

(version by Eamon Grennan)

OUD IN OVERIJSSEL

Twee op een brommer, leren jassen
tegen de wind. Eén lichaam zijn ze
dat zijn beste jaren gehad heeft.
Met mondvooraad onder haar dijen:

Tassen vol broodjes, een thermoskan
met koffie. Twee op een deken
in de berm, zij schenkt en snijdt
de worst op het brood met voorzichtige handen.

'We hebben het goed,' zegt ze, 'vroeger
had je geen boter maar reuzel, en worst
daar viel nog niet aan te denken.'

Ze reddert rond, een duif op het oude nest,
hij ziet het aan — de hond is dood,
hun dochters kwamen goed terecht.

OLD IN OVERIJSSEL

Two on one moped, leather-coated
against the wind. They are one body
which has had its best years.
With provisions under her thighs:

Bags of sandwiches, a thermos flask
of coffee. Two on one blanket
on the grass verge, she pours coffee, lays
the sausage on the bread with careful hands.

'We're well off', she says, 'in the past
you didn't have butter but lard, and sausage
was undreamt of.'

She puts things in place like a pigeon in the old nest
he looks on — the dog is dead,
their daughters turned out fine.

(version by Robert Greacen)

DE MOL

Aarde die 'k adem in den zwaren nacht,
voor honger aarde en aarde voor den dorst;
mijn zachte en warm met bloed gevulde borst,
mijn longen voor de lucht, met aard bevracht.

Oogen waarin het zonlicht vloeide lijk
de gouden gloed in Danaë's schoot, herboren
als gouden zoon uit de oogen om te gloren
met glans en wederglans, ontaard in slijk.

Aarde getorst door mij, gewicht van grond
met vingers doorgegraven tot een gang
en achter deze gang een andre gang zoo lang
dat hij in andren grond, in grond uitmondt.

Gedolven in een graf, sprakeloos en vaal,
gevoed met wortelen en worm en zaad,
terwijl de blauw-en-groene pauw bestaat,
het paard, 't hert met gewei, de nachtegaal.

THE MOLE

Earth which I breathe in the heavy night,
earth for hunger, earth for thirst;
my soft warm breast is filled with blood,
my lungs are clogged with earthen air.

Eyes in which the sunlight flowed
like the golden glow in Danae's womb, reborn
as a golden son whose eyes, destined to
gleam luminously, corrupted into mud.

Earth hauled by me, bulk of ground
scooped out with fingers to a corridor
behind which runs another corridor so long
that, in further soil, it ends in soil.

Dug in a grave, speechless, drab,
feeding on roots and worms and seeds,
while there are blue-green peacocks,
horses, deer with antlers, nightingales.

(version by Dennis O'Driscoll)

EPIFANIE

Heet ijs snelt (schijnt het) door
haar aderen, haar beenderen breken
vlees beeft, de adem stokt, de lenden steken
zweet parelt op poriën, zeker
vóór een dergelijk werk
vlees met vlees doorstoken en
beenderen gekneed, geraamtes krakend
getweeën aaneengeklonken, gebroken, één
smeltend stollend magma te maken.
Onder uw striemen en smaden begeeft zij 't
stom en schreeuwend, haar bloed keert
zij moet dat verdragen, knel, sper,
praam haar: zij boet uw slagen.
Beloon mij dan (roept zij), vertoon mij daarna
je fijnmechaniek
je allerinnerste rad waardoor
die zilveren trillende sperwer opschiet
kopschudt en klapwiekt
speel mij voor
je mommerij je muziek
zodat ik van lachen
telkens ontsta telkens verga.

EPIPHANY

Hot ice shoots (it seems) through
her veins, her bones fracture
flesh quakes, breath flags, loins pain
sweat pearls on pores, steadfast
before such a work
flesh pierced by flesh and
bones kneaded, skeletons splintering
two riveted together, broken, to make one
melting clotting mass.
Under your onslaughts and abuse she breaks down
dumb and screaming, her blood sours
she must endure this, squash, bar,
poke her: she suffers your attacks.
Reward me then (she shouts), show me afterwards
your precision instrument
your inmost cog through which
that silver trembling hawk shoots up
shakes its head, flaps its wings
rehearse for me
your masquerade your music
so that I with laughter
routinely come to life routinely die

(version by Dennis O'Driscoll)

DECEMBER

waarom liegt ze tegen mij
zei je aan de telefoon
ze heeft zo'n ziekte nooit
gehad, ze valt gewoon
van de trap, van haar fiets,
ze valt als je haar aanraakt

je haakte in en lachte
omdat ik alles had gehoord

ik zal er een gedicht
van maken, zei ik, nam mijn dochter
bij de hand en wachtte
op de bus naar huis

het was al tegen kerstmis
ik herinner mij gedwarrel
in het licht van auto's
komend uit de bocht
de winkels gingen dicht
we wisselden gedachten:
wat we morgen zouden kopen
hoestsiroop, gehakt, ze vroeg
waarom ik lachte, en ik loog:
omdat het sneeuwde
ik had er zo lang op gewacht

DECEMBER

why does she lie to me
you said on the line
she never had such an
illness, she simply falls
on the stairs, from her bike,
she falls if you touch her

you touched my arm and laughed
for I knew it all

I shall make a poem
out of this, I said, taking my daughter
by the hand, and waited
for the bus home

it was up on Christmas
I remember a whirling
in the light of cars
coming out of bends
the shops closed
we exchanged ideas
what we would buy tomorrow
cough mixture, minced meat, she asked
why I laughed, and I lied:
because it was snowing
I had, for this, waited so long.

(version by Joan McBreen)

MEEUWEN

Het krijsen van meeuwen wees de weg naar de zee;
een nauwe steeg, steil naar beneden, daar was de haven
maar niets dan boten, trage kranen, ijzerwaren. Geen vogel
vloog of liep te pikken of deinde op een golf.
Toch, het geluid hield aan; het geweld van machines
werd zelfs overstemd door het schreeuwen.
De kranen hevelden lichte, niet helemaal dichte kisten.
Tussen de brede spleten leefde opeens de lading: vlerken
en veren. Zo werden de meeuwen het ruim in gehesen.

SEAGULLS

The gull shrieks guided us
down a steep alley to the harbour
of boats, crawling derricks, ironworks, but
no bird flew, peck-walked or wave-bobbed.
Yet, the clamour continued: the machine din
was even drowned by the screeching.
Cranes hoisted light, poorly sealed crates.
Between gaps the cargo burst to life: wings
& feathers. Thus the gulls rose to the hold.

(version by Greg Delanty)

IK WOU WEL WEER EEN BEETJE ZIEK ZIJN

Ik wou wel weer een beetje ziek zijn,
en dat je dan een hete kop melk
met rum klaarmaakte voor elk

van mij, voor de kleine weemoedige
en de grote overmoedige, en wat ik maar wou wezen,
en dat ik dan nooit meer hoefde te genezen.

Je kon het altijd uitleggen:
je legde het terug in mij.
Ik moest slechts de ogen sluiten om te zien.

Hoe je er niet meer bent.
Hoe veel plaats er is.
Hoeveel minder verdriet.

Je huid doorschijnend als een glas
dat je tot de bodem hebt uitgedronken:
jezelf. En ik, die er niet was

om je handen los te laten, vingers tien,
toen je zo ver was, zo heel, heel ver.
En om ze te hebben vastgehouden, net voordien.

IF ONLY

If only I could be, just a little, sick again
with you stretching out to me
a mug of hot milk and rum —

a mug for the staggering child, one for
the swaggerer, whichever I'd like to be —
and never after have to be well again.

You could lay out the story,
carefully storing it up in me.
I close my eyes the better to see it unfold.

Now you are not
around any more, how much space there is,
how little sadness.

Your pale skin is a glass you
drained to the bottom, draining
yourself. And I wasn't even around

to let your hands float off, your ten fingers,
when you had sunk so very, very far.
If only I could have held them, before the end.

(version by Theo Dorgan)

PAALHOOFDEN

Dat palen soms in water wonen en zonder leven
elke golf doen omslaan is niet om te verbazen.
Als boom waren zij al bereid om dagen
lang de wind te breken of zon te zeven

door hun blad. Het is niet zo dat ik van
dode bomen hou. Maar palen in een rij in
zee geven soms een gevoel dat ook in
bed ineens kan komen: veiliger dan

overdag. Zoiets als oude namen tellen
van wie er niet meer zijn. Verhalen
maken van herinnering en langzaam dwalen
door een eigen land. Een beetje knielen

voor wat heilig is en zeker weten dat
wat al weg is toch niet wordt vergeten.

POST HEADS

That posts dwell at times in water and, lifeless themselves,
make each wave break is no surprise.
As trees they were ready for days on end
to block the wind or split up sunlight

through their leaves. It isn't that I love
dead trees. But a row of posts in sea-water
makes me feel at times
the way I feel in bed: safer

than by day. It is something
like reciting over the old names
of those who are no more. Out of your memory
fashion stories and slowly walk all over

a country of your own. Briefly kneel
for what is holy and know in your bones that
what's been taken away won't ever be forgotten.

(version by Eamon Grennan)

DE WEG VAN HET WATER

I

Wat niet bestaat kan er niet zijn.
We zagen de eenzaamheid van de zee
en de lange weg van het water.

Kleuren werden oud
wolken zeilden over
maar achter de grenzen leek alles wit.

GIVING WAY

What one wants from a letter is not an answer.
We saw the vast blue of the sea,
every inch of the water a different colour.

The purple stains gave way
to clear green waves when clouds
rested too long. But one white rose
glistened against a wall.

(version by Medbh McGuckian)

THE WAY OF THE WATER

I

What does not exist cannot be.
We saw the solitude of the sea
and the long way of the water.

Colours became old
clouds sailed over
but behind the borders all seemed white.

(version by Peter van de Kamp)

HUIS AAN ZEE

Het huis is ver verleden ligt
verborgen in een tuin.

Begraven dode mus
schelpen geven de plaats aan.

Schommel aan een tak
de moeder sprak van breken.

En overal de wind
van zee achter het duin

waarin het kind zich terugtrok
alsof het al van afscheid wist.

LANDSCHAP

Alles heeft zijn plaats
het water van de rivier
de oevers ernaast.

Hoe een landschap soms oplost
als zout in water

verdwijnt naar later
waar het weer aankomt en
uitdooft alsof het niet bestaat.

Zoals ook zee zich terugtrekt
en leegte achterlaat.

HOUSE BY THE SEA

The house in the long ago
lies hidden in a garden.

A buried dead sparrow
its place marked by a shell.

A swing from a branch
a mother spoke of breaking.

And everywhere the wind
from the sea behind the dune.

A child withdraws into itself
as though it knows of some leavetaking.

(version by Micheal O'Siadhail)

LANDSCAPE

Everything has a place,
the water in the river,
and those banks so close.

Sometimes a landscape liquifies
like salt in water

and vanishes into a future
where it arrives again, then
dies, as if it had never been,

a sea that shrinks into itself
leaving such a blank behind.

(version by Micheal O'Siadhail)

VOGELTREK

Nacht achter glas. Een vlucht werd uitgezet
in lijnen. De vogeltrek begint, legt open
wat niet eindigt.

Woord dat het zwijgen deelt, de taal verliest.
Om wat voorbijging zonder stem heb ik nog mensen lief.

BIRDS LEAVING

Night takes feelings to the window,
looks at them like a network
of international airlines. When the birds leave,
they throw all the blackness elsewhere.

When a word leaves the language, silence adopts it.
Some have gone without having ever sung.

(version by Medbh McGuckian)

PLAATS EN DATUM

Ik ben in België geboren, ik ben Belg.
Maar België is nooit geboren in mij.

Ik ben in Vlaanderen geboren voor altijd,
Maar niet in Vlaanderen stond mijn oudste wieg.

Vlaanderen is mijn moderne kunstmoeder nu
Van wie ik mijn kindertong niet kreeg,
Van wie ik de hartbrekende wartaal bestudeer.
Vlaanderen werd traag mijn historische vader
Wiens voorgeslacht het mijne niet is.

Ik ben geboren in Limburg, koud,
Een koude, koude provincie.
Ik heb het er heet gekregen.

Ik ben ook geboren in Bree, Loons
En Luiks, een dodenstad, een middenstand
Met een zangerig, klagerig plat
Dat me hardop droomt als ik slaap,
Als ik slapend word ondergedompeld
In langzaam Nederduits.
                    Dat is muziek
Die ouder, me vertrouwder is dan dit
En die ik hier probeer te transponeren.

En ten slotte, als gezonde zoon
Van veel kanonnevlees, ten slotte
Ben ik geboren in 1947,
Een rauwe datum, een hoopvolle tijd,
Een wereldwijd tekort dat groeit
In mij, in mij volwassen wordt.

PLACE AND DATE

I was born in Belgium, I am Belgian.
But Belgium has never been born in me.

I was born once and for all in Flanders
But Flanders is not where my first cradle was.

Flanders is now my modern substitute mother
From whom I didn't get my childhood tongue,
And whose heartbreaking double Dutch I study.
Slowly Flanders became my historical father
Whose ancestry is not mine.

I was born in Limburg, cold,
A cold, cold province.
It put a fire under me.

I was also born in Bree, Loons,
And Liege, a necropolis, a bourgeoisie
With a querulous, sing-song patois
Which dreams me out loud when I sleep,
As sleeping I am soaked
In slow low German.
                              That is music
More familiar, and for longer, than this
And the one I'm trying to transpose here.

And finally, as the healthy son
Of abundant cannon fodder, finally
I was born in 1947,
A harsh date, a hopeful era,
A worldwide shortage that grows
In me, in me comes to maturity.

(*version by Michael O'Loughlin*)

AFKOMST

Ik kom uit een familie van zakenlui, leraren, priesters,
Mannen die weten wat een woord berekent, een getal betekent.
De borderellen die sinds 1865 zwijgend worden doorgegeven
Vertellen mijn doorlopende seconde met dezelfde vaste hand.

Er is altijd wel een vleugel of een zus die Schubert zingt
Boven de blote cijfers uit, over hun seksuele bewerkingen heen—
Generaties muziek, bezig met beursberichten en mekaar bedenken
Er gaat in die eeuw geen dag voorbij of ik ben er al half.

Voor de leraren, vitterige doden, zeg en schrijf ik teksten op
In de bibliotheek die uitziet op het Vrijthof, op mijn leven,
Op mijn blijvende verwarring van kalligrafie, vrouwen en God.
Spiegeldeuren weerkaatsen het profiel waaruit ik weg wil.

De priesters leren me zo lang bidden totdat hij bestaat.

ADRES

De anderen zijn allemaal van hier.
Hun hoofden hebben overal vandaag de plattegrond.
Hun voeten vinden blind hun eigen straat
In hun eigen straat, hun handen grijpen de enige klink,
Het juiste nummer waarin ze werkelijk wonen.

Iets of iemand heeft mijn sleutels afgepakt,
Mijn vingerafdrukken gejat, mijn naam van de bel gehaald
En mijn verleden zonder koffers op straat gezet.
Nu moet ik op zoek naar de enige deur. Die zonder adres.
Laat iets weten als ik die gevonden heb.

ORIGINS

I come from a family of businessmen, teachers, priests,
Men who know the price of words, the meaning of numbers.
The ledgers silently handed down since 1865
Point to my continuous moment with the same fixed hand.

There is always a grand piano or a sister singing Schubert
Above the naked sums, transcending their sexual conditioning
Generations of music, busy with stock market news and schemes.
Not a day of that time passes but I'm already half present.

For the teachers, the nitpicking dead, I recite and rewrite texts
In the library which gives on to the Vrijthof, on to my life,
My persistent confusion of calligraphy, women and God.
Mirrored doors reflect the profile I want to escape from.

The priests teach me to pray until he exists.

(version by Michael O'Loughlin)

ADDRESS

The others are all from here.
Today they have the map of everywhere in their head.
Their feet blindly find their own street
In their own street, their hands grasp the only latch,
The right number in which they really live.

Something or someone has taken my keys,
Stolen my fingerprints, torn my name from the bell
And set my past on the street without luggage.
Now I must look for the only door. The one with no address.
Let me know if I find it.

(version by Michael O'Loughlin)

SINT-VITUSDANS IN OKTOBER *10*

Je moet gezond zijn om een koord te kunnen spannen
Over het zuigende gat aan je voeten.
Je moet waanzinnig worden om het woord te vangen
Dat je vogelvrij komt groeten
En verdwijnt als vrijheid een vuist maakt rond je tong.

Maar niet dit tussengebied! Niet dit schaduwenrijk
Van de mosselmens, je vlees vol spangen;
Niet die kou van platonische grotten, je blinde kijk
Op licht waaruit je wordt verbannen—
O die onstandvastige dingen, die zelfverzekerde pijn.

DICHTERLIJKE VRIJHEID

Tussen twee angsten, dus tussen twee liefdes
Heb ik mijn vruchtbaarste jaren verdeeld.
Tussen twee angsten, twee liefdes rijdt
De stadsbus met mijn doodste gewicht.

Ik woon in de Hertoginstraat 20
En kan er niet schrijven.
Ik schrijf in de Lentelei 20
En kan er niet wonen.

Ik leef maar heen en weer.
Mijn uren van 20 naar 20 en 20 naar 20
Zijn de duttende tijd van de klerk en de lasser,
De ochtendlijke droefheid van de minnaar.

Tussen twee angsten, twee liefdes verander ik
Dagelijks van naam, van thuis en tong.
Tussen twee angsten, twee liefdes reist
De bus met mijn afwezigste gezicht.

SAINT VITUS'S DANCE IN OCTOBER *10*

You have to be healthy to stretch a cord
Across the sucking chasm at your feet.
You have to go mad to catch the word
Which comes to greet you free as a bird
And disappears when freedom makes a fist around your tongue.

But not this foreshore of the mussel gatherer!
Not this Kingdom of Shadows, your flesh full of hooks,
Not this cold of Platonic caves, your blind gaze
At light from which you are banished—
Those insubstantial objects, this self-assured pain.

(version by Michael O'Loughlin)

POETIC LICENSE

Between two fears, that is, between two loves
I have divided my most fruitful years.
Between two fears, two loves, the bus moves
With my dead weight.

I live in Hertoginstraat 20
And can't write there.
I write at Lentelei 20
And can't live there.

My life is in the back and forth.
My hours from 20 to 20 and 20 to 20
Are the day dreaming time of the clerk and welder
The morning sadness of the lover.

Between two fears, two loves I change
Name daily, home and tongue.
Between two fears, two loves the bus journeys
With my most absent face.

(version by Michael O'Loughlin)

SCHATPLICHTIG

Ze slaapt en dat is stil. Dan sneeuwt het in de kamers
Van het huis waarin ik woon met mijn vriendin.
Ze ligt er naakt en wit, een ademende steen,
Een groot en lastig beeld waaraan ik mij moet stoten,
Een scherp gewicht dat ik moet dragen alle dagen,
Alle nachten dat haar slaap me uit de slaap houdt.

Ik ben met haar alleen. Alleen met haar kom ik
De jaren afgewandeld want haar naam wijst me de weg
En in haar blik zie ik mijn blinde tijd weerspiegeld.
Ze ligt er naakt en wit, een ademende steen
Waaraan ik heel mijn bot bestaan geslepen heb
En slijp, ook als ik slaap en roepend van haar droom.

TRIBUTARY

She is sleeping, so it's quiet. Then it snows in the rooms
Of the house where I live with my love.
She lies there naked and white, a breathing stone,
A big, awkward statue that gets in my way,
A trenchant weight I must carry each day,
Each night that her sleep keeps me from sleep.

I am alone with her. Alone with her I come
Striding out of the years because her name shows me the way
And in her eyes I see my blind time reflected.
She lies there naked and white, a breathing stone
On which I have honed all my rough existence
And hone it still, even in sleep when I cry out, dreaming of her.

(version by Michael O'Loughlin)

PARANOIA

Ze zeggen dat dichters hun tong in bedwang moeten houden.
Zij, dat zijn die modejournalisten die mijn kleren kraken
En morgen mijn ontwerpen dragen. Dat zijn die keukenmeesters
Die souperen van mijn vlees en in mijn pannen spuwen.
Dat zijn die onkruidverdelgers en dode dokters van de poëzie.
Maar wie heeft de naakten gekleed, de hongerigen gespijsd?

Nee, mijn door de wol geverfde tong van jullie is ook van mij
En wat ze doet is nu eenmaal vaak pathetisch gedacht.
Jullie metrische colbertjes en rijmbroeken, daar pas ik voor.
Jullie zoutloze sonnettenfoto's, nee, pardon, merci.

Ik kan het ook niet helpen, de subliemste prosodie
Komt uit de darmen, elke ziel denkt finaal intestinaal.
(Anders staat het met mijn Hoofdletter, hier komt ze:
Zij is de solsleutel van mijn dwarse notenbalken.)

Dit charmeert of epateert misschien. Het was niet zo bedoeld.
Veel van deze regels is met haat en nijd ineengetimmerd,
Ook met goede voornemens, mijn weg gaat naar de hel.
Wie lijdt gaat naar de hel, aan pijn is geen verdienste.

Woorden, zaad en centen zijn gemaakt om te rollen.
Zet ze nooit op het spaarboek van de evidente vorm.
De innigste vorm zit in het ritme van de vent—poëzie
Met kloten dus, zoals Pavese zei, en hij slikte zich dood.

PARANOIA

They say that poets should keep their tongue in check.
They, they are the fashion journalists who slate my clothes
and tomorrow wear my designs. They are the kitchen inspectors
who sup on my flesh and spit in my pans.
They are the weed killers and dead doctors of poetry.
But who has clothed the naked and fed the hungry?

No, the tongue you have stained on your slides is also mine
and what you do is actually pretty pathetic.
Your metrical jackets and rhyming britches, count me out.
Your salt-free sonnet snapshots, excuse me, no, merci.

I can't help it, the sublimest prosody
comes from the guts, ultimately every soul thinks intestinally
(Unlike my capital letter, here she comes:
She is the C clef of my horizontal staves.)

Perhaps this charms or startles. It wasn't meant to.
Many of these lines are hammered together with malice and hate.
Even with good intentions, my road leads to hell.
If you suffer you go to hell, there's no percentage in pain.

Words, seed and cents were made to spend freely.
Never put them in the savings book of the evident form.
The deepest form is in the fellow's rhythm — poetry
with balls, therefore, as Pavese said, and he gulped his death.

(version by Michael O'Loughlin)

ANDERS

Er hangt de laatste tijd
langer een waas over de landen
steeds vroeger
worden bossen blauw

de laatste takken breek je
minder graag
en minder gauw

dat wat de handen doen
smaakt bitterzoet
in de verleden tijd
vervoegen zich de dromen

de laatste bloesem
heeft de kleur van tederheid
en in je lijf stolt het verlangen
tot vruchtbegin
van eenzaamheid

de laatste jaren ruikt
de lente anders:
minder belofte
en meer spijt

DIFFERENT

A mist hangs of late
over the land
always woods
become blue earlier

the last branches you break
less ardently
and not so soon

what the hand does
tastes bittersweet
in the past
gather the trees

the late blossom
has the colour of tenderness
and in your body thickens the desire
to bear fruit
from loneliness

the last years smell
spring differently
less promise
and more regret

(version by Joan McBreen)

BASHŌ I

Oude man tussen het riet achterdocht van de dichter.
Hij gaat op weg naar het Noorden hij maakt een boek met zijn (
Hij schrijft zichzelf op het water hij is zijn meester verloren.
Liefde alleen in de dingen uit wolken en winden gesneden.
Dit is zijn roeping zijn vrienden bezoeken tot afscheid.
Schedels en lippen vergaren onder wuivende luchten.
Altijd de kus van het oog vertaald in de dwang van de woorden.
Zeventien het heilig getal waarin de verschijning bestemd word
Het voorbije verteren bevriest zo versteend als een vlinder.
In een marmer getij de geslepen fossielen.
Hier kwam de dichter voorbij op zijn reis naar het Noorden.
Hier kwam de dichter voor altijd voorgoed voorbij.

BASHŌ II

Wij kennen de poëtische poëzie de gemene gevaren
Van maanziek en zangstem. Gebalsemde lucht is het.
Tenzij je er stenen van maakt die glanzen en pijn doen.
Jij, oude meester, sleep de stenen
Waar je een lijster mee dood gooit.
Jij sneed uit de wereld een beeld dat je naam draagt.
Zeventien stenen als pijlen een school doodse zangers.
Zie bij het water het spoor van de dichter
Op weg naar het binnenste sneeuwland. Zie hoe het water het uitwist
Hoe de man met de hoed het weer opschrijft
En water en voetstap bewaart, de vergane beweging steeds stilzet,
Zodat wat verdween er nog is als iets dat verdween.

BASHO I

Old man in the rushes the poet's suspicion.
He sets off for the North he makes a book with his eyes.
He writes himself on water he has lost his master.
Love only in things hewn from wind and cloud.
This his vocation to visit his friends and then farewell.
Skulls and lips amass under swaying skies.
Always the eye's kiss translated under the duress of words
Seventeen the sacred number in which appearance is destined.
Time spent freezes petrified like a butterfly.
In a marble wave the engraved fossils.
The poet passed through here on his road to the North.
Here passed the poet for once and for always.

(version by Michael O'Loughlin)

BASHO II

We know poetical poetry the common dangers
Of moonstruck and serenade. It is perfumed air,
Unless you turn it to stones which glitter and hurt.
You, old master, hewed the stones
With which you fell a thrush.
From the world you carve an image that bears your name.
Seventeen stones like arrows a school of deathly singers.
See near the water the trace of the poet
En route to the upland snows. See how the water erases it
How the man with the hat writes it again
Keeping water and footstep, always halting the vanished movement,
So that which disappeared is still like something that disappeared.

(version by Michael O'Loughlin)

BASHŌ III

Nergens in dit heelal heb ik een vaste woonplaats
Schreef hij op zijn hoed van cypressen. De dood nam zijn hoed af
Dat hoort zo. De zin is gebleven.
Alleen in zijn gedichten kon hij wonen.
Nog even en je ziet de kersebloesems van Yoshino
Zet je sandalen maar onder de boom, leg je penselen te rusten.
Berg je stok in je hoed, vervaardig het water in regels.
Het licht is van jou, de nacht ook.
Nog even, cypressehoed, en ook jij zult ze zien,
De sneeuw van Yoshino, de ijsmuts van Sado,
Het eiland dat scheepgaat naar Sorēn over grafstenen golven.

BASHŌ IV

De dichter is een gemaal door hem wordt het landschap van woorden.
Toch denkt hij net als jij en zien zijn ogen hetzelfde.
De zon die verongelukt in de bek van het paard.
De buitenste tempel van Ise het strand van Narumi.
Hij vaart in het zeil van de rouw hij koerst naar zijn opdracht.
Zijn kaken malen de bloemen tot de voeten van verzen.
De boekhouding van het heelal zoals het zich dagelijks voordoet.
In het Noorden kent hij zichzelf een hoop oude kleren.
Als hij is waar hij nooit meer zal zijn lees jij zijn gedichten:
Hij schilde komkommers en appels hij schildert zijn leven
Ook ik ben verleid door de wind die de wolken laat drijven.

BASHO III

Nowhere in this world have I a home
He wrote on his hat of cypress. Death removed his hat,
as is fitting. The sentence remained.
His only home was in his poetry.
A little longer and you'll see the cherry blossoms of Yoshino.
Put your sandals under the tree, lay your brushes to rest.
Hide your stick in your hat, put the water into lines.
The light is yours, the night too.
A little longer, cypress hat, and you too will see them
The snow of Yoshino, the icehelm of Sado,
The island that embarks for Sorēn across tombstone waves.

(*version by Michael O'Loughlin*)

BASHO IV

The poet is a pumping-station turning the landscape into
words.
Yet he thinks just like you and his eyes see the same.
The sun which crashed in the mouth of the horse.
The outermost temple of Ise the beach of Narumi.
He voyages in the sails of mourning he heads for his task.
His jaws grind the flowers into the feet of verses.
Keeping the books of the world's everyday business.
In the North he knows himself a pile of old clothes.
When he is where he nevermore shall be you read his poems:
He peeled cucumbers and apples he paints his life.
I too have been lured by the wind which drives the clouds.

(*version by Michael O'Loughlin*)

DE SCHAATSER

weer is de plas een fraai cliché
voor oud en nieuw, een uit de gouden eeuw
gesneden prent, en stil alsof dit altijd blijft

maar dan is er de schaatser, donker grijs
krast hij z'n ijzers vloeiend in het ijs

hij past nauwkeurig in de snelheid van z'n lijf
en in het landschap dat hem licht omlijnt;

een landschap dat weer overgaat,
dat straks gestroomlijnd in zichzelf verdwijnt
zoals de schaatser—, die het zicht uit rijdt

THE SKATER

Again the lake is a pretty catchphrase
'ring out the old, bring in the new', a print
from a golden age: still, the same, and always.

But then there is the skater. Dusky and grayish,
he scratches the ice so fluently with his irons.

He and the speed of his body precisely match
to fit a landscape outlining him with light.

Again the landscape shifts
and now streamlined it fades into itself
just like the skater — riding out of sight.

(version by Micheal O'Siadhail)

DE LAATSTE TEKENS ZIJN VAN ZWAAR GEWICHT

de laatste tekens zijn van zwaar gewicht:
u stond vannacht voor opname gereed,
parmantig schuchter in het felste licht,
op z'n zondags in diepzeeblauw gekleed,
de bovenste knoop als vanouds strakdicht,
vertrouwder dan 't reclamepopgezicht
van zwartwitfoto's toen u minder leed;
de laatste tekens zijn van zwaar gewicht:
goed, ik kom, antwoord op uw spoedbericht
en kus de wangen, lippen, warm en schich-
tig, hoor hoe een manchestersterk profeet,
mijn vader, kalm de dood de das om deed:
de laatste tekens zijn van zwaar gewicht.

THE FINAL SIGNS

The final signs are weariness and might.
You stood this evening ready for your date,
timid in the ward's exposing light,
in Sunday best, a traveller at the gate,
your topmost button, as of old, closed tight.
Now, more familiar than the black and white
snapshots of a youngster, hardy, straight,
the final signs are weariness and might.
So keep your appointment, say, 'Yes, all right',
savour the kisses' warmth, however slight.
Hear now how my father, once a great
prophet, rib-cord strong, dressed up for fate.
The final signs are weariness and might.

(version by Pat Boran)

OP STAP MET EDVARD MUNCH

Wanneer je vanuit de andere wereld
in één van de lichtpaleizen komt,
dan zie je hoe de gedaantes van de mensen vibreren.
Ze krimpen en zwellen, ze gloeien op en doven
in een paar seconden.
Hun gezichten zijn slechts bleke vlekken.
De kleuren variëren van donkerblauw tot zwart
en vloeien in elkaar over.
Spiegel weerkaatst spiegel,
                  zodat de grenzen verdwenen zijn.
Het is het bal van de niet-doden,
                          spookachtig zijn ze al.

Wanneer je in één van de lichtpaleizen bent,
temidden van de geweldige sociale omgangsvormen,
dan zijn deze gedaantes
vele blauwe plekken
op het prachtige en begeerlijke
lichaam van een geliefde, waar je
heel voorzichtig je vinger op moet leggen.

STEPPING OUT WITH EDVARD MUNCH

When from the other world you
walk into the Grand Hotel,
you see the shades of people dancing.
They shrink and swell, they scintillate and fade
all in an instant.
Their faces are mere blotches.
They shade from cobalt to black
melding into one another.
Mirror reflects mirror,
                              so that the borders merge.
It is the ball of the living-dead,
                                        ghosts
already.

When you are part of this charade,
amid the awful pomp,
these shapes become
multiple bruises
on the luscious
body of your beloved, warning you
'handle with care'.

(version by Anne Kennedy)

OP STAP MET EDVARD MUNCH

Wanneer je vanuit de andere wereld
in één van de lichtpaleizen komt,
dan zie je hoe de gedaantes van de mensen vibreren.
Ze krimpen en zwellen, ze gloeien op en doven
in een paar seconden.
Hun gezichten zijn slechts bleke vlekken.
De kleuren variëren van donkerblauw tot zwart
en vloeien in elkaar over.
Spiegel weerkaatst spiegel,
                              zodat de grenzen verdwenen zijn.
Het is het bal van de niet-doden,
                              spookachtig zijn ze al.

Wanneer je in één van de lichtpaleizen bent,
temidden van de geweldige sociale omgangsvormen,
dan zijn deze gedaantes
vele blauwe plekken
op het prachtige en begeerlijke
lichaam van een geliefde, waar je
heel voorzichtig je vinger op moet leggen.

STEPPING OUT WITH EDVARD MUNCH

When from the virile grave
you waft into the weather of women,
you enter the atmosphere that is sprayed round everyone.

Their floating sounds connect with March, siphon off
into the thin pillar box.
Their childlessness is ash-green,
twilit and evening patches hook together.

The far-off snow of the ceiling
is not hurt by never meeting them,
there is no break in the fire talk
in this well-behaved dream.

When you have got used to being in the pillar-box,
then these much the same colours
form millions of closed buds cooling
all over the cornflower and rose
you re-christen your forever love,
into whose night you must sink like frozen water.

(version by Medbh McGuckian)

VAN TULPEN

Van tulpen houd ik niet, ze ogen
me te recht. Keukenhofpest.
Uit op applaus. Alleen soms, in een vaas
en bijna dood, zijn ze hun stijfheid kwijt:
zieltogend op hun best.

TULIPS

Tulips I do not love, they seem
too straight to me. Keukenhofpest
Out for applause. Only sometimes, in a vase
and almost dead, they shed their stiffness:
soul-sorrowing at their best.

(version by Joan McBreen)

CONSIDERING TULIPS

Tulips, like Americans,
feel they are the romance:
stars, fielders,
always certain that they matter.

Only when their juice
has been swallowed up by sand
in the angle of a tea-cup, where they stand
cold as wedding-cake,
theirs is the soul of the Nineties.

(version by Medbh McGuckian)

ZO VROEG

Zo vroeg zo moe en
niets te zien buiten
jezelf. Spiegel genoeg,
met krasjes en al lang
het weer erin. Hoe vreemd
je huid zo vroeg
met spinnen op je wang.

SO SOON

So soon, so tired,
Nothing to see outside
yourself. Mirrored enough
with scratches and long
weathered. How strange
the spider-webbed skin
on your cheek
so soon.

(version by Joan McBreen)

SO SOON

So soon — so without tomorrow —
your eye for months together
sees nothing but roofs.

Mirror written to by fog, by rain,
by rusty weather — scrap of wallpaper
scratched by weeks and seasons.

How pure child
your Tuesday skin,
now Friday is in your cheeks.

(version by Medbh McGuckian)

DE HERTOG EN IK 2

Twee mannen trokken een kar door het bos,
door de modder van lichtschuwe wegen,
in dienst van een vrouw die verdeelde
en heerste. Hun lust, hun last stond zij

naakt boven hen, de zweep in de hand,
trots, door geen man ooit bezeten
dan in het offer van een gespleten
bestaan. De ene man ik, de ander gezant

van de nacht die zijn angst door mij joeg.
Wij trokken samen, de hertog leidde,
hij kende het bos in al zijn geheimen.
De vrouw zag het onderscheid. Sloeg.

THE DUKE AND I 2

Two men were dragging a cart through the woods,
through the mud of light-shy avenues,
in the service of a woman. Dividing and
conquering, she stood, both burden and desire

naked above them, whip in hand
arrogantly — possessed by no man
unless by the sacrifice of a split
existence. I was one; the other, a servant

of the night who drove his fear through me.
Together we pulled, the duke in front
— he knew the forest in all its moods.
The woman saw the difference. Cracked.

(version by Desmond Egan)

HERENIGING

Daar verschijnt zij op het gouden pad
dat door de herfst is aangelegd.
Zoals toen, toen ik me in haar
begroef en nooit zo leefde, nooit

zo 'dood, dood' stamelde omdat
ik voelde dat ik haar alleen kon
houden als ik haar kon toevertrouwen
aan de bladeren waarin wij lagen.

Onveranderd jong lacht zij om
de grauwe man die ik geworden ben.
Hoe eerder je komt, zegt zij, hoe
minder we schelen. Stijf wankel ik
haar binnen, zij is warm gebleven.

RETURNING

There she looms on the golden path
yellowed by autumn. Inviting as then,
when I smothered myself in her waters —
not come to this, not exposed like this,

not stammering 'gone, gone',
as I sensed the one way to hold on
was forever to let her go
to the leaves beneath us.

There she looms, untouched by the years
mocking this grey-haired old man.
'The sooner you come,' she beckons,
'the sooner we are one.' Stiff-limbed, I wade
back in; there is warmth yet in her waters.

(version by Ruth Hooley)

TOGETHER AGAIN

I behold her there
on the path strewn gold by autumn
where I buried myself within her
and first began to live

so, 'dead, dead,' I stammered because
I knew I could not keep her
outside our bed of leaves.

Forever young she mocks
the gray man I have become.
The sooner you come, she says,
the closer we'll be. Stiffly I totter
inside her; she keeps me warm again.

(version by Anne Kennedy)

HERENIGING

Daar verschijnt zij op het gouden pad
dat door de herfst is aangelegd.
Zoals toen, toen ik me in haar
begroef en nooit zo leefde, nooit

zo 'dood, dood' stamelde omdat
ik voelde dat ik haar alleen kon
houden als ik haar kon toevertrouwen
aan de bladeren waarin wij lagen.

Onveranderd jong lacht zij om
de grauwe man die ik geworden ben.
Hoe eerder je komt, zegt zij, hoe
minder we schelen. Stijf wankel ik
haar binnen, zij is warm gebleven.

VUILNISZAKKEN

Zoals ze daar 's morgens
op de stoep tegen elkaar
aan geleund warmte zoekend
in hun plastic jassen
staan te wachten, grijs,
vormeloos, vol afgedankt
leven, tegelijk broos
en weerloos. Je zou ze
weer naar binnen willen
halen, je ouders
wachtend op de bus.

TOGETHER AGAIN

You get these thoughts in melancholy Autumn.
My beloved appears in this pathway yellow with quince.
I buried my happiest self in her. I never
enjoyed sex so much before or since.

'Dead, dead' I stammered and died myself
Love would remain although she could not stay.
I retained every detail and nuance on the shelf
of memory, the crinkly leaves on which we lay.

Now she intrudes on her own memorial
unchanged, undead, laughing at me, at the grey
old poet I have turned out to be.
'The sooner you come,' she says, kindly,
'the better, and the less we'll differ.
Get it up and get inside me, as warm as ever.'

(version by James Simmons)

RUBBISH BAGS

The way they wait there
on the pavement in the dawn
huddled against each other
seeking warmth in plastic coats,
grey, formless, full of spurned life,
feeble and helpless. You'd like
to take them in again, your
parents waiting for the bus.

(version by Dennis O'Driscoll)

FENOMENAAL

Soms komt de liefde
uit de diepte stijgt ze op

zoals een vrouw
per roltrap naar de mode

Later zie je haar ineens
op de voorplecht van een schip

schuift ze zingend
onder een brug uit

recht in de armen
van de zon

A PHENOMENON

Sometimes love comes,
from the deep it arises

like a woman on an escalator
on her way to fashion

Afterwards you spy her
on the forecastle of a ship

singing along, gliding
from under a bridge

right into the
sun's wide-open arms

(version by Aidan Sharkey)

HET IERSE SCHAAP

Langs de drooggevallen baai
weerkaatst de weg het morgengrijs

een kraai trekt aan de
wondkorst van de dag

Iemand vraagt hoe laat het is:
'Someone' ruist de wind, 'is getting
married, another will be buried'

We zien nog hoe de baai
begint te stromen, hoe zij
decor en figuranten aanpast

maar alles lijkt opeens herinnering
Vertraagd beweegt een meeuw zich
tot hij roerloos hangen blijft

'De tijd hebben we opgeborgen'
zwijgen de wazige heuvels ons toe,
'in oude verhalen, ruïnes, graven,
in hoe we willen dat het was'—

Op de klippen komt van eeuwen ver
een schaap, kauwt gras,
likt aan de dag

THE IRISH SHEEP

Around the dried-up bay the road
reflects the morning grey

a crow rips up the
wound scab of the day

Somebody asks what time it is:
'Someone' sighs the wind,
'is getting married, another
will be buried'

We just witness how the bay
starts filling, adjusting
scenery and puppets

but suddenly all seems a memory
A gull flying slower and slower
until suspended motionless

'Time we locked up,' the hills
silently speak, 'in old tales,
ruins, graves, in how we would like
things to be remembered'—

On the cliffs, from beyond the ages,
a sheep crops up, chewing grass,
munching away the day

(version by Aidan Sharkey)

DECEMBEROFFENSIEF

Alleen de allerergste wanhoop is zo koud
als deze slotgracht; dit verdraagt
geen mens die niet bevroren is.
Soldaten hebben pijn die zij niet voelen,
bloed dat niet vloeit, grimmig gevecht
met slechts een schijn van woede.

Krakend verscheurt een paard het ijs,
galop gestold. Alles zit klem en nooit
komt het meer goed. Zie het vuur
verwaaien zonder warmte op de torentrans.

Rug tegen kale muur, van voor
de vijand, voeten op bevroren
grond, de wind een zweep.

INVASIE

Op de kale helling, wind in mijn haar,
staan wij en je kijkt. Uit alle macht
kijk jij naar mij, beeld van liefde.

En ik, ik kruip door je betraande ogen
binnen, glijd langs zenuwbanen, huppel
over myelineknopen; synapsen
ruisen, RNA dwingt eiwitten
zich te groeperen naar mijn beeld:

Ik sta gekerfd, gebeiteld in je hersens
tot je sterft, totdat je sterft.

DECEMBER OFFENSIVE

Only the very worst despair is as cold
as this moat; no man
who is not frozen can bear this.
Soldiers have pain that they don't feel,
blood that does not flow, hideous fight
with only a shadow of rage.

Cracking, a horse tears up the ice,
gallop curdled. Everything is stuck and it will
never be right again. Watch the fire
blow about without warmth on the battlements.

Back against bare wall, in front
the enemy, feet on frozen
ground, the wind a whip.

(version by Peter van de Kamp)

INVASION

On the bare slope, wind in my hair,
we stand and you look. With all your might
you look at me, this image of love.

And I, I sneak in through your eyes
filled with tears, slither down nerve-tracks,
skip over myelin sheaths; synapses
rustle, RNA forces proteins
to group according to my image:

I stand carved, chiselled in your brains
till you die, until you die.

(version by Peter van de Kamp)

VERZWEGEN TIJD

Stilte doelloos
drijvend op dood water
woorden tot de
tanden gewapend

Eens zag ik in de schaduw
van elk jaargetijde
eilanden schitteren
aan een ketting zonnestralen

Nu mezelf gelijk aan ruimte
waaraan geen schakel
zich laat smeden dan wat
splijt en breekt en splijt

LANDSCHAP

Het landschap zoals het
onveranderlijk
in mijn geheugen stond verdween,
viel uit zijn kostbare omlijsting.

Vroeg of laat ruimt al het overbodige
zichzelf op,
brokkelt het moeizaam vergaarde af
en glijdt weg in ravijnen

daarna maakt elk beeld plaats
voor een glazen rivier
dichter bij de bron.

SILENT TIME

Silence aimlessly
floating on dead water
words
armed to the teeth

Once I saw in the shadow
of each season
islands glittering
on a necklace of sunbeams

Now I find myself
equal to space in which
no chain is forged
but one that cleaves
and breaks and cleaves

(version by Aidan Sharkey)

LANDSCAPE

The landscape as it stood
immutably in my mind
dropped out of its precious frame.

Sooner or later all superfluity
clears itself away,
wears away
what was collected with care
and slides down into ravines

afterwards each image gives way
to a glass river
closer to the source.

(version by Aidan Sharkey)

WINTERSPIEGEL

Zo'n eerste dag dat water
geen water meer is maar meer.
Het kind met beide voeten gestrand
vraagt naar ijs—glas—ijs
zo vraagt ze naar de chemie
van het simpele, gladde volmaakte
waarin zij haar doorzichtige drie jaren ziet.

De snelle schaatsers flitsen voorbij
Tekenen in de wind.

Het kind beweegt, schaduwloos
ze knielt, buigt zich over een verdriet:
een vis bloedt dood onder het ijs.
Ze wil hem redden, klopt en roept
het bloed sijpelt, kleurt
de vis ademt verdriet
dat zij daar in die winterspiegel ziet
niet zeggen, niet doen, niet.

WINTERSPIEGEL II

's Nachts in donker en dons verpakt
slaapt zij haar ijstijd uit
Het boekje dat je niet kan sluiten:
de vis is dood.
Ze denkt in slaaptaal door
dicht bij mijn oor hoor ik haar woorden smelten
Haar vuistjes spannen in gevecht op leven
Haar foenix is een bevend kuiken

In haar rode droom is de vis,
de vis zilver en vrij gevlogen.

WINTER MIRROR

The first day when water
is no longer mere water.
The child stranded with both feet
asks about ice: glass? ice?
she asks about the chemistry
of the simple, smooth perfection
in which she sees her transparent three years.

The speeding skaters flash by
signs in the wind

The child moves shadowless
she kneels, bends over a sorrow:
under the ice a fish bleeds to death
she wants to save him, knocks and calls
the blood seeps, colours
the fish breathes sorrow
which she sees in that winter mirror
say nothing, do nothing, nothing.

(version by Michael O'Loughlin)

WINTER MIRROR II

At night packed in darkness and down
she sleeps through her ice age
The books you cannot close:
the fish is dead.
She thinks on in the language of sleep
close to my ear I hear her words melt
Her fists clench in her fight for life
her phoenix is a trembling chick.

In her red dream the fish,
the fish is silver and has flown free.

(version by Michael O'Loughlin)

WILLEMSBRUG

Een oogwenk hing de zon
in een notenbalk van zwarte lijnen.
Bij dit laatste salvo van licht
hield zelfs de avondbries
zijn adem in.

Alleen de aarde draaide verder
en ook het verkeer raasde voort
van hot naar her over de kale kaden
alsof de volmaakte brug tussen
dag en nacht ons niet aanging.

Dat oogwenk scheurde de zon
in roodgloeiende draden.

WILLIAMSBRIDGE

Just an instant the sun hung
in a stave of black lines.
At this final salute of light
the very evening breeze held
its breath.

But the earth kept on turning
and also the traffic tore along
right and left over the bare quay
as if the perfect bridge between
day and night was none of our business.

That instant the sun tore up
to red-hot threads.

(version by Aidan Sharkey)

MOEDERVLEKJE

De leeuwerik
zingt de nacht aan scherven.

Een moedervlekje
aan de gevel van de hemel
brengt hij God een serenade
en waant zich de hemel
zijn ereboog.

In mijn ochtendnevel,
het hoofd vol scherven
waarvan de stukken voorgoed
een raadsel zullen blijven,
tast ik naar de grond. Met
geen voet kan ik die raken.

Mijn stem moet lager.

MOTHER'S MARK

The lark
sings the night to fragments.

A mother's mark
on the front of heaven
he brings a serenade to God
and thinks the sky
his triumphal arch.

In a morning mist,
my head falling to fragments
the pieces of which
are not up to the mark,
I grope for the ground
that my feet cannot reach

and come down a peg or two.

(version by Aidan Sharkey)

BIBLIOGRAPHIES OF DUTCH AND FLEMISH LITERATURE IN TRANSLATION

Prosper Arents, *De Vlaamse schrijvers in het Engels vertaald 1481-1949*, Ghent: Koninklijke Vlaamse Academie voor Taal- en Letterkunde, 1950.

"Bibliografie van het Nederlandstalige boek in vertaling", bibliographical section which appears regularly in the journal *Ons Erfdeel*.

Georg Hermanowski and Hugo Tomme, *Zuidnederlandse literatuur in vertaling: bibliografie*, Hasselt: Heideland, 1961.

A.J. van Huffel, *Nederlandsche schrijvers in vertaling (van Marcellus Emants tot Jan Eekhout): proeve van eene bibliographie*, Leiden: E.J. Brill, 1939.

A.J. van Huffel, *Nederlandsche schrijvers in vertaling (van Marcellus Emants tot Jan Eekhout): proeve van eene bibliographie. Supplement*, Leiden: E.J. Brill, 1946.

Yann Lovelock, *The Line Forward. A Survey of Modern Dutch Poetry in Translation*, n.p. [Amsterdam]: Bridges Books, 1984 [contains bibliographies of translations in magazines and anthologies (together with a few studies of contemporary Dutch poetry) and of volumes of poetry by individual poets between 1961 and 1984 compiled by Scott Rollins and James S. Holmes].

P.M. Morel, 'Translations of Dutch Literature, 1900-1957',in *Bibliographia Neerlandica*, The Hague: Martinus Nijhoff, 1962.

Het Nederlandse boek in vertaling. Bibliografie van vertalingen van Noord- en Zuidnederlandse werken, The Hague: Staatsuitgeverij. The following volumes have appeared: 1958-1967; 1968-1972; 1973-1977; 1978-1982 (from this volume on there is an extra subtitle:*The Dutch Book in Translation. Bibliography of Translations from Holland andFlanders*); 1983; 1984; 1985; 1986; 1987 (publisher: SDU).

C<small>OLLECTIONS OF</small> D<small>UTCH</small> A<small>ND</small> F<small>LEMISH</small> P<small>OETRY IN</small> E<small>NGLISH</small>
T<small>RANSLATION</small>

(For translations of collections of poems and prose by individual authors, published separately, see 'Biographies of Dutch Poets').

Barnouw, Adriaan, comp. & tr., *Coming After: An Anthology of Poetry from the Low Countries*, New Brunswick, New Jersey: Rutgers University Press, 1948.

E.M. Beekman, Scott Rollins, Clair Nicolas White, et al., trs., *Translation. Dutch Issue, Translation* XXIV (1990).

Jethro Bithell, ed. and trans., *Contemporary Flemish Poetry in Translation*, London and Felling-on-Tyne, New York and Melbourne: The Walter Scott Publishing Co., 1917.

Hugo Brems & Ad Zuiderent, ed., *Contemporary Poetry of the Low Countries*, Rekkem: Stichting Ons Erfdeel vzw, 1992.

Paul Brown & Peter Nijmeijer, eds., 'Modern Dutch Writing',*Chapman*, Vol. 2, Nos 5/6 (1974).

Jozef Deleu, chief ed., *The Low Countries: Arts and Society in Flanders and the Netherlands*. A Yearbook, Stichting Ons Erfdeel, 1994.

Delta. A Review of Arts, Life and Thought in The Netherlands, Vols: 1-16, Amsterdam, 1958-1974 [each issue contains English translations of Dutch poetry].

Dutch Crossing. A Journal for Students of Dutch, Nos. 1-.... (from August [April] 1986 entitled *Dutch Crossing. A Journal of Low Country Studies*), London, 1977-.... [most issues contain English translations of Dutch poetry].

From "the Low Countries". Poets from The Netherlands, Belgium and Luxemburg, intro. by Bradley R. Strahan & Shirley G. Sullivan (*Visions International Series* 34), Falls Church: Black Buzzard, 1990.

Joke Gerritsma and Martin Mooij, eds., Ko Kooman, tr., *En wie bent u? : zeven kunstenaars ontmoeten vijf Nederlandse en Vlaamse dichters/ And Who Are You? : Seven Artists meet Five Poets from The Netherlands and Flanders,* Rotterdam: Stichting Poetry International, 1992.

Glassgold, Peter, ed., *Living Space: Poems of the Dutch 'Fiftiers',* New York: New Directions, 1979.

Theo Hermans, ed., 'Dutch Issue', *Contemporary Literature in Translation,* No. 32 (1981).

James S. Holmes & Peter Nijmeijer, eds., *Modern Poetry in Translation* (London), Nos. 27/28, London, Summer 1976.

James S. Holmes & William Jay Smith eds., *Dutch Interior: Postwar Poetry from the Netherlands and Flanders,* New York, Columbia University Press, 1984.

Konrad Hopkins and Ronald van Roekel, eds., *Quartet: an Anthology of Dutch and Flemish Poetry,* Paisley: Wilfion Books, 1978.

Maria Jacobs, ed., *With Other Words: A Bilingual Anthology of Contemporary Dutch Poetry by Women,* Windsor, Ontario: Netherlandic Press, 1985 [dual language edition].

Reinder P. Meijer, *Literature of the Low Countries. A Short History of Dutch Literature in The Netherlands and Belgium,* The Hague/Boston: Martinus Nijhoff, 1978 (2nd. edn.) [contains translations from the classic canon of Dutch poetry, and offers a comprehensive literary history].

Reinder P. Meijer, ed., 'Post-War Dutch & Flemish Poetry,' *Poetry Australia*, No. 54, Five Dock N.S.W. Australia, 1974 [dual language edition].

Peter Nijmeijer, ed., *Four Dutch Poets: Lucebert, Gerrit Kouwenaar, Sybren Polet, Bert Schierbeek,* London: Transgravity Press, 1976.

Peter Nijmeijer, ed., *Four Flemish Poets: Hugo Claus, Paul Snoek, Gust Gils, Hugues C. Pernath,* London: Transgravity Press, 1976.

Peter Nijmeijer, 'Dutch Number', *Poet*, Vol. 11, No. 9, Madras, September 1970.

E. Prins & C.M. MacInnes, trs., *War Poetry from Occupied Holland,* Bristol: J.W. Arrowsmith, 1945.

Scott Rollins, ed., *Ten Lowlands Poets*, Amsterdam: Dremples, 1979.

Scott Rollins & Lawrence Ferlinghetti, eds., *Nine Dutch Poets*, San Francisco: City Lights Books, 1982.

Scott Rollins, ed., *6 Dutch Poets, The Greenfield Review*, Vol. 10, Nos. 3/4 (Winter/Spring 1983).

A.L. Snell, trans., *Flowers from a Foreign Garden. Selections from the Works of Modern Dutch Poets,* London: Love & Malcomson, 1902.

Paul Snoek & Willem M. Roggeman, eds., *A Quarter Century of Poetry from Belgium [1945-1970]*, intro. Eugéne van Itterbeek, tr. James S. Holmes, Brussels & The Hague: Manteau, 1970.

Clark Stilman & Frances Stilman, *Lyra Belgica: Guido Gezelle and Karel van de Woestijne in English Translation,* New York: Belgian Information Centre, 1950.

Garmt Stuiveling, *A Sampling of Dutch Literature. Thirteen Excursions into the Works of Dutch Authors*, tr. & adapted by James Brockway, Hilversum: Radio Nederland Wereldomroep, n.d. (ca. 1962).

Eddy van Vliet, ed., *Writing in Holland and Flanders*, No. 38 (Spring 1981).

Eddy van Vliet & Willem M. Roggeman, eds., *Poetry in Flanders Now*, Antwerp: Flemish PEN Centre, 1982.

Weevers, Theodoor, *Poetry of the Netherlands in its European Context, 1170-1930. Illustrated with Poems in Original and Translation*, London: University of London, The Athlone Press, 1960.

Manfred Wolf, ed. & tr., *Change of Scene: Contemporary Dutch and Flemish Poems in English Translation*, San Francisco: Twowindow Press, 1969.

DUTCH ANTHOLOGIES

Manfred Wolf, ed. & tr., *The Shape of Houses. Women's Voices from Holland and Flanders*, Berkeley: Twowindows Press, 1974.

C.J. Aarts and M.C. van Etten, eds., *Domweg gelukkig, in de Dapperstraat. De bekendste gedichten uit de Nederlandse literatuur*, Amsterdam: Bert Bakker, 1990.

Hugo Brems, ed., *Dichters van deze tijd. Veertig jaar Nederlandse ('50-'89) poëzie uit Noord en Zuid*, Ghent: Poeziecentrum, 1990 (24th rev. edn.).

C. Buddingh' and Eddy van Vliet, eds., *Is dit genoeg: een stuk of wat gedichten. Honderd jaar Noord- en Zuidnederlandse poëzie (1880-1980) in dertig thema's*, 2 Vols., Amsterdam/Brussels: Elsevier, 1982.

C. Buddingh' and Eddy van Vliet, eds., *Poëzie is een daad van bevestiging Noord- en Zuidnederlandse poëzie van 1945 tot heden*, Amsterdam/ Brussels: Elsevier, 1978.

Jozef Deleu, *Groot verzenboek: vijfhonderd gedichten over leven, liefde en dood. Een thematische bloemlezing uit de Noord- en Zuidnederlandse poëzie van de twintigste eeuw*, Tielt/Baarn: Lannoo/Anthos, 1992 (5th rev. edn.).

Marko Fondse and Peter Verstegen, eds., *Achter gewone woorden. De beste poëzie uit tien jaar De Tweede Ronde*, n.p. [Amsterdam]: Bert Bakker, 1990.

Gerrit Komrij, ed., *De Nederlandse poëzie van de negentiende en twintigste eeuw in duizend en enige gedichten*, Amsterdam: Bert Bakker, 1979 (9th edn., 1992).

Jan Kuijper, ed., *Dit is poëzie. 72 dichters van Querido met 104 gedichten*, Amsterdam: Em. Querido, 1990.

Martin Mooij, ed., *Woorden in Vrijheid. Nederlandse en Vlaamse dichters op Poetry International 1970-1990*, Amsterdam: Meulenhoff, 1990.

Paul Rodenko, ed., *Nieuwe griffels schone leien. van Gorter tot Lucebert van Gezelle tot Hugo Claus. Een bloemlezing uit de poëzie deravantgarde*, Antwerp/The Hague: De Sikkel/Daamen N.V., 1954 (4th edn. with Bert Bakker Publishing 1955).

Laurens Vancrevel, ed., *Spiegel van de surrealistische poëzie in het Nederlands*, Amsterdam: Meulenhoff, 1987 (1989).

Victor E. van Vriesland, ed., *Spiegel van de Nederlandse poëzie. Elfhonderd tot negentienhonderd*, Amsterdam: Meulenhoff, 1979 (7th ed.).

Hans Warren, ed., *Spiegel van de Nederlandse poëzie. Dichters van de twintigste eeuw*, Amsterdam: Meulenhoff, 1979 (6th rev. ed. 1992, under the title *Spiegel van de moderne Nederlandse poëzie*).

BIOGRAPHICAL DICTIONARIES OF DUTCH AND FLEMISH AUTHORS

A.G.H. Bachrach et al., eds., *Moderne Encyclopedie van de Wereldliteratuur*, 10 Vols., Weesp/Antwerp: De Haan/De Standaard, 1980–1984.

G.J. van Bork and P.J. Verkruijsse, eds., *De Nederlandse en Vlaamse auteurs van middeleeuwen tot heden met inbegrip van de Friese auteurs*, Weesp: De Haan, 1985.

Josien Moerman, ed., *Ik ben een God in 't diepst van mijn gedachten. Lexicon Nederlandstalige Auteurs*, Utrecht/Antwerp: Het Spectrum, 1984.

C.G.N. de Vooys & G. Stuiveling, *Schets van de Nederlandse Letterkunde*, Groningen: J.B. Wolters, 1966.

Winkler Prins lexicon van de Nederlandse letterkunde, Amsterdam - Brussels: Elsevier, 1986.

Ad Zuiderent, Hugo Brems and Ton van Deel, eds., *Kritisch lexicon van de Nederlandstalige literatuur na 1945*, Alphen aan den Rijn - Brussels/Groningen: Samson , Uitgeverij/Wolters-Noordhoff, 1980.

BIOGRAPHIES OF DUTCH AND FLEMISH POETS

Aafjes, Bertus (1914-1992)

Dutch poet and journalist. Trained for the priesthood and subsequently studied archaeology in Louvain and Rome. Gave up his studies to devote himself fully to his writings. For Aafjes, travelling is the 'most beautiful gift of God'. His lyrical travellogue *Een voetreis naar Rome* (*A Journey on Foot to Rome*, 1946) gained immense popularity in The Netherlands. On the merits of this troubadour-like romantic poem, Martinus Nijhoff hailed him as 'the youngest of [Dutch] masters'.

His verse expresses an impassioned love of life and an equally intense fear of death through a dexterous yet always unadorned style. Among his best work is *In den beginne* (*In the Beginning*, 1949) in which the story of Adam and Eve, and the notion of original sin, is compared to the poetic craft (Aafjes had depicted poetry as 'a fight with the Muse' in *Het gevecht met de muze*, 1940).

His travels are also central to his prose. Journeys to Japan, for instance, were the source for his popular crime stories about Judge Ooka (1677–1751).

Achterberg, Gerrit (1905–1962)

Achterberg made his debut in 1925 with traditional, religious poetry which was dominated by his Protestant background. He would later distance himself completely from this poetry of his youth, and it is not included in his *Collected Poems*. His second collection, *Afvaart* (*Sailing Away*, 1931) manifests his departure from traditionalism to a highly individual exploration of the regions between life and death, and the role of the artist in recreating that which has departed. His Orpheus is incapable of finding Eurydice, and wanders through the realm of the dead, giving a mythical dimension to everyday language.

Achterberg's mixture of the lyrical and the metaphysical is most hauntingly expressed in his later collections, *Ballade van de gasfitter* (*Ballad of the Gas Fitter*, 1953) and *Spel van de wilde jacht* (*Game of the Wild Chase*, 1957).

More than any Dutch poet, Achterberg struck the chord of the modern human condition. During his life, he received every important literary prize for Dutch poetry. After his death, his fame rose with the publication of his *Collected Poems*. Between 1963 (1st imprint) and 1991 (11th) over 50,000 copies of this book were sold. Shortly after his death, Dutch poet Simon Vinkenoog disclosed in a poem that 'Gerrit Achterberg has murdered a woman'. The news of Achterberg's obsessive love, and its tragic outcome (in December 1937), hit the front pages of the Dutch papers, and has tainted some critical interpretation of his work.

Translations: *A Tourist Does Golgotha and Other Poems*, selected and translated by Stan Wiersma. Grand Rapids, Michigan: Being Publications, 1972; *Hidden Weddings*, selected and translated by Michael O'Loughlin, Dublin: Raven Arts, 1987; *But This Land Has No End. Selected Poems*, selected and translated by Pleuke Boyce, Lantzville: Oolichan Books, 1989.

Andreus, Hans (J.W. van der Zant) (1926–1977)

Representative of the Fifties Movement who preferred "being" to "becoming". After a five-year sojourn from Paris through Italy, he decided to take up writing as a profession. His oeuvre is immensely varied, ranging from radio-plays to commercials and comprising songs and children's books. His earliest verse is playful, but with *Het explosieve uur* (*The Explosive Hour*, 1955), a melancholy, philosophical tone infused his poetry, balancing the figurativeness of experimentalism with a traditional form. His recovery from mental illness is impressively expressed in *De sonnetten van de kleine waanzin* (*Sonnets of Little Madness, 1957*).

Translations: *The Stilt Pedlar and Other Stories*, 1970 (*Straat op stelten*, 1967) [children's stories]; *The Bear who Stood on his Head*, 1977 (a selection of children's stories from *Maarten en Birro*, 1970); *The Story of Baldus Bear and Ivan Krasnovitch*, 1978 (*Het verhaal van Baldus Beer en Iwan Krasnowitsj*, 1976) [children's book]. A large number of Andreus' collections of children's stories about meester Pompelpoes (Master Bumblemoose) have been translated.

Arends, Jan (1925–1974)

The constricted form of his verse bears out his constrained and alienated way of life. Poems like "I Have a House" (I/know/whoever drinks coffee at my place/will later hang himself) are of biographical relevance. His work couples a heart-felt loneliness and disbelief in the human condition with supreme irony. On the day his second collection of poetry, *Lunchpauzegedichten* (*Lunchbreakpoems*, 1974) appeared, Arends committed suicide.

Beranová, Jana

Czechoslovakian by birth, Beranová fled with her parents from the com-
munist regime. Went to secondary school in Bexhill-on-Sea, Sussex. Has
lived in The Netherlands for over thirty years. She has translated the en-
tire oeuvre of Milan Kundera into Dutch, and has also translated poets like
Miroslav Holub and Jaroslav Seifert.

She has published two collections of Dutch poetry, *Geen hemel zo hoog*
(*No Sky as High*, 1983), and *Rozemarijn* (*Rosemary*, 1987). She made her de-
but as a prose writer with *Nu delen we een geheim* (*Now We Share a Secret*,
1992).

Bernlef, J. (Hendrik Jan Marsman) (1937)

Poet, novelist, playwright, and translator (from Swedish). Made his po-
etic debut in 1960 with *Kokkels* (*Cockles*), in which he explores the relation-
ship between text and reality. The extraordinariness of ordinary reality
informs his work in the 1960s. After 1970 his poetry expresses the prob-
lematic nature of language in a more formally controlled medium. This
concern with representation is also central to the sophisticated literature
and criticism of the structuralist journal *Raster*, which he has edited since
1977.

Bernlef's novel *Hersenschimmen* (1984), which deals with dementia, has
received much acclaim.

Translations: *The Phantoms of the Mind*, 1988 (*Hersenschimmen*, 1984) [novel];
Out of Mind, 1989 (*Hersenschimmen*, 1984) [novel], *Public Secret*, 1992 (*Publiek
geheim*, 1987), [novel]; *Driftwood House: Poems*, selected and translated by
Scott Rollins, Francestown N.H.: Typographeum, 1992; *Eclipse* (*Eclips*, 1993),
in preparation [novel].

Bloem, J.C. (1887–1966)

Bloem belonged, with Adriaan Roland Holst, to the generation of mas-
ter-craftsmen-poets. But where Holst, influenced by W.B. Yeats, ventured
into a mythic, grand otherworld, Bloem faces the fragmentation of contem-
porary Holland with a courage which allows him to transcend melancholy
and face reality, expressed in a vision induced through tragic joy.

Qualified as a lawyer, he held several administrative posts and an editorship
with Holland's quality newspaper, the *Nieuwe Rotterdamse Courant*, before
devoting his life fully to writing. His literary development bears out his
aphorism "Poetry is learning not to". His first collection, *Het verlangen* (*De-
sire*, 1921) is imbued with an ornateness which is absent in subsequent

collections, like *Media Vita* (1931), in which the "in morte sumus" threatens to take precedence over the poet's earthly yearning. From *De nederlaag* (*Defeat*, 1937) through *Sintels* (*Embers*, 1945) to "*Quiet though sad*" (1947) Bloem develops his poetic expression of tragic joy, throwing doubt even on his 'inspired rhetoric':

> Is this enough: some few poems
> As a justification of an existence....

His final work betrays his love of life when the heart is threatened "by autumn and old age, winter and death."

Bloem, Rein (1932)

Teaches at the academy of film and at a teacher training college, and is chairman of *Schrijvers op School* (*Writers in School*, founded in 1971). Contributes to *De Gids* (*The Guide*) and *Raster*. Poetry reviewer for *Vrij Nederland*, columnist for *De Groene*, his articles displaying the wide variety of his artistic interests and his erudition, as he moves from Gerrit Kouwenaar to the sixth century, from music in *The Antwerp Song-Book* to French painters.

In his verse, Bloem couples erudition with originality, in a style that is radically modern. His first collection is titled *Overschrijven* (*to Copy* or *Revise* or *Write again*, 1966). The book is a literary quest from the middle ages to Bloem's favourite Ezra Pound, with a host of literary quotations along the way.

Originality of form and meaning is an essential ingredient of collections such as *De bomen en het bos* (*The Trees and the Wood*, 1968), and *Scenarios* (1970), in which he attempts to "deconstruct the fixed frame of meaning of words", by an interplay of criss-cross references to which the reader is invited to contribute. His great example is the twelfth century with its birth of science, when science lived among the people, rather than being institutionalised.

I.K Bonset (Theo van Doesburg; pseud. of C.E.M. Küpper) (1883–1931)

One of the original members of *De Stijl* (*The Style*), an artistic movement which rigidly focused on the primary artistic expression. Van Doesburg fell out with Piet Mondrian over the introduction of diagonals in *De Stijl*'s paintings—Mondrian insisting on the exclusive use of verticals and horizontals. Contributed to the magazine *Het Getij* (*The Tide*), and later edited *De Stijl* (1917-31), to which Mondrian also contributed. His poetry fuses the visual and the verbal, and creates a monumental architecture with the aid of words. In the mainstream of Dadaism, van Doesburg rejected individualised expression, insisting that words should not be used to describe, but to lay bare an underlying universal interplay of content and form.

Boutens, P.C. (1870–1943)

At an early age, Boutens rejected the strict Protestantism of his Middelburg milieu. A sickly child, he spent his formative years in isolation. At the age of eighteen he translated Plato's *Symposium*. Platonism, and Platonic love, come to the fore in most of his work. He studied Greek and Roman, against the wish of his father, and was for a while employed as a teacher of classics.

Initially Boutens was influenced by the poetry of the Eighties. His first collection, *Verzen* (*Verses*, 1898) bears the mark of Gorter. But his poetic sensitivity led to a sumptuous refinement which is as idiosyncratic as it is unparalleled in Dutch poetry. *Stemmen* (*Voices*, 1907) exudes this refinement, in its exquisite prosody, lavish imagery and personal diction.

With his belief in the poet as prophet, as chosen partaker of the divine, Boutens is the last of the Dutch Romantics.

Bouwers, Lenze L. (1940)

Born in the month of the German invasion, Bouwers is a representative of the post-War generation that encapsulates solid pre-War values in the context of contemporary social issues. These he faces head-on in his novel *Lieve vader, vuile schurk* (*Dear Father, Dirty Scoundrel*, 1988), which deals with the traumas of incest.

Bouwers teaches Dutch and is Dean of *De Gereformeerde Scholengemeenschap*, a Protestant secondary school in Zwolle. Evangelical convictions lay at the basis of his first two collections, *Leven* (*Life*, 1976) and *Neem dit van me aan* (*Please take this for Granted*, 1978). His quest for a consistent form of expression led him to the haiku, in *Nieuws onder de zon* (*News under the Sun*, 1982) and in *IJssel en Vecht* (1982). Subsequently, he found crafted freedom in the rondel; *Rondelen* (*Rondels*; 1985) manifested his break-through, and put his poetry in line with Dutch neo-traditionalism.

Bouwers is literary editor of *Het Nederlands Dagblad*.

Buddingh', Cees (1918–1985)

Studied English. Edited the journal *Podium*. Gained fame with *Gorgelrijmen* (*Gurgle Rhymes*, 1953), a collection of nonsense poetry in the tradition of

Edward Lear. He has been called the Dutch Marcel Duchamp, and the Dutch Magritte. His surreality is characterised by a deadpan humour, reflected in titles like 'Six Manifestations of Lenin on a Piano'. Hi s collection, *Het houdt op met zachtjes regenen* (*It's Ceasing to Rain Softly*, 1976) contains gentle reflections on mortality.

Buddingh' was a zealous worker for popularising Dutch literature. He compiled several anthologies, and wrote the *Lexicon der poëzie* (*Lexicon of Poetry*, 1968)

Cami, Ben (1920)

Made his debut with the collection *In de tijd verloren* (*Lost in Time*, 1950). Co-founded the avant-garde magazine *Tijd en Mensch* (*Time and Man*, 1949–1955), the Flemish counterpart to the Dutch *vijftigers*, movement of the Fifties. Cami is not tied down by the "new style" of the Fifties, which dictated a "free" experimentalism; instead, he unambiguously communicates his protests against the cultural debasement of contemporary society.

Campert, Jan (1902–1943)

Journalist, drama critic, writer of short stories and poet. His early poems were part of the melancholy, romantic tradition after the 1880s. In July 1942 he was arrested by the Germans for helping Jews. In captivity, he translated Shakespeare and a novel by Joseph Conrad. He died in the concentration camp at Neuengamme on January 12, 1943. The poem 'De achttien dooden' ('The Eighteen Dead'), based on the execution of eighteen hostages on 13 March 1941, was published as an illegal broadsheet in 1943, and became the best known poem of the resistance. He is the father of Remco Campert.

Campert, Remco (1929)

Poet, translator and fiction writer. Son of the poet Jan Campert. In his poetry, he is one of the milder, less experimental of the poets of the Fifties, displaying an easy, conversational tone, not deplete of self-mockery, behind which one can sense the pathos of despair. Campert was one of the founding members of the literary journal *Braak* (*Fallow*, but also the first person singular and imperative form of *To Vomit*).

Translations: *No Holds Barred*, 1965 (*Liefdes schijnbewegingen*, 1963) [novell]; *The Gangster Girl*, 1968 (*Het gangstermeisje*, 1965) [novell]; *In the Year of the Strike: Poems*, translated by John Scott and Graham Martin. Poetry Europe Series, No. 8. London/Chicago: Rapp & Whitling/The Swallow Press, 1968.

Charles, J.B. (W.H. Nagel) (1910–1983)

Studied law in Groningen. Held administrative functions in several courts. Joined the underground movement in 1944. Published two clandestine collections of poetry. After the War, he became professor of criminology in Leiden. In 1953, he published a polemical essay, *Volg het Spoor Terug* (*Trace the Trail Back*), which starts starts with the trial of Van der Lubbe, Dutch scapegoat for the burning of the *Reichstag*, and concludes that the demon unleashed in Nazi Germany in the Second World War has not yet been exorcised.

Claus, Hugo (1929)

Painter, novelist, poet, playwright and translator. One of the most energetic and versatile Flemish writers. Claus has been associated with various styles and movements. His first collection, *Kleine reeks* (*Small Series*, 1947) contained the traditional confessional lyrics of a youthful poet. But one year later, with *Registreren* (*Registering*) he placed himself in the forefront of Flemish experimental poetry, and not long after became a member of COBRA. In *Oostakkerse gedichten* (*Oostakker Poems*, 1955) he combined straightforward expression with the secrecy of myth. In the 1960s, his work became less overtly experimental. The use of myth and the related intertextuality became a hallmark of his work. Much of his work focuses on his country's history and culture. He increasingly expresses critical opinions of contemporary Belgium.

Among Claus' translations, that of Dylan Thomas's *Under Milkwood* has received much praise.

Translations: Hugo Claus, *A Bride in the Morning*, 1960 (*Een bruid in de morgen*, 1955) [play]; *Sister of Earth*, 1966 (*De Metsiers*, 1950) [novel]; *Friday*, 1972 (*Vrijdag*, 1969) [play]; *Selected Poems 1953–1973*, ed. Theo Hermans, tr. Theo Hermans, Paul Brown and Peter Nijmeijer, Portree, Isle of Skye: Aquila Poetry, 1986; *The Sign of the Hamster*, ed. Paul Claes, tr. Paul Claes, Christine D'haen, Theo Hermans & Yann Lovelock. Louvain: Leuvense Schrijversaktie, 1986 [dual language edition]; *Sorrow of Belgium*, 1990 (*Het verdriet van Belgi.*, 1983) [novel].

de Coninck, Herman (1944)

Flemish poet and journalist, chief editor of *Nieuw Wereldtijdschrift* (*New World Magazine*). Contributor to the journal *Humo*. Makes an icon out of the urbane, with a colloquial yet highly controlled style. Shares Cees Buddingh's deadpan sense of humour, but is more vivacious and intimate than his

Dutch counterpart. Many of his poems come in long stretches of deceptively casual language. De Coninck couples New Realism with what is essentially a lyricism induced by romantic yearning.

Degenaar, Job (1952)

Born in Dubbeldam, near Dordrecht, the son of a general practitioner. Studied Dutch at the University of Amsterdam, and works as a teacher of Dutch. His poetry has been widely published in literary journals and anthologies in The Netherlands and Belgium. Made his poetic debut in 1976 with the collection *Bericht voor gelovigen* (*Notice for the Faithful*). Degenaar's poetry combines clarity with an enigmatic gleam. His most popular subjects are love, nature and transitoriness. In his most recent collection, *De helderheid van morgens* (*The Clarity of Mornings*, 1992), the poems inspired by Ireland have been singled out for praise.

Dèr Mouw, J.A. (Adwaita) (1863–1919)

Philosopher and classical scholar. Studied classics at Leiden University. Taught at a grammar school in Doetinchem, until his position became untenable, due to his rejection of Christianity. Became a private teacher in The Hague, where he led a somewhat eccentric life. Solipsism forms the cornerstone of his Indian philosophy, and is expressed, sometimes with irony, in the poetry which he began to write at around the age of fifty. His highly original sonnets, with a very subtle tone, earned the admiration of Albert Verwey and Frederik van Eeden.

de Vries, Hendrik (1896–1989)

Poet and painter. Contributed to the journals *Het Getij* (*The Tide*) and *De Vrije Bladen* (*The Free Magazines*). With Marsman, de Vries is associated with Dutch expressionism, but in form and diction his work is anchored in the tradition of 17c. Dutch poetry and of the emotive classicism of Willem Bilderdijk (1756-1831). His work is frequently invocatory, and presents in a complex of personal and mystical symbols a fear of death and of the apocalypse.

D'haen, Christine (1923)

Born in Saint-Amandsberg, Ghent. Graduated with a *licentiate* in Germanic Philology, worked from 1950 to 1970 as a teacher, and from 1969 to 1983, for the Gezelle Archive. She translated Guido Gezelle's poetry into English, and wrote a comprehensive biography about her precursor.

D'haen made her poetic debut in 1948 with the epic 'Abelard en Heloise', which appeared in the journal *Dietsche Warande en Belfort*. Her first collection of poetry, *Gedichten 1946-1958* (1958) was characterised by an intense and lofty passion, with allusions to mythology, restrained by its traditional form. In her subsequent collections, she explores the expression of passion through formal restraint in various manifestations, combining archetype with archaism, sensuous resonance with rhetoric. The collection *Onyx* (1983) contains frequently anthologised poems like 'De mol' and the sequence of elegies set to music by P. Cabus, together with new verse which bears out Yeats's dictum that 'Ancient salt is the best packing'.

Ducal, Charles (Frans Dumortier) (1952)

Flemish fiction writer and poet. Teaches Dutch and English. His first collection, *Het huwelijk* (*Marriage*, 1987), received instant acclaim. The book compares the pragmatic, non-poetic life of the spouse with the fragile existence of the poet, who has substituted imagination for reality. Where Remco Campert has called poetry 'an act of affirmation', Ducal calls it 'an act of negation', negating the reality of existence and clinging to the imagination of the soul.

The struggle of imagination and reality is also central to Ducal's second collection, *De hertog en ik* (*The Duke and I*, 1989). The child's world of the imagination is constantly compared with the adult world that has flung its nets over it, and that has made *Angst* the key term of existence. In this collection he pays homage to his poetic ancestor, Gerrit Achterberg.

du Perron, E. (1899–1940)

Indonesian-born (his father's family being French nobility), du Perron went to Paris, and supported by the family fortune, led a bohemian existence. Went to Belgium, and contributed to its left-wing, experimental arts. Gradually exerted an innovative influence in The Netherlands. After the dissipation of the family fortune, du Perron maintained himself and his second wife in Paris with his journalism. Went back to Indonesia in 1936, and settled in Holland in 1939.

His powerful, individualist personality exerted a notable influence on the Dutch literary tradition. With Gaston Burssens (1896-1965) and Van Ostayen he founded the magazine *Avontuur* (*Adventure*). He was also one of the founders of the influential journal *Forum* (1932-35), which offered a counterbalance to the "vitalism" of *Het Getij* (*The Tide*). Instead of the expressionism of *Het Getij*, *Forum* maintained that form had to be an extension of the poet's personality. His own poetry shows du Perron's personality as playful, colloquial and matter of fact. Together with essayist Menno ter Braak, du Perron is the prime example in Holland of the *littérature engagée*, wary of compromise.

His autobiographical novel, *Het land van herkomst* (1935) contains reminscences of his childhood in Indonesia. He was a friend of André Malraux, who dedicated *Le Condition Humaine* to him.

Translations: *The Country of Origin*, 1984 (*Het land van herkomst*, 1935) [novel].

Eijkelboom, J. (1926)

Journalist, poet and translator. Editor of Dutch quality left-wing newspapers, *Vrij Nederland* (*Free Netherlands*) and *Het Vrije Volk* (*The Free Nation*). Born in Ridderkerk, where his father worked as an insurance broker. During his secondary education in Rotterdam he befriended the poet Jan Emmens. After the War he joined the army, and saw active service in Indonesia. Studied in Amsterdam, first English, then Politics, but never finished his studies.

Together with Jan Emmens, he founded the journal *Tirade* in 1957. Made his debut with the collection *Wat blijft komt nooit terug* (*What Remains Never Returns*, 1979), a collection of beguiling, direct lyrics depicting apparently autobiographical themes with a gentle mixture of the anecdotal and the melancholic. Eijkelboom maintains that his poetry has not been influenced by the Dutch literary tradition. Instead, his work bears affinity with Robert Lowell, Philip Larkin, W.B. Yeats and Richard Murphy, all of whom he translated. These, together with his translations of John Donne, Spenser and Emily Dickinson, show his mastery of form. Intimations of death and decay form a constant theme in his poetry, and shine through the title of his most recent collection *Hora incerta* (1992).

Elburg, Jan G. (1919–1992)

Contributed before the War to the magazine *Criterium*, and published traditional poetry during the War. After the War, he was one of the most influential and innovative contributors to the magazine *Het Woord* (*The Word*). Came in contact with members of the COBRA movement, and with Lucebert, Kouwenaar and Lodeizen is considered one of the most important exponents of the experimentalist movement of the Fifties.

Puns lie at the basis of his attempt to destabilise language and thus expose unacceptable platitudes. His later verse displays a less playful, more restrained use of language.

Elsschot, Willem (Alphons J. de Ridder) (1882–1960)

Studied at the Higher Business School in Antwerp. Worked before the War in offices in Paris, Rotterdam and Brussels. After the War, he set up an advertising agency. Retained an interest in literature, and combined business with writing.

Trade plays a central role in his famous series of novels *Lijmen* (*Soft Soap*, 1924), *Kaas* (*Cheese*, 1933), and *Het been* (*The Leg*, 1938). Told in the first person singular, these books recount the affairs of Laarmans in the world of business corruption. In the first book, he develops from an impressionable office clerk to the scrupulous associate of the likable mountebank, Boorman; in the last, he regains his ethics. Elsschot's laconic style is distinguished by its sparkling cynicism.

Initially discouraged as a poet, Elsschot resumed writing verse after his poetry was published in *Forum*. A poet of the Thirties, Elsschot combines social commitment with personal sentiments which are often hidden behind a veneer of matter-of-fact statements.

Translations: *Three Novels: Soft Soap. The Leg. Will-o'-the-Wisp*, 1965 (*Lijmen*, 1924; *Het been*, 1938; *Het dwaallicht*, 1946) [novels]; *Three Tales from a Life*, 1991 (*Lijmen*, 1924, *Het been*, 1938, and *Het dwaallicht*, 1946), [novels]; *Villa des Roses*, 1992 (*Villa des Roses*, 1913) [novel].

Enquist, Anna (Christa Widlund) (1945)

Psychoanalyst. Studied psychology at Leiden, and piano at the Amsterdam Academy of Music. Then specialized in psychoanalysis in Amsterdam. Married to a Swedish cellist. Started writing poetry in 1988, and was initially published in the journal *Maatstaf* (*Gauge*). Her collection, *Soldatenliederen* (*Soldiers' Songs*, 1991) received unanimous praise for its 'discipline and insight, sense of language and emotional control'. Expresses everyday experiences with an argumentative thrust and within formal constraints. Her work has been compared with that of Vasalis.

Faverey, Hans (1934–1990)

Psychologist. Made his debut in 1968 with the collection, *Gedichten* (*Poems*), which displayed an innovative typography, reminiscent of Paul Van

Ostayen. A poet in the tradition of Van Ostaiyen, but also of Mallarmé, he aims at limiting the communicative value of language, particularly by manipulating coherence. Through a wide frame of reference Faverey postulates relationships between things which are beyond what our cognition considers to be coherent. The result is a poetry on the verge of paradox. Through repetition and variation he attempts to display the relativity of time in his poems. His work contains reminiscences of Japanese and classical art. Faverey's early work was considered idiosyncratic and unimpregnable. In *Chrysanten, roeiers* (1977) Faverey made his poetic frame of reference more accessible. The collection still thrives on paradox, but makes it subservient to the events which it focuses on. It also casts light on the imagery in his previous poems.

Translations: *Against the Forgetting*, tr. Francis R. Jones, London: Anvip Press, 1993.

Gerhardt, Ida G.M. (1905)

Taught Greek and Roman from 1939 to 1963; translated for her doctorate (1942) Lucretius' *De Rerum Natura*, books I and V. Stands out as the upholder of traditional Dutch Christian values, with Gorter and Leopold as her cultural predecessors (her "robust" translation of the psalms, in collaboration with Marie H. van der Zeijde, in 1972, has been called "of immeasurable importance for our culture").

Gerlach, Eva (Margaret Dijkstra) (1948)

Made her debut in *Hollands Maandblad* (*Holland Monthly*) in 1977, and brought out her first collection, *Verder geen leed* (*That Apart no Hurt*) in 1979. This collection proved very popular, and led to conjectures about the poet's identity. She shunned publicity for years. Eight years after her first publication, and after the publication of *Een kopstaand beeld* (*An Image Standing on its Head*; 1983) and *Dochter* (*Daughter*; 1984), she consented to an interview, in which she explained her desire for privacy as a *sine qua non* for inspiration ('I want to remain invisible, otherwise I can't write verse').

Achterberg and Nijhoff count as major influences in her work. Lines like 'With pencil and eraser I made what best I could: death' bear their imprimatura, as does her insistence on form—most notably the use of octaves. Like Achterberg's, her poetry frequently expresses the inability to communicate, but where her precursor projects this onto the autonomy of the poem proper, Gerlach confines it to the feeling of despondency this inability engenders in her verse, which hinges on words unspoken or unheard.

Gezelle, Guido (1830–1899)

Flemish nationalist, priest, journalist, linguist, ethnologist, and one of the most important lyrical poets in the Dutch language. The son of a gardener, he grew up in a working class area in Bruges. He developed an ambition to become a missionary in England. Began writing poetry at the Seminary at Roeselare, where he paid part of his college fees by doing chores. In 1854, just before he joined the priesthood, he began teaching Natural History and Modern Languages at Roeselare. But his unconventional teaching methods came in for much criticism. In 1860 he was appointed co-director of an English College in Bruges, and vice-rector at the Seminary Anglo-Belgium, but his unorthodoxy led to another transfer, to a parish in Bruges.

On the advice of his superiors, he took charge of the weekly *'t Jaer 30*, and contributed anti-liberal polemics. He was involved in several litigations, and in 1872 he was once again transferred, to a parish in Kortrijk, where he resumed his political journalism and his literary activities, translating Longfellow's *Hiawatha* (1886). In the 80s, his work began to receive acclaim, particularly in West Flanders. He died soon after being appointed rector of the English Convent in Bruges, and was given a royal funeral in Flanders.

Translations: *Guido Gezelle (1830-1899). Selection from his Poem s*, ed. and tr. Maude Swepston, Bristol: the Burleigh Press, 1937; *Poems/ Gedichten*, tr. Christine D'haen, Beurle a.d. Leie: Colibrant, 1971; Hermine J. van Nuis, *Guido Gezelle: Flemish Poet-Priest. A Critical Stud y*, contains poems selected and translated by Hermine J. van Nuis, Westport: Greenwood Press, 1986; *The Evening and the Rose: 30 Poem s*, tr. Paul Claes & Christine D'haen, Antwerp: Guido Gezellegenootschap, 1989 [4th rev. edn. of *Poems/ Gedichten*].

Gilliams, Maurice (1900–1982)

Flemish poet; worked as typographer, office stationer, teacher and librarian. For him, poetry is the attempt to reach the highest perfection in the "objective representation of very subjective situations." These he expresses through "soliloquies of the lonely", autonomous and sometimes *in vacuo*, at best voicing the "pathos of intelligence".

Gilliams is a poet-craftsman whose melancholic tone has been associated with that of Karel van de Woestijne. From his first collection, *Elegieën* (*Elegies*, 1921) he consistently moved towards greater simplification. His *personae* are onlookers rather than participants. This distanced perspective is also manifest in his other writings, including his diaries, *De Man voor het Venster* (*The Man in Front of the Window*, 1943).

Greshoff, Jan (1888-1971)

Dutch poet, essayist and critic. Began his career as a journalist in The Hague, became editor in chief of *De Nieuwe Arnhemse Courant* (1920-1924), and, from 1927, correspondent of Dutch and Dutch Indies journals in Brussels. An impassioned opponent to fascism, he moved to Capetown in 1939. Journeyed to the Dutch Indies and the States before settling in South Africa after World War II. From 1947 he contributed literary chronicles to the Dutch newspaper *Het Vaderland*.

He made his debut with *Aan den verlaten vijver* (*By the Deserted Lake*, 1909) which was followed by *Door mijn open venster* (*Through My Open Window*, 1910). With their melancholic tone and classical form, both collections betray the influence of Boutens and van de Woestijne. The latter served as an example to many exponents of the generation that included Adriaan Roland Holst and Martinus Nijhoff. They reinstated rhetoric. Their poetics are manifest in Greshof's *De Ceder* (*The Cedar*, 1924) and, ten years later, in *Voces Mundi* (1934). Greshoff may have shared the rhetoric of his contemporaries, but his voice had a modernist inflection. In *Aardsch en hemelsch* (*Earthy and Heavenly*, 1926), he expresses irony through the understanding of human failings and the acceptance of the human condition. This voice contributed to Greshof's evolving into a truly modern writer, invigorating his poetry with the cadences of everyday speech.

Like his friend, du Perron, Greshoff gave vent to his anti-bourgeois attitudes. In his later work, death becomes a prime motif. With his repulsion of dogmas and -isms, his capacity for friendship, his support of young authors, Greshoff became one of Holland's staunchest custodians of traditional literary values.

Hanlo, Jan (1912–1969)

Born in Indonesia. Like his contemporary, Cees Buddingh', Hanlo made an art out of trivia. His novel, *Zonder geluk valt niemand van het dak* (*It Takes Luck to Fall off a Roof*, 1972), juxtaposes philosophical reflections, absurdity and experiences in mental hospitals. Hanlo was claimed by the Fifties movement for his experimentalism. Yet in essence he was an individualist who endeavoured to 'construct poetry out of its own materials', and who imbued his verse with a tender, and sometimes even romantic, music. His tone poem *Oote* was so controversial that it formed a topic of debate in the Dutch parliament.

Herzberg, Judith (1934)

Dutch poet and dramatist, living in Tel Aviv and Amsterdam, where she was born. Contributor to the journal *Tirade*. Worked for the Institute of Research for Dutch Theatre, and teaches filmscript writing at the College of Dutch Film and Television.

Made her poetic debut with the collection *Zeepost* (*By Slow Boat*, 1963). She has published eight volumes of poetry, including *27 Liefdesliedjes* (*27 Love Songs*, 1971), an adaptation of *The Song of Songs*, and most recently, *Zoals* (*Just As*, 1992). Through the anecdotal she balances personal experiences with an impersonal, quasi-objective stance, allowing scope for the reader's imagination. The power of interpersonal relations, and the distress these can cause forms a frequent theme in her work, which is always characterized by a deeply felt humaneness.

Internationally, Judith Herzberg's is one of contemporary Holland's most established poetic voices. She has contributed to various English poetry magazines. In English, her poetry has been anthologized in, among others, *A Book of Woman Poets* (1980) and *Voices within the Ark* (1980).

Judith Herzberg has also written several plays that have been produced in the theatre and on television in Holland and Germany. Her film scripts include *Charlotte*, a dramatization of the diaries of Charlotte Salomon, a young German Jewish painter who died in Auschwitz.

Translations: *That Day May Dawn. A Play*, 1977 (*Dat het 's ochtends ochtend wordt*, 1974) [television play]; *But, What*, 1987 (*En/of*, 1985) [play].

Hoekstra, Han G. (1906–1988)

Poet and journalist. Together with Ed. Hoornik and Cola Debrot, Hoekstra edited the literary journal *Criterium* in 1940. After World War II he became editor of *Het Parool*, a national Dutch daily newspaper. In his poetry he celebrates the role of the imagination through simple, everyday language, with gentle irony and melancholy. Also wrote humorous verse and stories for children.

Hoornik, Ed. (1910–1970)

Journalist and editor of *Werk* (*Work*, 1939), *Criterium* (*Criterion*, 1940–1942) and, after 1945, of *De Gids* (*The Guide*). Worked for the foundation for the cultural cooperation with Surinam and the Dutch Antilles. Was imprisoned in a concentration camp in Dachau from 1943 to 1945.

Made his debut in 1936 with *Het keerpunt* (*The Turning Point*), a collection of *engagé* poems coupled with verses about religious motives and about the mother-child relationship. The latter is central to *Mattheus* (*Matthew*, 1938), an epic poem about the wanderings of a psychopath who has escaped from the asylum.

After the War, his poetry and fiction gave vent to a confrontation with death and the guilt of the survivor. In this respect, his work is related to that of Achterberg, who was his friend and mentor. In *De overweg* (*The Crossing*, 1965), Hoornik describes his visit to the dying Achterberg. Hoornik felt indebted to Nijhoff, a fellow-wanderer whose Eliot-like world view he shared.

Translations: *The Fish: A Long Poem*, tr. Koos Schuur, Amsterdam: Delta, 1965.

Jooris, Roland (1936)

Flemish poet and art columnist. Studied Germanic languages. Made his debut in 1956 with *Gitaar* (*Guitar*), a collection of experimental verse. He developed into one of the most important exponents of Flemish New Realism, with collections like *Een konsumptief landschap* (*A Consuming Landscape*, 1969) in which the self-reflexive plays an important role in an attempt to breach the gap between art and reality. The primary role which visual perception plays in this verse is reflected in his publications on modern art.

Kloos, Willem (1859–1938)

One of the leaders of the poets of the Eighties. It is generally believed that Kloos launched this movement with his introduction to the poems of *Perk* (1882), which became the movement's manifesto. In 1885 he founded the journal *De Nieuwe Gids* (*The New Guide*), together with, among others, Albert Verwey, whom he befriended in 1882. In 1885 their friendship became more intimate, as is borne out by Verwey cycle of sonnets *Van de liefde die vriendschap heet* (*Of the Love Called Friendship*). In 1888 Verwey got engaged, and this was seen by Kloos as a betrayal of their "higher friendship".

As with many of the poets of the Eighties Movement, Kloos's poetry cannot be considered in isolation from his personal philosophy. From his reading of Kant, Schelling, Schopenhauer and Von Hartmann, he distilled his theory of "De Onbewustheid" ("The Unconscious"), the inner force from which life emanates and to which it will return. This Unconscious is the creative force in Man, his claim to divinity. In line with post-symbolists like Yeats and Mallarmé, Kloos believed that the reasoning power in man had gradually disowned our human claim to divinity. His ideal world, where the Unconscious reigned supreme, was represented by Greek Antiquity, where civilization and art were in complete harmony (as in Yeats's Byzantium). Like Yeats and Wilde, Kloos venerated "moods" as the realizations of the Unconscious, the movements of the "eternal Soul".

Knibbe, Hester (1946)

Grew up in picturesque Harderwijk; its surrounding meadows and hayfields are represented in her poetry. Worked for several years as a medical analyst in Rotterdam.

Began writing poetry at the age of fourteen, but started seriously in 1979. In 1982 she opened the Rotterdam Poetry International Festival. She has been a regular contributor to journals like *WAR* and *De Tweede Ronde*, and has been anthologised. Her poetry expresses a fundamental and impregnable loneliness which is an essential part of human existence.

Komrij, Gerrit (1944)

Poet, playwright, translator and columnist. Studied Literary Theory. Emigrated to Portugal. Regular contributor to several Dutch newspapers. TV critic for the daily *De Nieuwe Rotterdamse Courant*. As a columnist, Komrij is the staunchest defender of style; he is renowned for the biting wit with which he delivers his formidable attacks on pretentiousness. Editor of the journal *Maatstaf (Gauge)*.

Made his debut with *Maagdenburgse halve bollen en andere gedichten* (*Magdeburg Hemispheres and Other Poems*, 1968), a collection of skillfully crafted verse with a wry sense of humour, contrasting sharply with the experimental poetry of the time. This was followed by the surrealist *Fabeldieren* (*Mythical Animals*, 1975) and the more melancholic *Capriccio* (1978).

Insistence on traditional forms infuses his neo-romantic poetry (he is Holland's most gifted contemporary sonneteer). His gift of irony is manifest in the different stances he adopts. Underneath the stances he affords us glimpses of melancholy.

Among the many writers he has translated are Shakespeare, Wilde, Kleist, Schiller, Molière, Alfred Jarry, Emmanuel Rhoidis and Poggio Bracciolini. He has compiled and edited two very significant anthologies of Dutch poetry from the 17th century to the present.

Translations: *The Comreigh Critter and Other Verse*, tr. Jacob Lowland. Amsterdam and New York: C.J. Aarts, 1982 [dual language edition].

Kool, Marga (1949)

Teacher and author. Born in Beekbergen. Descended from agricultural families. Lives in Zuidwolde, in the rural province of Drenthe. Is politically active for the retention of Drenthe dialect, and is a member of the *Gedeputeerde Staten (Provincial Council)* of Drenthe.

From '84 to '89 Marga Kool produced and presented the Drent Cultural programme of Radio Noord (North). She is founding and board member of *Stichting Het Drentse Boek (Foundation for the Drent Book)*, and chairperson of the Federation for Regional Language Organisations in the Low-Saxon Area.

Her publications include an early TV drama, *Niemandsland (No Man's Land)*, and a collection of poetry, *Achter Oen Ogen (Behind Your Eyes)*. Her collection *Hoogspanning (High Voltage)* contains Drent and Dutch poetry. She has also written several plays, and compiled an anthology of women's poetry. Her poems have appeared in various journals, including *Roet (Soot)*, *Maatstaf (Gauge)*, *WAR*, *Literama Magazine*, *Oeze Volk (Our People)* and *Maandblad Drenthe (Drent Monthly)*.

Kopland, Rutger (pseud. Rutger Hendrik van den Hoofdakker) (1934)

Psychiatrist; since 1983 professor of biological psychiatry at the University of Groningen. His department has made significant contributions in the research of fighting depression by altering sleeping patterns. Author of two controversial collections of essays on ethics in medicine. Contributor to journals such as *Tirade* and *Raster*. Made his debut with *Onder het vee (Among the Cattle*, 1966), but received recognition with the collection *Het orgeltje van Yesterday (The Little Barrel Organ of Yesterday*, 1968) and *Alles op de Fiets (Everything on the Push-Bike*, 1969).

Most typical of Kopland's verse is his tone, always modest, sometimes furtive. In an unadorned, and often understated style, he pits human desires for one's childhood and its protectiveness, against the demands of everyday reality. In his later work Kopland often expresses directly a single human emotion as it is experienced. Kopland's poetry has been widely translated.

Translations: *An Empty Place to Stay & Other Selected Poems*, tr. Ria Leigh-Loohuizen. San Francisco: Twin Peaks Press, 1977; *The Prospect and the River*, tr. James Brockway, London: Jackson's Arm, 1987; *A World Beyond Myself*, selected and translated by James Brockway, London: Enitharmon Press, 1991.

Korteweg, Anton (1944)

Studied Dutch and Literary Theory. Head-conservationist of the Literary Museum in The Hague. His first collection *Niks geen Romantic Agony* (*None of that Romantic Agony*, 1971) depicts his stance with regard to Dutch Neo-Romanticism. Not wary of self-mockery, Korteweg wrenches his own childhood in a Protestant and sexually repressive atmosphere into perspective. In his later work, mockery begins to give way to melancholy.

Compiled an anthology of nineteenth-century Dutch preacher-poets.

Koster, Edward B. (1861–1937)

Essayist and poet. Studied Greek and Roman at Leiden University, and obtained a doctorate for his *Studia Tragico-Homerica*. Koster wrote several studies of Shakespeare, and translated many of his plays; also translated from the Italian, Greek, Latin and German.

Was influenced by the Movement of the Eighties. His second collection, *Liefde's dageraad en andere gedichten* (*Love's Dawn and Other Poems*, 1890), was however slated by Lodewijk van Deijssel, one of the movement's foremen. Koster's lyrics, though imbued with his sensitive love of nature, were less exultantly romantic than those of his compatriots. In fact, his romanticism was more directly informed by English Romantics like Blake, whose daimon makes several appearances, and more nuanced. Koster's universe is antinomous; behind his description of the homeliness of the day lies the impending anguish of the night. Overshadowed by the Eighties' confident, but steam-rolling revolution, Koster never received the attention his subtle work deserves.

Kruit, Johanna (1940)

Born in Zoutelande, Zeeland, the Dutch province that has consistently battled with the North Sea (its weapon bears the motto *Luctor et Emergo*), and that forms the *genius loci* of her poetry. Made her debut in 1976 with the collection *Achter een glimlach* (*Behind a Smile*), and has since published seven more books of poetry. Since 1989 she also writes poetry for children. Her poems are accessible to a wide public, and are frequently autobiographical. Nature plays a major part in her work.

Lasoen, Patricia (1948)

Born in Bruges. Studied Germanic Philology at the University of Ghent. Was on the editorial board of the New-Realist journals *Yang* and *Kreatief*

(*Creative*). Lasoen's poetry is eminently accessible in its focus on common human experiences. These she depicts in objective, business-like descriptions behind which lies an emotional, deeply personal, involvement, forever threatening to break through.

Leeflang, Ed (1929)

Poet and teacher of Dutch. Started writing poetry at an early age, but his first collection, *De hazen en andere gedichten* (*The Hares and Other Poems*) was not published until 1979. It was an instant success. Leeflang calls himself "drenched in poetry". His view of the humanitarian function of poetry is apparent from his own verse; using a mixture of sensitivity and scepsis, he tries to preserve in words the few remaining comforts against the vicissitudes of life. He combines the use of everyday language with neologisms and original imagery.

Lodeizen, Hans (1924–1950)

Studied biology at Amherst, Massachusetts, where he befriended the poet James Merrill. Suffering from leukemia, he terminated his studies and spent the last months of his short life at a sanitarium in Switzerland.

Lodeizen may be called the Keats of the Fifties Movement. His work is poignant with romantic longing and implicit complaint. An eminently visual poet, he incorporates imagery with a freedom and freshness reminiscent of Frank O'Hara and Paul Eluard.

Translations: *A Ship of Leaves. Twelve Poems*, ed. and tr. Geert Lernout, Toronto: Aliquando Press, 1982.

Lucebert (Lubertus Swaanswijk) (1924)

Painter and poet. Has been called "Emperor of the Fifties Movement". A member of COBRA. Lucebert wishes to restore the primary physical forces, which through the ages mankind has suppressed. He tries to recreate this original vitality by treading the boundaries of coherence, with great leaps in imagery, syntactic anomalies and imaginative compounds, while at the same time attaching great importance to sound associations.

In the '60s, Lucebert devoted himself fully to painting, gaining a considerable international reputation. In the '80s, he returned to poetry.

Translations: *Lucebert Edited by Lucebert*, tr. James S. Holmes & Hans van Marle. London: Marlborough Fine Art, 1963; *The Tired Lovers They Are Machines*, tr. Peter Nijmeijer. New Selection Series. London: Transgravity Press, 1974.

Marsman, Hendrik (1899–1940)

After a brief career in law, Marsman devoted himself fully to his writing. Edited several magazines, and contributed columns to the paper *Nieuwe Rotterdamse Courant*. Translated Gide's *The Immoralist* and, in collaboration, Nietzsche's *Thus Spoke Zarathustra*.

In his early work, Marsman espouses the values of German expressionism. These he presents in his "Vitalism", a cult of intensity which infuses the Dionysiac energies of his *Paradise Regained* (1927). In the '30s these energies became constrained in a poetry which has been accused of "wordiness" and of lacking spontaneity. Yet in these poems, Marsman, more than any other Dutch poet, captures the atmosphere of the Dutch landscape ("space" is a key-word in these poems), as he carefully places the emblems of the Dutch landscape in perspective.

A seasoned traveller, Marsman was constantly in search of an ideal perspective. The ship that was bringing him to freedom in England at the outbreak of WWII was torpedoed by the Germans; his wife and one other passenger were the sole survivors.

Michaelis, Hanny (1922)

Made her debut in 1949 with *Klein voorspel* (*Short Prelude*), a collection reminiscent of the poetry of Vasalis. She avoided the experimentalism and radicalism of her contemporaries, opting instead for an individually modern style, marked by a quality of reticence. She writes simple, refined personal poetry about loss and loneliness, in which a sensitive heart clashes with a realistic mind. The underlying theme in her work is the realisation of the uncertainty of human relations.

Translations: *Against the Wind. Selected Poems*, tr. Manfred Wolf and Paul Vincent. Berkeley: Twowindows Press, 1987.

Min, Neeltje Maria (1944)

Min wrote poetry from an early age, and was discovered in 1966 by Dutch publisher Bert Bakker, who published an interview with her in *Maatstaf* (*Gauge*). In that year he published her collection *Voor wie ik liefheb wil ik heten* (*For Those I Love I Want to Have a Name*), which was a bestseller.

In this collection she pits the alien, outside world—often the world of parents—against a self incapable of communicating its thwarted innermost feelings, thus higlighting the failure of language to effect communication.

Her collection *Een vrouw bezoeken* (*Visiting a Woman*, 1985) pursues this confrontation further in the implicit war of the sexes. The book manifests

Min's growth into a skilled poet, adept at handling complex emotions through a seemingly objectified reportage of symbolic events.

Mok, Judith (1958)

Born in Bergen, 1958. Her father, Maurits, was a well-known poet. She has made a career as a classical singer, and tours the world. She recorded *Cosi Fan Tutti* for EMI. She has made her first feature film, *Hoffmann's Hunger*, with Eliot Gould and Jacqueline Bisset.

Made her poetic debut in 1982, with *Sterk Water* (*Formaldehyde*), which couples music with vigorous language, and has been described as 'not typically feminine'. Her second collection, *Materiaal* (*Material*) shows her growing engagement. Her involvement with social issues is also evident in her latest collection, *Kinderspel* (*Child's Play*).

Morriën, Adriaan (1912)

Studied and taught French until 1941 before becoming a full-time writer in 1945. Was one of the founders of *Literair Paspoort* (*Literary Passport*) in 1946, a journal of foreign literature, which he edited until 1964. His own translations include work by Freud, Böll, de Maupassant, Camus and de Laclos. Edited *Criterium*, and, in the sixties, was literary editor of *Het Parool*.

Made his poetic debut with *Hartslag* (*Heartbeat*, 1939), a collection of gentle lyrics with the relationships of man, woman and child as its theme, and nature as its backdrop. Love and life are lyrically expressed in *Landwind* (1942). *Het vaderland* (*The Fatherland*, 1946) expresses nationality kindled by war experiences. In the early Fifties, Morriën's poetry becomes more imagistic in such collections as *Moeders en zonen* (*Mothers and Sons*, 1962) and *Het gebruik van een wandpiegel* (*The Use of a Wall Mirror*, 1968), which are more erotic than his earlier work yet as gently lyrical. They introduce insinuations of personal unease—through a form of impending bereavement—which lies at the core of *Avond in een tuin* (*Evening in a Garden*, 1980).

As a critic, Morriën has been acclaimed for his essays on poetry, *Concurreren met de sterren* (*Competing with the Stars*, 1959). His prose is playful and sometimes erotic, and includes *Een slordig mens* (*An Untidy Individual*, 1951 reprinted as *Mens en engel* [*Man and Angel*, 1964]).

Translations: *The Use of a Wall Mirror*, tr. Ria Leigh-Loohuizen, San Francisco: Twowindows Press, 1970.

Nijhoff, Martinus (1894–1953)

Came from a family of publishers. Studied law and Dutch. Nijhoff shared Bloem's fascination with the gloominess of urban life in such works as *De*

Wandelaar (*The Wanderer*, 1916) and *Het Uur U* (*Zero Hour*, 1937). In these Nijhoff presents a lost soul within a lost society. The same alienation informs *Awater* (1934), with its motto, "ik zoek een reisgenoot" ("I am looking for a travel companion"). Awater is the name of that companion (the name might be derived from that of a canal in the South of Holland called "De Wijde Aa"). "Awater" was to be "an arbitrary human being with whom I had no personal ties...a fellow man who was a representative of the multitude and who approached me along the slenderest thread of contact." The poem is highly reminiscent of the desolateness of Eliot's *The Waste Land;* Nijhoff admitted his indebtedness to Eliot (in 1951 he translated *The Cocktail Party*).

Nijhoff forms a bridge between the poets of the journal *De Beweging* (*The Movement*) and the generation of poets that emerged around 1935. He published a number of the poems that were to appear in his first collection in *De Beweging* in 1916. In bridging the gap between two generations, Nijhoff belongs to neither the traditionalists of *De Beweging* nor to the modernists that were to succeed them. *De Wandelaar* already indicates his affiliation with modernism, while the collection entitled *Vormen* (*Shapes*, 1924) is written in a traditional, neo-classical and eminently lyrical style.

Eliot's influence on Nijhof has been the subject of critical study; Yeats's influence, however, has largely escaped critical attention. Like Yeats and Roland Holst, Nijhoff, at one stage, escapes into the magic of words, stating that "the essence of a word is not its meaning, but the thing of the word itself." That "thing of the word" is ever-present, Nijhoff believed, as "latent language", and can be evoked if the poet objectifies himself into the experience of an imagined human being. Thus the poem is in fact "not a product of the human mind, but already exists as 'latent language'." Writing poetry is "but the hewing of a super-personal shape that is already present."

Nolens, Leonard (1947)

Flemish poet, born in Bree. Works as a free lance translator. Made his debut with *Orpheushanden* (*Orpheus Hands*, 1969). As for Beckett, for Nolens writing is existing, an attempt at expressing one's identity, which is inevitably thwarted by the final full stop. Hence themes like self-expression, language, the existentialist isolation of the self, and death abound in his work. His incantatory style derives much of its rhetorical force from abundant images and tonal associations. In *Alle tijd van de wereld* (*All the Time of the World*, 1979) a less rhetorical, more musing, note enters into his work.

Nooteboom, Cees (1933)

Was educated at convent schools in the South of The Netherlands. Worked as a foreign correspondent for the Catholic left-wing newspaper, *De Volkskrant*, and received a newspaper prize for his report on the Paris revolution of '68. Works as poetry editor for the glossy journal *Avenue*.

Built up his reputation as a writer with the novel, *Phillip en de anderen* (*Phillip and the Others*, 1955) and the play *De zwanen van de Theems* (*The Swans of the Thames*, 1959), which was adapted for TV in 1973. While his first collection of poetry, *De doden zoeken een huis* (*The Dead Are Looking for a House*, 1956) is still quite conventional in its lyricism, his next collection, *Het zwarte gedicht* (*The Black Poem*, 1960) already manifests his personal poetics, based on the poem as an autonomous construct, hermetically sealed. This notion is exemplified in titles of collections like *Gesloten gedichten* (*Closed Poems*, 1964) and *Open als een schelp, dicht als een steen* (*Open Like a Shell, Closed Like a Stone*, 1978).

Translations: *A Song of Truth and Semblance: A Novel*, 1984 (*Een lied van schijn en wezen*, 1981) [novel]; *Mokusei!: A Love Story*, 1985 (*Mokusei! een liefdesverhaal*, 1982) [novella]; *Rituals*, 1983 (*Rituelen*, 1980) [novel]; *In the Dutch Mountains*, 1987 (*In Nederland*, 1984) [novel]; *Philip and the Others; A Novel*, 1988 (*Philip en de anderen*, 1955) [novel]; *The Knight Has Died*, 1990 (*De ridder is gestorven*, 1963) [novel].

Otten, Willem Jan (1951)

Born in Amsterdam in a family of musicians. Grew up in the North Holland town of Laren and in Hilversum, the Dutch town associated with broadcasting. Studied philosophy and English in Amsterdam. Worked as a drama and opera critic before becoming a playwright. Also wrote and translated song lyrics.

Made his debut as a poet in 1973 with the award-winning *Een zwaluw vol zaagsel* (*A Swallow Full of Sawdust*). Other successful verse includes *Ik zoek het hier* (*I Look for it Here*, 1980). A distinctive prosody, with emphasis on internal rhyme and repetition of single words, reinforces the symbolic intensity of his poetry. Nature imagery, often indicative of human moods, dominates his early poetry.

Ouwens, Kees (1944)

Born in Zeist. Full-time writer and poet. Made his poetic debut with *Arcadia* (1968), in which he sets off on his quest for the unusual, the 'Absolute','the

Eternal Woman'. The poems manifest a mixture of romanticism and real-
ism, combining the grotesque and the anecdotal, with masturbation as a
recurrent theme. In the same year, he published *De strategie*, a novel which
deals with eroticism and immaturity. Ouwens' later work is progressively
less romantic and less anecdotal, and moves towards greater abstraction.

Peaux, Augusta (1859–1944)

Daughter of a preacher. On the fringe of the poets of the Eighties. De-
scriptions of nature abound in her work. But where Perk and mainstream
Eighties poets present nature as a manifestation of the liberated self, Peaux's
poetic self is more covert in nature descriptions that confine, as much as
imply, its existence.

Peaux's output was small, consisting of one collection of stories, two
collections of verse and some single publications. For a long time, she was
delegated to obscurity. The anthologist and poet Hans Warren is compil-
ing a collected edition of her work.

Perk, Jacques (1859–1881)

Born in Dordrecht, the son of a preacher with literary interests. Studied
Law in Amsterdam. During a trip through the Ardennes in 1879 he met,
and fell in love with, the Walonian girl Mathilde Thomas. Within three
months he had eternalised her in a cycle of 106 sonnets, which was ini-
tially titled *Een ideaal* (*An Ideal*) but which was later named after her: *Mathilde,
een sonnettenkrans* (*Mathilde, a Wreath of Sonnets*). Some of these sonnets
were placed in *De Nederlandsche Spectator*, a journal. In the spring of 1881
Perk fell in love with Joanna C. Blancke, the sister of his future brother-in-
law. To her he dedicated *Eene Helle- en Hemelvaart* (*A Journey to Hell and
Heaven*), a cycle published in *De Nederlandsche Spectator*, consisting of seven
sonnets based on *Mathilde*, with three additions, including "Hemelvaart",
which deifies Beauty. "Iris", a poem that displays Shelley's influence, ap-
peared shortly before his death. Although Perk only saw the publication of
a handful of his sonnets, he exerted a major influence. Within a year of
Perk's death, his close friend Willem Kloos edited *Mathilde*, rearranged
the cycle, and published it, with some other additions from Perk's poetry.
The publication caused a considerable stir, for Perk's Keatsian devotion to
beauty, which had made him adopt the most complex of sonnet forms, was
seen as a radical break from the formula of rhetorical poetry and its con-
ventional rhythms; this was more than reinforced by Kloos' Introduction,

which became the manifesto of the Movement of the Eighties.

Rodenko, Paul (1920–1976)

Son of a Russian, who had fled in the revolution of 1917. Studied Slavonic Languages at the University of Leiden; switched to Psychology at Utrecht. In the War, he contributed 'unorthodox surrealist' poetry and prose to journals of the resistance. After the War, he studied Comparative Literature and Psychology at the Sorbonne, and became deeply influenced by Sartre's existentialism. In Paris, he formulated his conviction that in modern art destruction and creation are inseparable. Never finished his studies, and returned to The Hague, where he was active in literary circles. Befriended Gerrit Achterberg. Made translations and compiled anthologies for Bert Bakker Publishing, including *Nieuwe griffels schone leien* (*A New Broom Sweeps Clean* [literally, *New Slate Pencils, Clean Slates*] 1954), which served for many as the introduction to experimental verse.

Rodenko is most renowned for his commentaries on the poetry of the Fifties Movement, of whom he formed an exponent as much as a precursor. Among his commentaries is his study of Hans Lodeizen (1954). His own poetry bears out his observation that 'real poetry is associated with madness and death; one must have the feeling that the poet at any moment might go mad or commit suicide'. He also wrote erotic fiction. His work is enjoying renewed interest.

Roggeman, Willem M. (1935)

Poet, art critic and novelist, Willem Maurits Roggen was born in Brussels. Studied economics at the University of Ghent before turning to writing. His first poems were published in *het Kahier* (*The Cahier*), the organ of the literary society *De Nevelvlek* (*The Nebula*) in Antwerp, which awarded him a prize for his first collection, *Rhapsody in Blue*, when the poet was 21.

In all he has published 12 volumes of poetry and in 1985 his selected poems, *Memoires* (*Memories*), appeared. He is also the author of two novels, a collection of stories and five volumes of conversations with artists and fellow writers. He himself was the subject of a major interview in the Irish magazine *Comhar* in 1990.

He has worked as a journalist with *Het Laatste Nieuws* in Brussels (1959-81) and on the editorial staff of *De Vlaamse Gids* (*The Flemish Guide*) and *Kentering* (*Reformation*). He was associated with the COBRA movement and his work has been widely translated.

He was one of the driving forces behind the Flemish Cultural Centre in

Amsterdam, *De Brakke Grond* (*The Brackish Soil*).

Translations: *The Revolution Begins in Bruges*, tr. Dorothy Howard and Hendrika Ruger. Windsor, Ontario: Netherlandic Press, 1983; Willem M. Roggeman, *A Vanishing Emptiness: Selected Poems*, ed. Yann Lovelock, London/Boston: Forest, 1989.

Roland Holst, Adriaan (1888–1976)

Studied Celtic Languages in Oxford; lived from 1918 in Bergen. From 1920 to 1934 he was editor of *De Gids* (*The Guide*). After WW II, he made a literary journey through South Africa.

Published his first collection, *Verzen* (*Verse*) in 1911; this was followed by *De belijdenis van de stilte* (*The Confession of Silence*, 1913). In these collections he introduces the solitude which is typical of his work, and which formed the centre of an almost visionary creed expressed in collections like *Voorbij de wegen* (*Past the Roads*, 1920) and *De wilde kim* (*The Wild Horizon*, 1925). With *Een winter aan zee* (*A Winter by the Seaside*, 1937) his work grows terser without losing any of its lyricism. With the threat of an impending war, his poetic voice becomes less distanced from the facets of everyday reality, for instance in *Onderweg* (*Along the Way*, 1940). After the War, his intimations of old age and death become manifest in collections like *In gevaar* (*In Danger*, 1958), *Omtrent de grens* (*Concerning the Border*, 1960), and *Uitersten* (*Extremes*, 1967).

For many years Roland Holst was the Nestor of Dutch poetry; he was known as "the prince of the Dutch poets." He has been called, by Desmond O'Grady, a "high priest in the church of Yeats." The influence of Yeats is indeed unmistakable, in contents (Helen, Troy, Deirdre, fools by the roadside recur), in purport (there is the same yearning for the otherworld, which Roland Holst names the "Elysian desire"), and in style (his rhyme and metre have Yeats's resonance); he shared Yeats's celebration of peasantry and aristocracy and clung to the values of ceremony and innocence, describing art as the vertical, the oak. He translated Yeats, and brought out an anthology of Yeats's poems. The narrative voice in such prose works as *Deirdre en de zonen van Usnach* (*Deirde and the Sons of Usnach*, 1920) and *De dood van Cuchulainn van Murhevna* (*The Death of Cuchulainn of Murhevna*, 1916) is reminiscent of Yeats in *The Secret Rose*.

Yet it would be a mistake to claim that Roland Holst simply followed in Yeats's footsteps. During his formative years, as a student in Oxford, he assimilated elements from the work and poetics of Yeats and Oscar Wilde into his own individual passionate lyrical intensity, a mythological lyricism with the poet as prophet.

Ross, Leo (1934)

Studied Dutch and teaches at the Institute of Dutch Literature in Amsterdam. Was a regular contributor t o *De Gids* (*The Guide*). Translated Thomas Erpenius' Latin fables of Lokman (1964).

His poetry has been called 'somewhat academic'; it juxtaposes the everyday and the poetic. Ross has published several collections and one anthology.

Rouweler, Hannie (1951)

Born in Goor, one of a Catholic family of seven. Started writing poetry when she was fifteen, but did not make her poetic debut until 1988, with the collection *Regendruppels op het water* (*Raindrops on Water*). Since then she has published a collection each year.

On her travels, from an early age, she has been in the thick of many perils, including the Yom Kippur War in Israel. These have formed the basis of her poetry. As a painterly poet she speaks in a whisper before a canvas on which she has depicted the reality of experience in a few brushstrokes.

Schippers, K. (Gerard Stigter) (1936)

With Bernlef, Schippers formed the driving force behind the journal, *Barbarber*. They co-authored *Een cheque voor de tandarts* (*A Cheque for the Dentist*, 1967), a documentary of New Realism. Schippers plays with reality in a way reminiscent of Dada. He focuses on the relationship between reality, language and observer, reference and referent. The visual arts, in particular the *Verfremdungseffekt* of the 'ready made', play an important role in his verbal pictures, not unlike Pop Art and Conceptual Art.

Schippers' poetry has been described as iconoclastic; he exposes art's bogus elevated status, and the personality cult accompanying it, by means of uninhibited and original observations.

Slauerhoff, Jan Jacob (1898–1936)

His adventurous life informs his literature. Graduated in medicine in 1923, and worked as a ship's doctor in the Far East. Returned, dissipated, but still restless, and went, again as ship's doctor, to South America. Came back, married a dancer, returned to South America, and came back, once again ill. The pattern would be repeated until ill-health made it impossible for him to make any more arduous voyages.

for him to make any more arduous voyages.

Undoubtedly, Slauerhoff's reputation has contributed to the criticism that his work is careless, sloppy even. However, his restless, impulsive spirit imbues his poetry with a *sprezzatura* that takes the attention away from form and focuses it on the man behind the verse. With his highly individual life-style and his exotic, imaginative, intensely melancholic poetry, Slauerhoff became the leading poet of his generation. After a period of relative silence, his work has recently been revived.

Sontrop, Theo (1931)

Poet and publisher. Studied French, and was a teacher for six years. Made his debut with *Langzaam kromgroeien* (*Slowly Growing Crooked*, 1962), a collection of short lyrics, remarkable for their punning. His poetry is characterized by its idiosyncracy, and its precision.

Sontrop established a reputation as scholar and critic. He was editor of the journal *Tirade*, and now edits *Maatstaf* (*Gauge*). He became an editor of *Meulenhoff* in 1970. In 1972 he joined *De Arbeiderspers* as director.

The poet Jaap Harten described Sontrop as 'a poet with a complex male brain, playing a sparring match with words which is not for slow-working brains'. He has translated Beckett.

Soudijn, Karel (1944)

Teaches psychology at the University of Tilburg. Made his debut in 1967 with *Dreunende kabouters* (*Droning Goblins*). His poetry is anecdotal and is understated. His earlier poetry presents memories of his youth and travels in a sober fashion. His later work has more absurdist touches.

Tellegen, Toon (1941)

Born in Den Briel, where his father worked as a GP. His mother had fled from St. Petersburg after the Russian Revolution, and was bilingual in Russian and Dutch. Tellegen went to the U.S. to study Liberal Arts at the University of Virginia. Back in Holland, he studied medicine at Utrecht. Began to write drama. Went to Kenya in 1970, and worked as a doctor among the Massai tribe. Returned in 1973, and set up medical practice in Amsterdam. Contributed to *De Gids* (*The Guide*), *Tirade* and *Hollands Maandblad* (*Dutch Monthly*). His first collection of poetry, *De zin van een liguster* (*The Sense of a Privet*, 1970) introduced him as a lyrical poet with a subtle ambivalence to romanticism. In *De aanzet tot een web* (*The Outset of a Web*, 1981), Tellegen anchors his poetry in the literary tradition of the antiquities, with Ovid as his precursor, and exile as a recurrent theme.

Tellegen is wary of publicity. In 1981, he resolved to leave behind the 'writerly side of this existence'. By 1987 he had published six collections of poetry in which the human condition is frequently described in what may seem an absurdist dreamworld, sometimes approaching nightmare. He is known among the larger public as a writer of children's stories.

ten Berge, H.C. (1938)
Made his debut in 1964 with the collection, *Poolsneeuw* (Polar Snow). Was influenced by Ezra Pound, whom he has translated. Especially in his early collections he makes use of montage techniques, juxtaposing different times and cultures. He is greatly interested in "primitive" cultures, and has translated Eskimo and North American Indian myths and fables. His later poetry is less hermetic and slighty more autobiographical. In 1967 he founded the literary magazine *Raster*, which has featured contemporary literature, criticism and literary theory.

Translations: Theo Hermans, ed., *The White Shaman. Selected Poems*, tr. Theo Hermans, Greta Kilburn, Yann Lovelock & Paul Vincent, London-Boston: Forest Books, 1991.

T' Hooft, Jotie (1956–1977)
Drug addict from the age of fourteen, T' Hooft's colourful life has formed the subject of a play and a film. After two unsucessful suicide attempts, he died from an overdose. Fascination with death shines through his verse.

T' Hooft was associated with the Flemish New Romantics. His poems deal with the paraphenalia of contemporary culture: pop music, science fiction, drugs—these are presented in a highly metaphorical setting. He became a cult figure for the seventies generation.

Tillema, Mieke (1944)
Born in Rotterdam. Teaches Dutch at a Grammar school in Haarlem. Started writing poetry at around the age of forty, receiving encouragement from Jan Elburg. He wrote about her work: 'One must have observed everyday things to the bone in order to visualise them in writing the way Mieke Tillema does'. Her poetry is beguilingly simple, hiding subtle poetic allusions, coupling playfulness with paradox, and containing a host of implicit, conflicting emotions.

Tillema made her poetic debut in 1984, and has been published in literary journals like *De Tweede Ronde* (*The Second Round*), *Het Nieuw Wereld Tijdschrift* (*The New World Magazine*) and the long-running *De Gids* (*The*

Guide). Several collections of her poetry have appeared, including *Het genot van het surplus* (*The Delight of Surplus*, 1988) and *Overzetttingen* (*Transcriptions*, 1990). In her most recent collection, *Wandeling* (*Stroll*, 1992), she wanders through her memories in search of her father. Her most recent publication, *Druk Bedrijf* (*Printing Business*, but also, *Busy Act*, 1992) describes an excursion through KLM documentation and repro.

Vancrevel, Laurens (1941)

Dutch surrealist, director of Meulenhoff publishing, and translator. With Willem Wagenaar and Frida Vancrevel, Laurens composed the *cadavre exquis*, made up of phrases the contributors jotted on a sheet of paper which was each time folded over to hide the previous contribution. Vancrevel was one of the editors of *Surrealist Encounters. Documents and Manifestos* (1989), and edited *Spiegel van de surrealistische poëzie* (*Mirror of Surrealist Poetry*, 1989).

He has translated Octavio Paz, Max Ernst and Samuel Beckett. *Speculatieven* (*Speculatives*), his own collection of verse was published in 1981, and was followed in '84 by *Vitrine* (*Showcase*).

van den Bergh, Herman (1896–1967)

Born in Amsterdam, where he received a doctorate in Law. Worked as a violinist in the Concertgebouw Orchestra. Was a foreign correspondent in Paris and Rome for the daily *De Telegraaf*, and for his work traveled to Asia and Africa. Returned to Amsterdam in 1945, and taught Italian Cultural History and Literature at the University of Amsterdam.

Van den Bergh was instrumental in introducing expressionism in the journal *Het Getij* (*The Tide*), of which he was editor for several years. His collections of expressionist poetry, *De boog* (*The Bow*, 1917) and *De spiegel* (*The Mirror*, 1925) had a great influence on poets like Marsman, with their vitality and their passionate love of nature. The experimental nature of his work also shines through the collection of prose , *Nieuwe tucht* (*New Discipline*, 1928), in which he argues for a new life-style to accompany a new form of poetry. In the 20s, van den Bergh also devoted four essays to Guillaume Appolinaire.

After a silence of about thirty years, van den Bergh returned to poetry in 1954 with his *Verzamelde gedichten* (*Collected Poems*). This was followed by several collections, from *Het litteken van Odysseus* (*The Scar of Odysseus*, 1956) to *Niet hier, niet heden* (*Not here, not presently*, 1962), in which he uses his expressionist style to describe the human predicament.

Van de Woestijne, Karel (1878–1929)

Became a prime Flemish exponent of *symbolisme*. His work contains the trappings of *fin de siècle* art; it presents an inner dialogue between clashing moods, emotions and intentions—notably a sensuous communion with nature vs. a withdrawn ascesis.

Gradually, van de Woestijne's poetry became more an expression of his spirituality, an attempt to transcend the everyday self. Formally his work grew more terse, and poetically more powerful. Like Yeats, van de Woestijne wrote books rather than individual poems. He grouped the poems thematically, and allowed for images to influence each other through cross references. Each of his separate collections presents a different poetic identity, with a different awareness.

Translations: *The Peasant, Dying*, 1965 ("De boer die sterft" from *De bestendige aanwezigheid*, 1918) [short story].

van Eeden, Frederik Willem (1860–1932)

Van Eeden studied medicine in Amsterdam, where the lurid aspects of the study affected his sensitive nature. Received his doctorate in 1886, and worked as a General Practitioner. Became an influential psychiatrist before he decided to devote himself completely to writing and realising his socialist ideals.

He became influenced by Tolstoy and Thoreau, and founded his own 'Walden', with the assistance of his family fortune. After the unsuccessful Dutch railway strike of 1903 van Eeden founded a cooperative movement, which failed through financial mismanagement. The family fortune was lost, and the colony disbanded in October 1907. Before the outbreak of WWI, he endeavoured to establish an international network of intellectuals, among them Freud and Upton Sinclair.

In 1913, his son died and van Eeden became obsessed with death. He embraced Catholicism in 1922, and died ten years later, a broken and disappointed man.

Van Eeden is one of the most versatile Dutch writers. His prose works include *Van de koele meren des doods* (*From the Cool Lakes of Death*, 1900), a psychologically informed depiction of the melancholy life of a mentally unstable woman.

In 1885, with Kloos and Verwey, van Eeden founded *De Nieuwe Gids* (*The New Guide*), in which his novel *De Kleine Johannes* initially appeared. Within ten years he had distanced himself from this journal and most of its contributors. Van Eeden's poetry, as collected in *Van de Passielooze Lelie* (*Of the Dispassionate Lily*), exemplifies his abhorrence of the rhetorical patriotic tradition of the mid-19th century, and his desire to capture essences.

Translations: *Little Johannes*, 1895 (*De kleine Johannes*, 1887)[novel]; *The Bride of Dreams*, 1913 (*De nachtbruid*, 1902) [novel]; *The Deeps of Deliverance*, 1902 (repr. 1974) (*Van de koele meren des doods*, 1900) [novel]; *Ysbrand*, 1910 (*IJsbrand*, 1908) [play]; *The Quest*, 1911 (*De kleine Johannes*, 1887; *De kleine Johannes II*, 1905; *De kleine Johannes III*, 1906); *Paul's Awakening*, 1979 (*Paul's ontwaken*, 1913) [novel].

van Haren, Elma (1954)

Born in Roosendaal; attended the College of Art in Den Bosch (1972–77). Left the province of Brabant to become an artist in Amsterdam. Now combines painting and writing poetry. Her first collection, *De Reis naar het welkom geheten* (*The Voyage to Welcome*, 1988) was considered the most important poetry debut of the year.

With a flawless technique, van Haren depicts the 'mystery behind the recognizable which makes recognition interesting', and which allows her, for instance, to make a connection between Spinoza and an egg.

Van hee, Miriam (1952)

Flemish poet and translator. Studied Slavonic languages at the University of Ghent (1970–1975). She teaches Russian at the Higher Institute for Interpreting and Translating in Antwerp.

Her first publications, in the literary journal, *Koebel* (*Cow Bell*), date from 1973. She has contributed to various magazines, such as *Yang, Restant* (*Remainder*), *Literair Akkoord* (*Literary Accord*), *De Gids* (*the Guide*), *Dietsche Warande & Belfort* (*Dutch Verandah & Belfort*), *Nieuw Vlaamsch Tijdschrift* (*New Flemish Journal*) and *Het Nieuw Wereldtijdschrift* (*New World Journal*).

Van hee's poems are almost invariably set in a wintry landscape which derives its sombre suggestiveness from its imagistic eye for detail, its simple diction, and its elliptical expression. She compares the horrors of the past with the hope for the future, whereas in the present 'the wind already upsets us/ when it tugs at the ladders/ the ropes the sunchairs shut tight'.

She has translated various Russian writers, such as Achmatova, *En de nacht belooft geen dageraad* (*And the Night Does Not Promise a Dawn*, 1981), Mandelstam, *Zwarte aarde* (*Black Earth*, 1986), Kuprianov, *De voelhorens van de aarde* (*The Feelers of the Earth*, 1988) and Chlebnikov, *Zaoem*, 1989.

Van Ostaijen, Paul (1896–1928)

One of the most remarkable innovators of modern poetry. Born in Antwerp, where he studied and worked as a clerk. Had to leave Belgium after the War because of his activist sympathies. Went to Berlin, where he became acquainted with expressionist artists; returned to Belgium in 1921, but had to serve in the Belgian Army in Germany until early 1923, after which he went back to Belgium. Befriended experimentalist writers like E. du Perron and artists like Oscar and Floris Jespers. Contributed to several journals, and founded, late in life, the magazine *Avontuur* (*Adventure*), with du Perron.

In rapid development, Van Ostaijen was influenced by such movements as "dilletantism", "unanism" and "humanitarian expressionism" before he developed his "organic" expressionism. Van Ostaijen rejected lyrical effusion as well as communicative poetry, striving instead for an individual art in which the poem unfolds organically. He believed that within this autonomous construct even the simplest word is endowed with a revelatory power that through its resonances in our unconscious calls forth the Platonic Idea. This invocation was aided by repetition and free association.

The dilletantism of a Laforgue and the unanism of Jules Romains inform his first collection, *Music-hall* (1916). In the title poem, the word "Music hall" is sprawled over one page, horizontally and vertically, in various fonts and colours. The effect is a unanimist merging of the visual and verbal. With its humanist expressionist themes, the individual vs. the Big City, need for faith, hope and love, his next collection, *Het sienjaal* (*The Signal*, 1918) became the credo of a group of young Catholics.

Bezette stad (*Occupied City*, 1921) was written in occupied Germany, and makes use of Dadaist typography. The collection contrasts with the joyful *The Signal* in its focus on violence and desolation. It chronicles the history of Antwerp from the German advance, through the occupation, to the German retreat, ending with the vague hope of bourgeois society's self-destruction. Van Ostaijen wished to title his next collection, *Het eerste boek van Schmoll* (*The First Book of Schmoll*) to bear out his move towards simplicity and music (the title refers to an elementary piano book). He died of consumption before the book was finished.

Translations: *Patriotism inc. and Other Tales*, 1971 [a selection of the prose]; *Homage to Singer & Other Poems*, tr. Peter Nijmeijer. London: Transgravity Press, 1974; *Feasts of Fear and Agony*, tr. Hidde Van Ameyden van Duym. New York: New Directions, 1976; *The First Book of Schmoll: Selected Poems 1920-1928*, tr. Theo Hermans, James S Holmes, Peter Nijmeijer, and Paul Vincent. Amsterdam: Bridges Books, 1982 [dual language edition].

van Riessen, René (1954)

On the blurb of the collection *Jagend Licht* (*Haunting Light*; 1984), van Riessen describes herself as 'living and working amidst realities that make me speechless.' She tries to give a local habitation to these 'daunting realities' by means of a personal diction which is sometimes majestic, sometimes idiosyncratic, and which can be stylistically unsettling. In her best poems, the combination of the majestic and the urbane contributes to a gentle irony, expressing both astonishment and endearment.

Vasalis, M. (M. Droogleever Fortuyn-Leenmans) (1909)

Psychiatrist. Studied at the University of Leiden (medicine, anthropology, psychiatry and neurology). Worked in Amsterdam and Groningen. With Hoornik and Hoekstra, she was associated with the literary circle of the journal *Criterium*. Made her debut with the novella *Onweer* (*Thunderstorm*) in 1940; in the same year she published her first collection of vers e, *Parken en woestijnen* (*Parks and Deserts*), which had vast appeal. In her poetry she presents the individual in quiet desperation trying to understand the coherence of heart-rending reality. The juxtaposition of romanticism and realism, typical of *Criterium* writers, is enhanced by a gentleness of tone which has made her one of the best-loved and most frequently reprinted of 20c. Dutch poets.

Verwey, Albert (1865–1937)

Poet and critic. By and large a self-taught man, Verwey received an honorary doctorate from the University of Groningen (1914) and held the chair of Dutch Literature at the University of Leiden (1925–1935).

Verwey was a leading force in the Movement of the Eighties. He was a close friend of Kloos', and from 1885 to 1889 he was one of the editors of *De Nieuwe Gids* (*The New Guide*). In '89 he fell out with the dominant Kloos. With Lodewijk van Deyssel, he founded and edited *Het Tweemaandelijksch Tijdschrift* (*The Bi-Monthly Journal*, 1894–1905). He subsequently founded and edited *De Beweging* (*The Movement*, 1905–1919).

His early, romantic verse expresses an adoration of Kloos. In his mature poetry this idolization is transformed into a devotion for the inner, spiritual forces, which he calls 'the Idea'. This notion, based on the philosophy of Hegel and Spinoza, Verwey sees as a deity which induces the poet to create, and which is given its form by the poet.

With this belief that the poet's task in life was to show awareness of the 'Idea', Verwey distanced himself from the adoration of indivdual beauty of the '80s. Verwey's 'collective, pantheistic' aesthetics first come to the fore in *Aarde* (*Earth*, 1896), where he states that life is all and in all.

Verwey translated Shelley, Dante, Shakespeare, Marlowe and Milton.

Translations: Manfred Wolf, *Albert Verwey and English Romanticism. A Comparative and Critical Study, with Original Translations*, The Hague: De Nederlandsche Boek- en Steendrukkerij v/h H.L Smits, 1977. *Vision and Form in the Poetry of Albert Verwey 1865–1937. Poems from the Oorspronkelijk Dichtwerk with renderings in English Verse*, ed., tr. and intr. by Theodoor Weevers, London: The Athlone Press, 1986.

Voeten, Bert (1918-1992)

Lambertus Hendrikus Voeten was born in Breda on 6 July 1918. Made his debut with a children's novel in 1940, and contributed to resistance magazines during the war years. After the War, Voeten quickly rose to fame with his collection, *De blinde passagier* (*The Blind Passenger*, 1946), and in particular with his war-diary, *Doortocht* (*Passage Through*, 1946).

An active contributor to, and editor of, poetry magazines, Voeten played a significant role in reconstructing Dutch poetry after the War. In 1950, he joined the editorial staff of *De Gids* (*The Guide*). His collection *Met het oog op morgen* (*With an Eye on Tomorrow*, 1953) displays his skillful virtuosity.

In the '50s Voeten proved his ability to renew himself. His early work was of great imaginative scope, while his later, 'parlando' poetry was more anecdotal.

Voeten received recognition as a translator, especially of drama. Among his translations are plays by Molière, Shakespeare, Fry, Miller, and Wilder.

Vroman, Leo (1915)

During World War II Vroman was interned in a Japanese prison camp. After the War he moved to the United States, where he still lives and works as a hematologist.

Vroman made his debut as a poet in 1946, when he published *Gedichten* (*Poems*); he soon became an important figure in helping to establish the post-war climate in which the "new poetry" of the Fifties could develop. Although Vroman maintained traditional aspects of form (rhyme, stanza, meter) in much of his poetry, his language is highly individual and innovative, and his tone both intimate and playful. His poems range from the intensely personal (about the War, his wife) to the highly fantastical and at times almost nonsensical. Much of his imagery (the human body, biological processes) derives from his profession, while his main themes concern the fear of death and life, the threats to one's personal (dream) world, and the creative process itself, which is seen as the poet's playing with (im)possibilities which also involve the reader. Poetry with Vroman is never detached from the everyday world.

Leo Vroman also writes poetry in English; this, however, is of a different nature than his poems in Dutch in that it is linguistically less creatively idiosyncratic.

Poems in English: *Poems in English*, Amsterdam: Querido, 1953 (included in *262 gedichten*, Amsterdam: Querido, 1974); *Just One More World*, Amsterdam: Querido, 1976; *Love, Greatly Enlarged*, ed. Stanley H. Barkan, Merrick, N.Y.: Cross-Cultural Communications, 1991.

Vroomkoning, Victor (Walter van de Laar) (1938)

Son of a Belgian mother and Dutch father. He grew up in a protective middle class *milieu* and subsequently studied Dutch Literature and Language. He has two children. Apart from being a poet, he is also a teacher of Dutch. He lives in Nijmegen (The Netherlands).

His first poems appeared in 1981. Since then he has been published in various literary magazines, both in The Netherlands and in Belgium. His work frequently contains autobiographical references, and by its use of accessible language and familiar imagery it is suited to a large public. Important themes in his work are: death, love of parents, eroticism.

Four collections of his poems appeared; the last, *Echo van een Echo* (*Echo of an Echo*) was published in 1990. Vroomkoning is a regular contributor to such poetry readings as the *Dutch Night of Poetry*.

Winkler Prins, Jacob (1849–1904)

Studied Classics. Painter in Paris; teacher in England. Finally settled in Beekbergen, where he devoted himself to gardening. Precursor of the poets of the '80s. His sensitive and mystical impressions of nature are reminiscent of Shelley, with whose work he felt affinity. His intimately melancholic poems have the impressionistic quality of water-colours, and were praised by Willem Kloos for their 'realistic expressiveness, which approximates the purity, but not the intensity, of Jacques Perk'.

Under the pseudonym of Kasper Brandt, Winkler Prins wrote fiction and essays. He died on board of the S.S. Andrew on the Irish sea, south of Ireland.

BIOGRAPHIES OF IRISH CONTRIBUTORS

Pat Boran was born in Portlaoise in 1963 and lives in Dublin where he was recently Poet-in-Residence with Dublin City Libraries. His collection, *The Unwound Clock* (Dedalus, 1990) won the 1989 Patrick Kavanagh Award for poetry and was followed by a chapbook, *History and Promise* (International University Press, 1990) and a collection of stories, *Strange Bedfellows*, (Salmon Publishing, 1991). Selections of his poems have appeared in *12 Bar Blues* (Raven Arts Press, 1990), *The New Younger Irish Poets* (Blackstaff, 1991) and *Dedalus Irish poets* (Dedalus, 1992). His new collection, *Familiar Things*, was published by Dedalus in April 1993. In 1988 he was chosen as a BBC Young Playwright, and in 1991 he received a Bursary in Literature from the Irish Arts Council. He is presently editor of *Poetry Ireland Review*.

Tony Curtis was born in Dublin in 1955. He was educated at Essex University in England and Trinity College Dublin. His two published collections are *The Shifting of Stones* (Beaver Row Press 1986) and *Behind The Green Curtain* (Beaver Row Press 1988). Last year his poem 'Siren off Inisheer' was included in *Leabhar Mor nah Eireann* (*The Great Book of Ireland*) a *magnum opus* celebrating the contemporary Irish imagination. A new collection of Curtis' poems, entitled *This Far North* will be published shortly.

Seamus Deane was born in Derry in 1940. He received B.A. and M.A. degrees from Queen's University, Belfast and a Ph.D. from Cambridge. He is Professor of Modern English and American Literature at University College, Dublin. One of Ireland's leading scholars and critics, he has contributed extensively to the study of Anglo-Irish literature, with books like *Celtic Revivals* (1985) and *A Short History of Irish Literature* (1986). He was chief editor of the *Field Day Anthology of Irish Writing* (1991).

Made his debut as a poet with *Gradual Wars* (1972). Subsequent collections include *Rumours* (1977) and *History Lessons* (1983). *Selected Poems* appeared in 1988.

Greg Delanty was born in Cork in 1958 and now lives in Vermont. He has been published widely in and outside Ireland, and was the recipient of the Patrick Kavanagh Award in 1983. In 1986 he was awarded an Allan Dowling Poetry Fellowship, a major award for a poet outside the U.S. writing in English, adjudicated by Christopher Ricks.

He has been Visiting Poet at several American universities and was Poet-in-Residence at the Robert Frost Place. His poetry has appeared in various anthologies, including the *Field Day Anthology of Irish Writing* (1991).

His first book, *Cast in the Fire,* was published by Dolmen Press in 1986. His latest collection, *Southward* (1992) is published by Louisiana State University Press in the United States and by Dedalus Press in Ireland.

Theo Dorgan was born in Cork in 1953. He took an M.A. in English at University College Cork. He taught at the university when he was Literary Officer at Triskel Arts Centre. He has been Co-Director of Cork Film Festival and is Director of Poetry Ireland.

His poetry has been published in various journals and broadcast in Ireland, England and Denmark. A collection of his verse, *The Ordinary House of Love,* was published by Salmon in 1991. John Montague has described Dorgan as 'an Irish urban voice which can reach far into Russia as well as into the enchanted garden of Sufi love.'

Dorgan was joint editor of *The Great Book of Ireland*, a modern-day Book of Kells with contributions from all leading Irish authors and artists. He is presenter of IN PRINT, RTE Radio 1's book programme.

Sean Dunne was born in Waterford in 1956 and now lives in Cork where he works as a journalist with the *Cork Examiner*. His books include *Against the Storm* (Dolmen Press, 1986) and the anthology *Poets of Munster* (Brandon Books, 1985). He has also written a prose memoir entitled *In My Father's House* (Anna Livia,1991), a novel about growing up motherless.

He has made many broadcasts on literary matters and has contributed essays and reviews to many publications in Ireland and the US. In 1991, he edited a major issue of the *Cork Review* devoted to the life and works of Sean O'Faolain. He is a member of the board of directors of the Triskel Arts Centre in Cork and he has also run a number of workshops for writers, including the poetry workshop at Listowel Writers' Week, which he directed in 1990.

Desmond Egan was born in 1936 in Athlone, and has spent most of his life in the Irish Midlands. He studied in Maynooth, Co. Kildare, and at University College Dublin, where he received an M.A. in English in 1965. He taught Greek and English in Mullingar, Navan, and at Newbridge College, Co. Kildare. In 1987 he became a full-time poet.

In 1972 Egan was one of the three founders of The Goldsmith Press, publications of which include Kavanagh's *Collected Poems*, and, in translation, Yannis Ritsos' *Corridor and Stairs*.

Among his prizes are the 1983 National Poetry Foundation of U.S.A. Award. He was poet in residence in U.C.D. and in Osaka. His poetry publications include *Midland* (1972), *Leaves* (1975), *Siege!* (1977), *Woodcutter* (1978), *Athlone* (1980), *Snapdragon* (1983), *Poems for Peace* (1986), *A Song for my Father* (1988), and *Collected Poems* (1983). He has published a translation of Euripides' *Medea* (1991), and a collection of essays, *The Death of Metaphor* (1990). His poetry has been translated in various languages, including French (*Terre et Paix*, 1988) and Dutch (*Echobogen*, trsl. Peter Nijmeijer, 1990). Together with Michael Hartnett, he compiled an anthology of contemporary Irish poetry, *Choice* (1973).

Patrick Gallagher was born in Egypt in 1934. He received a Jesuit education in Clongowes Wood College. Studied Spanish and French in Trinity College, Dublin, and at the Ecole Normale Supérieure. He taught Spanish in Trinity College, Dublin, Queen's University Belfast and the University of Sheffield. He has been Professor of Spanish at University College Dublin from 1969.

Gallagher is the author of books and articles on 15th and 16th century Spanish poetry, on the modern Spanish novel and on contemporary poetry. His own poetry has been published in *Poetry Ireland Review*, *The Honest Ulsterman*, *Manxa* and in the *Bulletin of Hispanic Studies*.

Robert Greacen was born in Derry (Londonderry) in 1920, grew up in Belfast and moved to London in the late 1940s. He was educated at Methodist College, Belfast, and Trinity College, Dublin.

Primarily a poet, Greacen was also involved in editing some influential anthologies in the 1940s, among them *Lyra: A Book of New Lyrics*, co-edited with Alex Comfort, and the Faber *Contemporary Irish Verse*, co-edited with Valentin Iremonger. In 1944 he published his first collection of poems, *One Recent Evening*, followed in 1948 by *The Undying Day*.

In the early 1950s he produced a critical study, *The Art of Noel Coward*, and then *The World of C.P. Snow*, published in 1962. The latter was a response to, as well as the occasion of, controversy surrounding the novelist. From the late 1950s to the 1970s Greacen combined careers as writer and teacher of English in London, and this led to a decline in output. In 1969 he published a volume of autobiography, *Even Without Irene*, which covers his early life.

The mid-70s saw the re-emergence of Greacen as a poetic force with the publication of *A Garland for Captain Fox*, poems which combine humour with that evocative lyricism which characterized the earlier work. Three further volumes, *Young Mr. Gibbon* (1979), *A Bright Mask* (1985) and *Carnival at the River* (1990) have reiterated this renewed vigour. *Brief Encounters*, a volume of essays dealing mainly with Irish writers of the 1940s appeared in 1991.

In 1986 Greacen was elected to membership of Aosdna. He was writer in residence at Gordonstoun School in Scotland, a Hawthornden Fellow (also in Scotland) and has twice been a Poetry Consultant (in 1988 and 1990) at Winthrop College, South Carolina. He is one of the Governors of the Irish Writers' Centre in Dublin.

Eamon Grennan was born in Dublin in 1941. Studied at University College, Dublin and Harvard. He teaches in the English Department of Vassar College, and divides his time between the U.S. and Ireland.

Made his poetic debut with *Wildly for Days* (1983). This collection was followed by *What Light There Is* (1987) and *As If It Matters* (1991). In 1991 Grennan received a Fellowship from the National Endowment for the Arts and was writer-in-residence at University College, Dublin.

Michael Hartnett was born in County Limerick in 1941. Studied at University College, Dublin and Trinity College, Dublin. Has worked as a civil servant, postman, housepainter, telephonist and as teacher at the National College of Physical Education, Limerick. Editor, with James Liddy and Liam O'Connor of *Arena* (1963-1965).

Made his poetic debut with *Anatomy of a Cliché* (1968).He has published over a dozen collections of poetry since, including *Selected Poems* (1970) and *A Farewell to English* (1975), which bore testimony to his resolve to write only in Irish.

In 1975, he was the recipient of the Irish-American Cultural Institute's Award for Irish writing and of the Arts Council of Ireland Award. His collections of Irish poetry include *Adharca Broic* (1978), and *Do Nuala: Foighne Chrainn* (1984); *A Necklace of Wrens* (1987) is a selection of Irish poems translated by Hartnett. Among his Irish translations are *The Hag of Beare* (1969) and *Selected Poems: Nuala Ni Dhomhnaill* (1986). He has also translated from other langauges, e.g. versions of *Tao* (1963), from the 6th Century Chinese, and Lorca's *Gipsy Ballads* (1972).

Returned to English poetry with *Inchicore Haiku*, which appeared in 1985. His *Collected Poems* appeared in two volumes (1984 & 1986). Together with Desmond Egan, he compiled *Choice: An Anthology of Contemporary Irish Poetry* (1973). He is a member of *Aosdna*.

Seamus Heaney. Ireland's most lauded poet since W.B. Yeats. Born in Castledawson in 1939. Studied English at Queen's University, Belfast. Taught at St. Thomas Secondary School, Belfast; lectured at St. Joseph's College of Education, Belfast and at Queen's University. Moved to the Republic of Ireland in 1972, and worked for three years as free-lance writer. Taught at Carysfort Training College, Dublin. Allott Lecturer at University of Liverpool. Since 1982 Visiting Professor, later Boylston Professor of Rhetoric and Oratory, at Harvard University. Since 1989 Professor of Poetry at Oxford University.

Made his debut in 1965 with *Eleven Poems*. This was followed by *Death of a Naturalist*, for which he received the Somerset Maugham Award in 1967 and the Cholmondeley Award in 1968, the first in a long list of major literary prizes. Subsequent publications include *Door into the Dark* (1969), *Wintering Out* (1972), *North* (1975), W.H. Smith Award; Duff Cooper Prize, *Bog Poems* (1975) *Field Work* (1979), *Preoccupations; Selected Prose, 1968–1978* (1980), *Selected Poems, 1965–1975* (1980), ed., with Ted Hughes, *The Rattle Bag* (1982), *Sweeney Astray* (1984), *Station Island* (1984), *The Haw Lantern* (1987), Whitbread Award, *The Government of the Tongue* (1988), *New Selected Poems 1966–1987*, *Seeing Things* (1991).

Ruth Hooley was born in Belfast where she still lives, writes and works in adult education. She edited an anthology of Northern Irish women writers entitled *The Female Line*, is co-editor of *The Honest Ulsterman* and has had poems published in various journals and anthologies. She is one of the contributors to a forthcoming book of Irish and Romanian poets which will contain translations of one another's work and is currently working on a collection of poems.

Anne Kennedy was born in Los Angeles. She studied writing with Yvor Winters at Stanford University and with Mark Schorer at UC Berkeley. Her work has appeared in publications in Ireland and the U.S. She is currently working on a project for the Smithsonian.

She has lived in Galway since 1977. She is a photographer, writer and broadcaster. Her *Buck Mountain Poems* was first broadcast on Radio Telefis Eireann as a documentary and subsequently published by Salmon Press. She leads the Barna's Writers Workshop and gives workshops in the Galway Arts Centre. She is currently Associate Editor at Salmon Publishing.

She wishes to acknowledge the textual discussions with Marianne ten Cate on her versions in this collection.

James Liddy, born in 1934 on the Night of the Long Knives from Limerick, Clare, and New York parentage. He was given a vision of terrestial paradise by summers spent in the resort of Kilkee and a vision of the eternal city by academic years at Glenstal Abbey. His years in U.C.D. were a long march towards poetry. He was published by The Dolmen Press during this period and founded *Arena* magazine. He became Writer-in-Residence at San Fransisco State College in 1967 and is currently Professor of English at the University of Wisconsin-Milwaukee.

His most recent books are *In the Slovak Bowling Alley, Art Is Not for Grown-Ups* and *Trees Warmer than Green: Notes towards a Video of Avondale House* (International University Press), which was launched to the sound of piano accordions in Avondale on August 24, 1991. He intends to find the noblest Irish pub in the Midwest for the hundredth Ivy Day. There he will lift a glass to Kate O'Brien, a cousin on his father's side, and to Edna O'Brien, a cousin on his mother's side, while he pursues a more obscure strategy.

Michael Longley was born in Belfast in 1939. Studied at the Royal Belfast Academic Institution and Trinity College, Dublin. For a few years he taught at schools in London, Belfast and Dublin. From 1970 to 1991 he was Director for Literature and the Traditional Arts at the Arts Council of Northern Ireland.

Made his poetic debut in Belfast at the Festival in 1965 with *Ten Poems*. This was followed by *Room to Rhyme*, a co-publication with Seamus Heaney and David Hammond. His first book-length collection, *No Continuing City: Poems 1963–1968* appeared in 1969; a number of the poems in this collection dated back to his undergraduate years. With *An Exploded View: Poems*

1968–1972, he established himself as a lyric craftsman of genius. Longley's harmoniously pitched, intimate voice is always imbued with compassion, whether he writes love poems, as in *Fishing in the Sky* (1975), or about the troubles in Northern Ireland. In 1975, his poetry was included in *Penguin Modern Poets 26*. Since then he has published several collections of poetry, of which the last, *Gorse Fires* (1991), was hailed as 'an unusual artistic blend: darkly austere, yet abundant in images, catalogues, and syntactical virtuosity.' It won the Whitbread Prize for Poetry. His *Poems 1963–83* was published in 1985.

Longley has edited *Causeway: The Arts in Ulster* (1971), and *Under the Moon, Over the Stars: Young People's Writing from Ulster* (1971). He has received several literary awards. He has also edited *Selected Poems: Louis MacNeice* (1988) and *Selected Poems: W.R. Rodgers* (1993).

Sen Lysaght was born in Cork in 1957; grew up in Limerick. Studied English Literature at University College, Dublin, where he received an M.A. in 1980. Teaches English and American Literature at St. Patrick's College, Maynooth. His critical and scholarly work has centred in the main on contemporary Anglo-Irish literature.

Made his poetic debut with *Noah's Irish Ark* (1989). This was followed by *The Clare Island Survey* (1991), which has received praise for its 'bright and sharply focused imagery'. He is currently writing a study of Robert Lloyd Praeger. His poetry has appeared in various journals, including the *Times Literary Supplement*.

Joan McBreen was born in Sligo and now lives in Tuam, County Galway. She trained as a primary teacher in Dublin and taught for many years. She is currently taking the WERCC (Women's Education Research and Resource Centre) course in Women's Studies, under the direction of Ailbhe Smyth, at University College Dublin.

McBreen has been widely published in poetry magazines and literary journals in Ireland, Britain, the U.S. and Canada. A selection of her work has been translated into Italian and appeared in Spring 1992 in *La Collina*. She has been broadcast on Radio Eireann and on BBC Radio 4, and has contributed to various literary manifestations, like the Yeats Summer School, Writers' Week Listowel, and The Poet's House at Islandmagee.

Her first collection, *The Wind Beyond the Wall*, was published by Story Line Press in 1990. A second collection has recently been completed. A poet of great control, both in her rhythms and in her almost logically structured meaning, she presents intimations of emotions of lyric intensity.

Medbh McGuckian was born in Belfast in 1950. She studied Anglo-Irish Literature at Queen's University, Belfast, from which she received an M.A. and a diploma in education. Taught English at St. Patrick's College, Knock, Belfast.

Winner of the National Poetry Competition in 1979 with 'The Flitting', she published two pamphlets, *Single Ladies: Sixteen Poems* and *Portrait of Joanna* (1980), and was included in *Trio Poetry 2* (1981) before her first collection, *The Flower Master*, appeared in 1982. This was followed by *Venus and the Rain* (1984), and *On Ballycastle Beach* (1988), which was a Poetry Book Society recommendation. Her poetry, highly original, has been described as 'mysterious' and 'unsettling'. It is as sensuous as it is imaginative, and derives its force from its firm stance in the feminine subconscious. McGuckian edited poems by young Irish people, as *The Big Striped Golfing Umbrella* (1985). She has been writer-in-residence at Queen's University, and has received various literary prizes, including the Eric Gregory Award (1980), Rooney Prize (1982), Arts Council Award (1982) and the Alice Hunt Bartlett Award (1983). In 1992 her book *Marconi's Cottage* was short-listed for the Aer Lingus Poetry Award.

Paula Meehan was born in Dublin in 1955. She has published three collections of poetry, *Return and no Blame*, (1984), *Reading the Sky*, (1986), *The Man Who Was Marked by Winter*, (1991), and *Pillow Talk* (1994). She has twice received bursaries in Literature from the Arts Council.

She has been writer-in-residence both in Trinity College and University College Dublin, and conducts workshops in the prisons and with community groups.

Mary O'Donnell was born in Monaghan in 1954. Educated at St. Patrick's College, Maynooth. She has been living in Maynooth since 1977, and has taught at a Dublin secondary school. Her poetry has been published in various Irish journals and in the USA. Her *Reading the Sunflowers in September* (1990) was nominated for the *Irish Times*/Aer Lingus Literary Award. Other publications include *Strong Pagans and Other Stories*, 1991, and a novel, *The Lightmakers*, 1992. She has been anthologized in Irish and English publications, and is a regular contributor to Irish broadcasts.

Sean MacReamoinn, an Irish critic, singled out her poetry for its 're-markably dual gift for objectifying the personal and appropriating the external, the "other". The self-studies, the evocations of experience, erotic and otherwise, are stripped of self-indulgence'.

Her translations from the German include poems by Ingeborg Bachmann.

Gregory O'Donoghue was born in Cork, 1951. Educated at University College, Cork, and Queen's University at Kingston, Ontario. Returned to live in Cork in 1990 after fifteen years abroad, mainly in Lincolnshire. His poetry has been published widely and a volume, *Kicking*, appeared in 1975 (Gallery Books). He is currently completing a new collection.

Dennis O'Driscoll was born in Thurles, County Tipperary in 1954. Studied Law at University College, Dublin. He has published three collections of poetry: *Kist* (Dolmen, 1982) and *Hidden Extras* (Anvil/Dedalus, 1987) and *Long Story Short* (Anvil/Dedalus, 1993). A long poem is in preparation.

He has edited *Poetry Ireland Review* and is a regular reviewer of poetry for publications in Ireland and the U.K. He was poet-in-residence in University College, Dublin in 1987. He works as a civil servant in Dublin Castle.

Michael O'Loughlin, poet and essayist, was born in Dublin in 1958. He is a graduate of Trinity College, Dublin. Is currently living in Amsterdam. He has published four collections of poetry, *Stalingrad: The Street Dictionary*, *Atlantic Blues*, *The Diary of Silence*, and, most recently, *Another Nation: New and Selected Poems* (1994). Among his numerous critical prose writings is a pamphlet, *Frank Ryan: Journey to the Centre* (1987) and an essay, *After Kavanagh*. Also published a collection of short stories. He has translated various modern Dutch poets, including Gerrit Achterberg, a selection of whose poetry, *Hidden Weddings*, he published with Raven Arts in 1987.

Micheal O'Siadhail was born and lives in Dublin. He is a full-time poet, and author of seven collections of poetry, including *Springnight* (1983), *The Image Wheel* (1985) and *The Chosen Garden* (1990). His latest collection, *The Middle Voice*, is contained in *Hail! Madam Jazz: New and Selected Poems* (Newcastle upon Tyne/ Chester Springs: Bloodaxe Books/ Dufour Editions, 1992). He has lectured and read his poetry widely in North America, and is a recipient of the Irish American Cultural Institute Prize for Poetry.

He was formerly a lecturer at Trinity College, Dublin, and professor at the Dublin Institute for Advanced Studies. His academic works include *Learning Irish* (Yale University Press, 1988) and *Modern Irish* (Cambridge University Press, 1989). He is a member of the Arts Council and the Advisory Committee on Cultural Relations and of Aosdna.

Gabriel Rosenstock was born in 1949. He is chairman of Poetry Ireland, and an honorary life-member of the Irish Translators' Association. Works as an assistant editor with a publications branch of the Department of Education, Dublin.

Author of "thirty something" books in Irish; his own selected poems were translated by Michael Hartnett and Jason Sommer in *Portrait of the Artist as an Abominable Snowman* (Forest Books, UK, 1989).

A prolific translator into and out of Irish, winner of the 1990 DuQuesne translation prize, awarded a Translation Bursary two years in a row (under the European Community's Pilot Scheme) for Willem M. Roggeman's *De Vorm van een Mens* (*Cruth an Daonna 2*, Coiscéim, 1990) and for the selected poems of Georg Trakl, *Craorag* (Carbad, 1991).

He has translated the selected poems of Seamus Heaney into Irish, and tales from Aran writer, Dara Conaola, into English, *Night Ructions*. Other titles include *Cuerpo en Llamas*, *Colainn ar Bharr Lasrach*, Irish versions of Chicano poet Francisco X. Alarcon, from Clo Iar-Chonnachta, and, also by Alarcon, *De Amor Oscuro/Um an nGr Dorcha*, homo-erotic sonnets, from Clo Iar-Chonnachta and The Yeats Club, Florida. Rosenstock has twice been nominated for the European Translation Prize.

He is currently working on a book-length series of erotic haiku. He also co-edited a volume of Yeats into Irish.

Aidan Sharkey was born in Drogheda in 1948, the son of a marine electrician. He grew up in Killybegs, Co. Donegal. After secondary school, he studied for two years at the seminary in Kilkenny. He has worked as a fisherman, manager of a bookstore, data-processor and electrician. In 1992 he settled in Haarlem, Holland.

Sharkey was one of the founders of the Killybegs Writers Group, which encourages cooperation between Northern Ireland and the Republic. His poems and stories have appeared in the American *The Southern Review*. *Making Waves*, his most recent collection appeared in 1993, both in book form (Amsterdam: E.M. Querido) and on CD.

James Simmons was born in Londonderry in 1933. Worked as a barman in Portrush, Co. Antrim, after spending some years in London. Was educated at Leeds University, and taught at Friends School in Lisburn, Co. Antrim, and at Ahmadu Bello University in Nigeria. Returned from Africa in 1967, and in 1968 took up a post teaching Drama and Anglo-Irish Literature at the New University of Ulster at Coleraine.

He began publishing in magazines like *The Listener* in the mid 50s, but his first pamphlet did not come out till 1966. 1967 saw the publication of his first full-length collection, *Late But in Earnest*. Subsequent collections include *In the Wilderness* (1969), *Energy to Burn* (1971), *The Long Summer Still to Come* (1973), *West Strand Visions*, 1974, *Judy Garland and the Cold War* (1976), *Constantly Singing* (1980), which was a Poetry Book Society Recommendation, and *From the Irish* (1985), a substantial number of poems of which are based on famous Irish originals. *Poems 1956/86* was Poetry Ireland Choice, a Book Society Recommendation and won the Irish Publishers' Award.

He has edited *Ten Irish Poets* (1974) and *Soundings 3* (1976), and, with T.W. Harrison, he has written a play, *Aikin Mata: The Lysistrata of Aristophanes* (1966). Among his critical work is an important study of Sean O'Casey (1983). He was founding editor of the *Honest Ulsterman* (1968).

Simmons has been called a lyricist of infectious sincerity who has stripped 'Ireland's madness of all its shabby pretence and excuses'. There are three LPs of his singing his own songs. Simmons has performed frequently on radio and TV, and was the subject of an edition of *Omnibus* on BBC TV, and a recent TV documentary on his early life, 'Now and Then' (1991), was shortlisted for several prizes. He is the recipient of the Eric Gregory Award (1962) and the Cholmondeley Award (1977).

PROVENANCE OF DUTCH AND FLEMISH POEMS IN TURNING TIDES

In this bibliography we have listed the collections from which the anthologised poems were taken. The year in brackets behind the title of a poem is the year of publication of the poet's collection in which the poem first appeared. If two years are given, the first is that of an earlier publication in a journal or anthology (where known to us). For untitled poems, the first line is given, printed in italics.

AAFJES, BERTUS
    De laatste brief (1940)
Verzamelde gedichten 1938 - 1988, Amsterdam: Meulenhoff, 1990.

ACHTERBERG, GERRIT
    Aan het roer dien avond stond het hart (1929/1930; 1931)
    Over de Jabbok (1939; 1941)
    Pinksteren (1940; 1941)
    Instrument (1940; 1941)
    Triniteit (1946/1947; 1947)
Verzamelde gedichten, Amsterdam: Em. Querido, 1988 (1963).

ANDREUS, HANS
    Liedje (1951)
    Voor een dag van morgen (1950; 1959)
    De lege kamer blijft de lege kamer (1973)
Verzamelde gedichten, ed. Gerrit Borgers, Jan van der Vegt and Pim de Vroomen, Amsterdam: Bert Bakker, 1983.

ARENDS, JAN
    Ik (1974)
    Ik heb (1975)
Verzameld werk, ed. Thijs Wierema, Amsterdam: De Bezige Bij, 1984.

BERANOVÁ, JANA
    Willemsbrug
Read at *Poetry International*, June 1993.
    Moedervlekje
Unpublished.
(from the poet's own selection).

BERNLEF, J
    Oom Karel: een familiefilmpje (1965)
Gedichten 1960-1970, Amsterdam: Querido, 1977.
    Verontrustend voorwerp (1980)
De kunst van het verliezen, Amsterdam: Em. Querido, 1980.
    Beatrice (1988)
Geestgronden, Amsterdam: Em. Querido, 1988.

BLOEM, J.C.
    Grafschrift (1931; 1931)
    Zondag (1931; 1931)
    Kamperfoelie (1937; 1937)
    Na de bevrijding (1945)
    De Dapperstraat (1945; 1946)
Verzamelde gedichten, Amsterdam: Athenaeum - Polak & Van Gennep, 1991 (10th edn.).

BLOEM, REIN
    Kroniek van Amsterdam (1970)
Scenarios, Amsterdam: Meulenhoff, 1970.

BONSET, I.K. (THEO VAN DOESBURG) [C.E.M. Küpper]
    X-Beelden (1920; 1975)
    X-Beelden/Herinnering der nachtfonteinen 1 (1920; 1975)
Nieuwe Woordbeeldingen. De gedichten van Theo van Doesburg met een inleiding van K. Schippers, Amsterdam: Em. Querido, 1975.

BOUTENS, P.C.
    Eenzame nacht (1902)
Verzamelde lyriek. Vol. I: 1898-1921, Amsterdam: Polak & Van Gennep, 1968.

BOUWERS, LENZE L.
    De laatste tekens zijn van zwaar gewicht (1988)
De schaduw van de buizerd, Amsterdam: Em. Querido, 1988.

BUDDINGH', CEES
    Enkele biografische gegevens (1957)
    De hyena (1968)
Gedichten 1938 - 1970, Amsterdam: De Bezige Bij, 1970.

CAMI, BEN
    Gij staat geleund op uwe spaad' en rust (1954)
Het land Nod, Amsterdam/Antwerp: C.P.J. van der Peet/'De Sikkel', 1954.

CAMPERT, JAN
 De achttien doden (1943; 1947)
Het onontkoombaar lied, ed. Harry Scholten, Amsterdam: De Bezige Bij, 1985.

CAMPERT, REMCO
 Zilver praten (1951)
 Een vergeefs gedicht (1952)
 Boodschap over de tijden (1970)
Alle Bundels Gedichten, Amsterdam: De Bezige Bij, 1976.
 Wandeling naar Parvondeval (1977; 1979)
 Theater (1979)
Theater, Amsterdam: De Bezige Bij, 1979.

CHARLES, J.B. (Willem Hendrik Nagel)
 Een pools meisje staande op een stoel (1966)
Topeka. De gedichten van 1963 tot 1966, Amsterdam: De Bezige Bij, 1966.

CLAUS, HUGO
 Een vrouw 12 (1954)
 De man van Tollund (1962)
Gedichten [(1948 - 1963)], Amsterdam/Antwerp: De Bezige Bij/Contact, 1965.

DE CONINCK, HERMAN
 Je truitjes en je witte en rode (1969)
De lenige liefde, 1969
 Ballade van de traagheid (1975)
Onbegonnen werk. Gedichten 1964-1982, Antwerp: Manteau, 1984.
 Ik wou wel weer een beetje ziek zijn (1984; 1985)
De hectaren van het geheugen, Antwerp: Manteau, 1985.

DEGENAAR, JOB
 Fenomenaal (1983; 1992)
 Het Ierse schaap (1988; 1992)
De helderheid van morgens, Amsterdam: Thomas Rap, 1992.
 (from the poet's own selection)

DÈR MOUW, J.A. (ADWAITA)
 'k Ben Brahman. Maar we zitten zonder meid (1919)
 Kent iemand dat gevoel: 't is geen verdriet (1919)
 Nog hoorbaar, heel heel ver, is de avondtrein (1919)
Volledig dichtwerk, ed. H. van den Bergh, A.M. Cram-Magré and M.F. Fresco,
Amsterdam: G.A. van Oorschot, 1986.

DE VRIES, HENDRIK
    Mijn broer (1919; 1920)
Keur uit vroegere verzen, Amsterdam: G.A. van Oorschot, 1962.

D'HAEN, CHRISTINE
    De mol (1958)
Onyx, Amsterdam: Athenaeum - Polak & Van Gennep, 1983.
    Epifanie (1989)
Mirages, Amsterdam: Em. Querido, 1989.

DUCAL, CHARLES
    De hertog en ik 2 (1989)
De hertog en ik: gedichten, Amsterdam: De Arbeiderspers, 1989.

DU PERRON, E.
    De zieke man (1927)
Mikrochaos, Maastricht & Brussels: A.A.M. Stols, 1932.

EIJKELBOOM, J.
    Soms (1982)
De gouden man, Amsterdam: De Arbeiderspers, 1982.
    Zo oud als toen (1987)
    A nos glorieux morts (1987)
De wimpers van de dageraad, Amsterdam: De Arbeiderspers, 1987.
    De stad een vogelreservaat (1993)
Hora incerta. Gedichten, Amsterdam: De Arbeiderspers, 1993.

ELBURG, JAN G.
    willen (1951; 1952)
    niets van dat alles (1958)
Gedichten 1950 - 1975, Amsterdam: De Bezige Bij, 1975.

ELSSCHOT, WILLEM
    Moeder (1932; 1934) [signed: 'Paris 1907']
Verzameld werk, Amsterdam: Em. Querido, 1976.

ENQUIST, ANNA (CHRISTA WIDLUND)
    Decemberoffensief (1991)
    Invasie (1991)
Soldatenliederen, Amsterdam: De Arbeiderspers, 1991.

FAVEREY, HANS
    In dienst van het wiel (1977)
    Van lieverlede; zo (1977)
Chrysanten, roeiers, Amsterdam: De Bezige Bij, 1977.

GERHARDT, IDA G.M.
Verwachting (1947)
De teruggewezen gave (1966)
Dodenherdenking (1970)
Verzamelde gedichten, Amsterdam: Athenaeum-Polak & van Gennep, 1989 (4th edn.).

GERLACH, EVA (M. Dijkstra)
Beurtelings (1982; 1987)
De Tweede Ronde (Autumn 1982); *Domicilie*, Amsterdam: De Arbeiderspers, 1987
[version as in *De Tweede Ronde*].

GEZELLE, GUIDO
Moederken (1901) [written 4 May 1891]
Ego Flos... (1901) [written 17 Nov. 1898]
Verzameld dichtwerk, Vol. VII, ed. J. Boets, Kapellen: De Nederlandsche Boekhandel;
Pelckmans, 1987.

GILLIAMS, MAURICE
Tristitia Ante (1929) [written in 1927]
Herfst (1937; 1938) [written in 1936]
Vita Brevis. Verzameld werk, Amsterdam: Meulenhoff, 1984.

GRESHOFF, J.
Ik groet u (1926)
De vriendschap voor een uitgelezen vrouw (1933)
Verzamelde gedichten 1907-1967, The Hague: Nijgh & Van Ditmar, 1981 (12th edn.).

HANLO, JAN
Vers per 7 Juni '51 (1951; 1958)
Verzamelde gedichten, Amsterdam: Van Oorschot, 1979 (4th edn.).

HERZBERG, JUDITH
Ochtend (1963)
Zeepost, Amsterdam: G.A. van Oorschot, 1963.
Slijtage (1968)
Beemdgras, Amsterdam: G.A. van Oorschot, n.d. [1968].
Meeuwen (1984)
Dagrest, Amsterdam: G.A.van Oorschot, 1984.

HOEKSTRA, HAN G.
De ceder (1941; 1946)
Verzamelde gedichten, Amsterdam: Em. Querido, 1972.

HOORNIK, ED
   Pogrom (1938; 1939)
   Een vrouw beminnen (1952; 1952)
Verzamelde gedichten, ed. K. Lekkerkerker, Amsterdam: Meulenhoff, 1972.

JOORIS, ROLAND
   Wat doet men anders (1969)
Een konsumptief landschap, Ghent: Yang Poeziereeks, 1969.
   Een dorp (1974)
Gedichten 1958-87, Antwerp: Lotus, 1987.

KLOOS, WILLEM
   Avond (1886; 1894)
   Sonnet (1886; 1894)
   De boomen dorren in het laat seizoen (1889; 1894)
   Zelf-verandering (1889; 1894)
Verzen, 4th edn., Amsterdam: Mij. tot verspr. van goede en goedkoope lectuur,
1932.

KNIBBE, HESTER
   De schaatser (1989; 1992)
De Tweede Ronde (Winter 1989); *Meisje in badpak*, Baarn: De Prom, 1992 [version as
in *De Tweede Ronde*].

KOMRIJ, GERRIT
   Dodenpark (1969; 1969)
Alle vlees is als gras/Ik heb goddank twee goede longen, Amsterdam: Meulenhoff, 1981.
   De dichter (1972; 1972)
Het schip De Wanhoop. Gedichten 1964-1979, Amsterdam: De Arbeiderspers, 1979.

KOOL, MARGA
   Anders (1987) [read at *Poetry International, Rotterdam* 1984]
Hoogspanning. Nederlandse en Drentse gedichten , Zuidwolde: Stichting het Drentse
Boek, 1987.

KOPLAND, RUTGER (R. H. van den Hoofdakker)
   Ontologie (1966)
Onder het vee, Amsterdam: G.A. van Oorschot, 1966.

KORTEWEG, ANTON
   Sed non frustra (1971)
Niks geen Romantic Agony, Amsterdam: Meulenhoff, 1971.

KOSTER, EDWARD B.
Een school van zilv'ren maanlichtvissen (1895)
Verzamelde gedichten, Rotterdam: W.L. Brusse, 1903.

KRUIT, JOHANNA
Paalhoofden (1985; 1987)
De Tweede Ronde (Winter 1985); *Voorheen te Orisande*, Amsterdam/Brussels:
Thomas Rap, 1987 [version as in *De Tweede Ronde*].
De weg van het water 1 (1988; 1990)
Huis aan zee (1989; 1990)
Landschap (1989; 1990)
Vogeltrek (1989; 1990)
De weg van het water, Middelburg: Zeeuws Kunstenaarscentrum, 1990.

LASOEN, PATRICIA
Die ochtend in april (1975)
Landschap met roze hoed. Een Keuze uit Gedichten 1965-1980 , Antwerp/Amsterdam:
Elsevier Manteau, 1981.

LEEFLANG, ED
1945 (1979)
De hazen en andere gedichten, Amsterdam: De Arbeiderspers, 1979.

LODEIZEN, HANS
De buigzaamheid van het verdriet (1949)
Op een paar uren (1949)
Het innerlijk behang en andere gedichten, Amsterdam: Van Oorschot, 1980 (12th edn.).

LUCEBERT (L.J. Swaanswijk)
ik draai een kleine revolutie af (1951; 1952)
visser van ma yuan (1953; 1953)
Verzamelde gedichten, ed. C.W. van de Watering, C.A. Groenendijk, Aldert Walrecht
and Lucebert, Amsterdam: De Bezige Bij, 1974.

MARSMAN, HENDRIK
'Paradise Regained' (1925; 1927)
Holland (1934)
Herinnering aan Holland (1937; 1938)
Landschap (1937; 1938)
Polderland (1937; 1938)
Verzameld Werk. Poëzie, proza en critisch proza, Amsterdam: Em. Querido, 1979
(4th edn.).

MICHAELIS, HANNY
    Briljant filosoferend (1969)
    Drie jaar was ik ongeveer (1969)
De rots van Gibraltar, Amsterdam: G.A. van Oorschot, 1969.

MIN, NEELTJE MARIA
    Mijn moeder is mijn naam vergeten (1966; 1966)
    Diep in de put waar haar gebeente ligt (1985) [read at Poetry International,
Rotterdam, 11 June 1975]
De gedichten, Amsterdam: Bert Bakker, 1989.

MOK, JUDITH
    Winterspiegel
    Winterspiegel II
Kinderspel [forthcoming].

MORRIËN, ADRIAAN
    Afscheid (1968)
Oogappel. Gedichten, Amsterdam: De Bezige Bij, 1986.

NIJHOFF, MARTINUS
    Het licht (1916)
    De laatste dag (1916)
    De troubadour (1916; 1916)
    De soldaat die Jesus kruisigde (1917; 1924)
    De danser (1919; 1924)
    Aan een graf (1930; 1934)
Verzamelde gedichten, ed. W.J. van den Akker & G.J. Dorleijn, Amsterdam: Bert
Bakker, 1990.

NOOTEBOOM CEES
    Bashō I (1989)
    Bashō II (1989)
    Bashō III (1989)
    Bashō IV (1989)
Het gezicht van het oog, Amsterdam: De Arbeiderspers, 1989.

OTTEN, WILLEM JAN
    Wad (1973)
Een zwaluw vol zaagsel, Amsterdam: Em. Querido, 1973.
    Allerzielen (1976)
    De dichter duikt (1976)
Het ruim: gedichten 1973-1976, Amsterdam: Em. Querido, 1976.

OUWENS, KEES
      Nieuwe trui (1973)
      Enige tranen, (1973)
      De boer (1973)
Intieme Handelingen, Amsterdam: Polak & Van Gennep, 1973.

PEAUX, AUGUSTA
      Koud landschap. (1918)
Gedichten, Haarlem: H.D. Tjeenk Willink & Zoon, 1918.
      Oude huizen aan de kade. (1926)
      Voorjaarslandschap. (1926)
Nieuwe gedichten, Haarlem: H.D. Tjeenk Willink & Zoon, 1926.

PERK, JACQUES
      Iris (1881; 1882)
Verzamelde gedichten, ed. G. Stuiveling, Amsterdam: De Arbeiderspers, 1957.

RODENKO, PAUL
      Bommen (1950; 1951)
      Februarizon (1951)
Orensnijder tulpensnijder. Verzamelde gedichten, Amsterdam: De Harmonie, 1975.

ROGGEMAN, WILLEM M.
      Een fata morgana in Vlaanderen (1979)
      Archeologische vondst (1982)
Al wie omkijkt is gezien. Gedichten 1974 - 1987, Antwerp/Amsterdam: Manteau, 1988.
      African Queen (1989; 1990)
De Tweede Ronde (Autumn 1989); with translations by Gabriel Rosenstock: *Cruth an Daonnai/De vorm van een mens*, Dublin: Coiscéim, 1990.

ROLAND HOLST, ADRIAAN
      Het leven (1911; 1911)
      Ik, die geboren ben (1913)
      De nacht (1913; 1929)
      Zwerversliefde (1913; 1920)
      De tussenkomst (1925; 1925)
      Kwatrijn (1936; 1940)
Poëzie I, ed. W.J. van den Akker, L.H. Mosheuvel and A.L. Sötemann, Amsterdam: G.A. van Oorschot, 1981.
      Herfstweer (1958/59; 1960)
      Naar buiten (1970)

Hoogste tijd (1976)
Poëzie II, ed. W.J. van den Akker, L.H. Mosheuvel and A.L. Sötemann, Amsterdam: G.A. van Oorschot, 1981.

ROSS, LEO
Requiescat (1962)
L'amour vert, Amsterdam: Em. Querido, 1962.

ROUWELER, HANNIE
Verzwegen Tijd (1993)
Reiziger naar het woord, Groningen: Holmsterland, 1993.
Landschap (1994)
Rivieren en ravijnen, Groningen: Holmsterland, 1994.
(from the poet's own selection)

SCHIPPERS, K.
No, No Nanette (1964; 1965)
Een leeuwerik boven een weiland. Een keuze uit de gedichten , Amsterdam: Em. Querido, 1980.

SLAUERHOFF, JAN JACOB
Columbus (1928)
In mijn leven... (1930)
Verzamelde gedichten, ed. K. Lekkerkerker, Amsterdam: Nijgh & Van Ditmar, 1990 (14th. edn.).

SONTROP, TH.
De eikel spreekt (1962)
Park (1962)
Langzaam kromgroeien, Amsterdam: G.A. van Oorschot, 1962.

SOUDIJN, KAREL
Schoonmaak (1970)
Het kruidenboek, Amsterdam: Athenaeum, Polak & Van Gennep, 1970.

TELLEGEN, TOON
Als ik eens één keer één dag een nijlpaard zou kunnen zijn (1980)
De zin van een liguster, Amsterdam: Em. Querido, 1980.
Het bezoek (1981)
De aanzet tot een web, Amsterdam: Em. Querido, 1981.

TEN BERGE, H.C.
from De Lusitaanse variant (1977)
Va-Banque, Amsterdam: De Bezige Bij, 1977; selection as read at Poetry International, Rotterdam, 1977.

T' HOOFT, JOTIE
    Chanson (1981)
    Dood, donkere dader en zachte hand (1981)
Verzamelde gedichten, ed. Fil Hantko, n.p. [Brussels]: Elsevier Manteau, 1981.

TILLEMA, MIEKE
    Van tulpen (1988)
Het genot van het surplus, Haarlem: Uitgeversmaatschappij Holland, 1988.
    Zo vroeg
Unpublished.

VANCREVEL, LAURENS (D.M. VAN KREVELEN)
    Over tijd (1981)
Speculatieven, Amsterdam: Marsyas, 1981.

VAN DEN BERGH, HERMAN
    Nocturne (1917)
Verzamelde gedichten, ed. W. Zoethout, Amsterdam: Em. Querido, 1979.

VAN DE WOESTIJNE, KAREL
    Koorts-deun (1896; 1903)
    De riemen, zwaar van wier (1910)
    Ik ben de hazel-noot (1928)
Verzamelde gedichten, Brussels & Amsterdam: Elsevier Manteau, 1978.

VAN EEDEN, FREDERIK
    De noordewind.(1886; 1898)
Enkele verzen, Amsterdam: W. Versluys, 1898.

VAN HAREN, ELMA
    Op stap met Edvard Munch (1988; 1988)
De Reis naar het welkom geheten, Amsterdam: De Harmonie, 1988.

VAN HEE, MIRIAM
    December (1988)
Winterhard, Amsterdam: De Bezige Bij, 1988.

VAN OSTAIJEN, PAUL
    Huldegedicht aan Singer (1928; 1928) [written 10 March 1921]
    Landschap (1924; 1928)
    Alpejagerslied (1928; 1928)
    Souvenir (1929)
Verzameld Werk. Poëzie [II], ed. Gerrit Borgers, Amsterdam: Bert Bakker, 1979 (6th edn.).

VAN RIESSEN, RENÉE
    Oud in Overijssel (1983; 1984)
Jagend licht, Amsterdam: Bert Bakker, 1984.

VASALIS, M (M. DROOGLEEVER FORTUYN-LEENMANS)
    De idioot in het bad (1936; 1940)
Parken en Woestijnen, Amsterdam: G.A. van Oorschot, 1983.
    Sotto voce (1947; 1954)
Vergezichten en gezichten, Amsterdam: G.A. van Oorschot, 1984.

VERWEY, ALBERT
    De Noordzee (1904)
Oorspronkelijk dichtwerk I, Amsterdam/Santpoort: Em. Querido/v.h. C.A. Mees, 1938.
    De schone wereld (1922)
    De ziel en de liefde (1924)
Oorspronkelijk dichtwerk II, Amsterdam/Santpoort: Em. Querido/v.h. C.A. Mees, 1938.

VOETEN, BERT
    De zon op mijn hand (1956)
Gedichten 1950 - 1980. Een keuze, Amsterdam: De Bezige Bij, 1988.

VROMAN, LEO
    Bloemen (1949)
    Regeneratie (1956)
    Een klein draadje (1960)
    Samen rimpelen (1960)
Gedichten 1946-1984, Amsterdam: Em. Querido, 1985.

VROOMKONING, VICTOR (Walter van de Laar)
    Hereniging (1989; 1990) [with an alteration by the poet]
    Vuilniszakken (1990; 1990)
Echo van een echo, Antwerp/Amsterdam: Manteau, 1990.

WINKLER PRINS, JACOB
    Bui (1885)
Verzamelde gedichten, ed. Joannes Reddingius, Amsterdam: Maatschappij tot verspreiding van goede en goedkope lectuur, 1929.

About the Editor

Peter van de Kamp was born in The Hague, The Netherlands in 1956, the youngest of three. After a Jesuit secondary education, he studied English and Literary Theory at the University of Leiden. He received a Ph.D. in Anglo-Irish Literature from University College, Dublin. Here he taught Anglo-Irish Literature for several years before taking up a permanent post as lecturer in Language Acquisition in the English Department at Leiden University, where he also taught translation theory. In 1989 he was awarded the Ireland Fund Newman Scholarship in Anglo-Irish Literature at University College Dublin. A Newman Scholar under T. Augustine Martin at U.C.D. from 1989 to October 1992, he did full-time research for a biography of Katharine Tynan, which he is currently writing. At present, he is a lecturer in English and Communications at the Regional Technical College in Tralee. He is the founder of the Kerry Summer School of Living Irish Authors.

His publications include various articles on English-language literature, particularly on Irish poets and novelists of the Nineteenth and Twentieth Century, and on developing tools for teaching literature and writing. Co-authored, with Peter Costello, *Flann O'Brien. An Illustrated Biography* (London: Bloomsbury, 1987), edited *Katharine Tynan. Irish Stories 1893-1899* (Leiden: Academic Press, 1993), co-edited *Yeats and Politics* (Amsterdam: Rodopi, 1994), collaborated with Gabriel Rosenstock and Dutch illustrator, Piet Sluis on *Netherverse. 24 Dutch Poems in English and Irish*. His own poetry has been published in journals in Belgium, The Netherlands and Ireland. He is working with Peter Costello on an Almanac of the Irish Literary Renaissance. In collaboration with Professor Augustine Martin, he is editing the prose of James Clarence Mangan. He is a member of the Irish Translators' Association and the Irish Writers Union.

ABOUT THE ASSOCIATE EDITOR

Frank van Meurs studied English and Middle Dutch Literature at the University of Leiden, and Translation Studies at the University of Amsterdam. He taught Philology and Language Proficiency at the Department of English, University of Leiden. He now teaches Language Proficiency at the Departments of English and Business Communication Studies at the University of Nijmegen. He collaborated on the Dutch translation of Jonathan I. Israel, *Dutch Primacy in World Trade: 1585 –1740* .

As Associate Editor, he traced the original publications and verified the source texts, suggested additions, deletions and emendations in both the biographical section and the main body of the anthology. He was also responsible for the bibliographical sections.